Romans

INTERPRETATION

A Bible Commentary for Teaching and Preaching

Most Scripture translations are those of the author. The Scripture quotations from the Revised Standard Version of the Holy Bible, copyright, 1946 1952, and © 1971, 1973 by the Division of Christian Education, National Council of the Churches of Christ in the U.S.A. are so noted and are used by permission.

Library of Congress Cataloging in Publication Data

Achtemeier, Paul J.
  Romans.

  (Interpretation, a Bible commentary for teaching and preaching)
  Bibliography: p.
  1. Bible. N.T. Romans--Commentaries. I. Title.
II. Series.
BS2665.3.A28 1985   227'.107   84-47796
ISBN 0-8042-3137-0

11 12 13 14 15 16 17 18

Printed in the United States of America
John Knox Press
Louisville, Kentucky 40202-1396

SERIES PREFACE

This series of commentaries offers an interpretation of the books of the Bible. It is designed to meet the need of students, teachers, ministers, and priests for a contemporary expository commentary. These volumes will not replace the historical critical commentary or homiletical aids to preaching. The purpose of this series is rather to provide a third kind of resource, a commentary which presents the integrated result of historical and theological work with the biblical text.

An interpretation in the full sense of the term involves a text, an interpreter, and someone for whom the interpretation is made. Here, the text is what stands written in the Bible in its full identity as literature from the time of "the prophets and apostles," the literature which is read to inform, inspire, and guide the life of faith. The interpreters are scholars who seek to create an interpretation which is both faithful to the text and useful to the church. The series is written for those who teach, preach, and study the Bible in the community of faith.

The comment generally takes the form of expository essays. It is planned and written in the light of the needs and questions which arise in the use of the Bible as Holy Scripture. The insights and results of contemporary scholarly research are used for the sake of the exposition. The commentators write as exegetes and theologians. The task which they undertake is both to deal with what the texts say and to discern their meaning for faith and life. The exposition is the unified work of one interpreter.

The text on which the comment is based is the Revised Standard Version of the Bible. The general availability of this translation makes the printing of a translation unnecessary and saves the space for comment. The text is divided into sections appropriate to the particular book; comment deals with passages as a whole, rather than proceeding word by word, or verse by verse.

Writers have planned their volumes in light of the requirements set by the exposition of the book assigned to them. Biblical books differ in character, content, and arrangement. They also differ in the way they have been and are used in the liturgy, thought, and devotion of the church. The distinctiveness and use of particular books have been taken into account in decisions about the approach, emphasis, and use of space in the commentaries. The goal has been to allow writers to develop the format which provides for the best presentation of their interpretation.

The result, writers and editors hope, is a commentary which both explains and applies, an interpretation which deals with both the meaning and the significance of biblical texts. Each commentary reflects, of course, the writer's own approach and perception of the church and world. It could and should not be otherwise. Every interpretation of any kind is individual in that sense; it is one reading of the text. But all who work at the interpretation of Scripture in the church need the help and stimulation of a colleague's reading and understanding of the text. If these volumes serve and encourage interpretation in that way, their preparation and publication will realize their purpose.

The Editors

PREFACE

This book represents the end product of a long period of reflection on Paul's letter to the Christians in first century Rome. Those reflections began some thirty years ago when I began to think seriously about my doctoral dissertation and have continued unabated since that time. As a result, there are many to whom my thanks are due for such wisdom as I may have found. That need is all the more urgent since the format of the INTERPRETATION commentary series does not give its authors a chance to indicate, in the form of extensive footnotes, all those scholars to whom they are indebted. While the bibliographies at the end of the book give some small indication, the absence of references to books in foreign languages gives a distorted picture. To the reader acquainted with the current debate on Romans, my debt to Pauline scholars here and abroad will be immediately apparent. I take this opportunity to acknowledge my debt to the scholarly "guild" from whose work on Paul in general, and Romans in particular, I owe an immeasurable debt.

In addition to my debt to my scholarly colleagues, there are others who have helped in the conception and writing of this book. James Mays, the general editor of this commentary series, has provided encouragement and guidance to me as I undertook to write a commentary so different from one's usual and accustomed scholarly form. Martha Aycock, Union Seminary's peerless reference librarian, has performed her usual feat of making herself indispensable in a project such as this. Leander Keck has shared with me his thoughts as he prepares his own work on Romans, and I have profited greatly from his generosity and sharp insights. My wife has patiently, gently, and helpfully borne with me in the writing of this book and has read through both first and second drafts. I have benefited greatly from her gifts as scholar and preacher. Much of what is good in this book—and none of what is bad—is due to these friends who have given me the benefit of their scholarly insight and clarity of thought. Unless otherwise indicated, all translations are my own, and I must take responsibility for them.

Finally, the dedication of the book indicates my gratitude to the students who, in three theological schools over the past twenty-five years, have been my companions on this journey of theological discovery. Their insight, patience, support, and developing scholarly acumen have helped me greatly in shaping my own thinking about Romans; and I happily take this opportunity to thank them as a group. To have had such students is more than any teacher has a right to expect.

CONTENTS

To the Students of my Romans Seminar
1958–1983
In Whose Company I Learned Much
This Book Is Gratefully Dedicated

Introduction

Paul was on fire to preach the good news of the gracious lordship of God expressed in Jesus Christ, and nowhere more so than in Romans. Because God as creator is Lord over the whole of created reality, reflections on that lordship encompass the full range of human problems, and nowhere is that more the case than in Romans. Paul deals with problems as contemporary as tomorrow's newspaper. They are problems as global as the headlines and as intimate as those discussed in "Dear Abby." The fate and future of the Jewish people, the role of the individual in the total sweep of history, the responsibilities of the citizen to the government of the country with which he or she may not always agree, the morality of actions in which adults engage, sexual and otherwise—all these and more occupy Paul in his letter to the Christians in Rome. It could not have been otherwise, because a letter to Rome was a letter to the political, military, and economic capital of Paul's world; and he could no more avoid such problems than could a Christian author in our day writing to Christians in Washington, D.C. One may come to Paul's letter to the Romans therefore with great expectations.

The history of the dialogue between the church and this letter confirms that such expectations are well placed. Its impact on the church at critical times in the church's life shows that plainly enough. When the Roman empire was tottering and the foundations of a civilization that had learned to value the Christian church were crumbling, Augustine learned from Romans how one can construct a view of human nature and of the state which can survive the breakdown of civilization. When the church exalted itself too highly in its own understanding of the ways of God with humankind, Luther and Calvin learned from Romans how a church could be structured which allowed the gracious lordship of God in Jesus Christ to come to clearer expression. When faith and culture were too uncritically combined in the nineteenth century, so that the development of human culture and the purposes of God were naïvely assumed to be identical, Karl Barth learned from Romans that God's lordship embodies a No to human pretension and pride which is the healing judgment of God's saving mercy.

That power to shape lives and heal one's perception of reality remains alive within the Christian faith, and the shape of that faith has the contours of Paul's thought indelibly impressed upon it. Fully one quarter of the New Testament is made up of writings bearing his name. One touches the roots of one's Christian faith when one deals with Paul, and nowhere more so than in Romans. To confront Romans is to confront one's faith at its source, to have it judged and healed, to have it called into question and renewed, to have it shattered and restored in stronger and more vital form.

Yet this epistle can prove to be as puzzling as any book in the Bible to many of its readers. A part of the problem lies in the epistle itself. If Paul warned the Christians in Corinth that he could give them only the milk of Christian thinking fit for babes in the faith (I Cor. 3:1–2), it is clear that he felt the Christians in Rome were ready for solid food. How could it be otherwise when Paul was dealing with so vast and intimate a problem as the relationship of creation to its Creator and Lord? The letter is unabashedly theological in its approach, and less serious perspectives have difficulty coming to terms with Paul. Yet Paul meant his letter to be read or heard and understood by "lay" men and women in the church in Rome. It is intended as a letter for practicing Christians, and that is the approach this commentary will take.

We will, in the pages that follow, undertake a fresh reading of the text which will be of value primarily to those who look to Romans as they look to the rest of Scripture, for guidance in their teaching and preaching as well as for guidance in their personal lives. Since the letter is unabashedly theological, the comments will have theology as their primary concern. Since it is a letter of the apostle Paul, the comments will have as their primary concern the intention motivating the apostle to write the words he did. We will assume that Paul said what he meant and that what he meant was important. Rather than our calling into question what Paul says from the "modern" point of view, we will find ourselves being called into question by what he writes. The results of such an approach will enable us to understand what Paul is about and will show that what he is about is useful to the contemporary tasks of preaching God's grace to modern people and teaching them the ways of God with humankind.

This is not to disparage the work of technical scholarship nor to discount or deny importance to the study of those scholars who probe the intellectual and religious history of Paul's time for clues to his language and his meaning. Modern biblical scholarship has made great contributions to our understanding of the New Testament in general, and of Paul in particular, and a commentary like this one would be impossible without that work. Much insight has come and will continue to come from that scholarly research, and many of the results already achieved will be assumed in the comments on the pages of this book. There is, in fact, much work being done currently to which we will need to pay careful attention in these pages. Some new avenues of investigation have been opened, and in some cases reopened, which have thrown light into some shadowy places.

One of those new avenues is the recognition that the framework of Paul's thought may be more significantly influenced by his thinking about historical problems, for example, the problem of the place of the Jews as chosen people within God's larger plan for human salvation, than had often been suspected by those who saw in Romans primarily the explication of the doctrine of justification by faith. Reading Romans from an awareness of Paul's own historical perspective will often yield clarity where otherwise the yield tended to be confusion.

A second and related avenue of investigation concerns the recovery of the insight that such Pauline reflections on the nature of God's plan for salvation drew on a kind of Jewish historical reflection that sought to come to terms with the conflict between the observable course of history and God's promise of final redemption. The recognition of that element in Paul's thought, enlarged and deepened by new sources (Dead Sea Scrolls) and by new avenues of approach (fresh reading of Rabbinic sources), enables us to see in Romans some things which before were difficult to see, if they were not totally obscured. We will have more to say about the significance of this kind of eschatological, apocalyptic thinking for Paul's argument in Romans later on in this introduction.

3

Our reading of the text will take advantage of these advances in New Testament research and will apply them to an exposition of Paul's discussion in his letter to Rome, but we will not enter into the lists of that debate in the pages of this commentary. One will of course continue to learn from that debate in the future as one has in the past, as one will continue to be indebted to scholars past, present, and future who work at the problems posed by that perspective on Romans. This commentary, however, is an attempt at another kind of reading, gaining from the insights of technical scholarship but not burdened with the necessity of focusing on the problems which occupy such scholarly debate. What we intend is not to correct but rather to supplement that kind of approach. Commentaries like those of C. K. Barrett and Ernst Käsemann are of great value to scholar and preacher alike, and familiarity with their content will make a reading of Romans, and of this commentary, all the more illuminating. If such familiarity is not essential for the usefulness of this commentary, it will nevertheless make what follows all the more useful for preacher and teacher alike. This commentary does not make all others dispensable; it presumes their results and enters into a theological dialogue with the text of Romans, a dialogue rendered clearer by their work.

Before that dialogue can be attempted in detail, however, it is necessary to gain a broader purchase on the form of Paul's thought as it takes shape in Romans. It is to that consideration that we must now turn.

The Background of Paul's Thought

It would be a mistake to imagine that Paul wrote Romans, or that any biblical author wrote any other book or portion of a book, in complete isolation from the culture within which he lived. As God in the Incarnation used human flesh to embody his Son, so in the biblical books the authors used their contemporary language and thought forms to embody what they had to tell their readers. As God spoke through the human flesh of Jesus, so he continued to speak through the human languages and cultures within which the biblical message was framed.

The same is true of Paul's letter to Rome. It is framed within the cultural and linguistic possibilities open to him. It will aid us in our understanding of what he is writing if we are aware of the choices he made from among the cultural options open to him as he sought to communicate his understanding of God's gracious act for sinful humanity in Christ.

There were in the Greco-Roman world of which Paul was a part a number of philosophies that were widely used and respected as means for the expression of religious and moral truth. Among the most important of these were two:

1. A popularized kind of Platonism, in which the world was divided into two realms of reality, the material and the spiritual. The material realm was transitory and the locus of evil, while the spiritual realm embodied unchanging perfection and was therefore the locus of God. Human nature was a mixture of these two elements. This philosophy later became the structuring element in Gnosticism, which sought to interpret the Christian faith in terms of a material realm which was unredeemably evil and a spiritual realm to which one sought to flee. As we will see, although Paul uses language that seems to reflect such a view, he does not in fact share it.

2. Along with such popularized Platonism, there was a kind of Stoicism which sought to achieve a truly moral life through the renunciation of dependence on anything beyond a person's control, lest such dependencies force one into actions contrary to one's will to do the good. Only an attitude of utter emotional detachment will enable one to stay free of the evil one might otherwise be tempted to do. Again, although Paul at times sounds much like a Stoic (e.g., I Cor. 7:29b–31a), he would not have agreed that one should avoid any real concern for one's fellow human beings.

In addition to such modes of understanding the nature of reality which were popular in the Greco-Roman world, the Jewish milieu, where the roots of Paul's family and his religion lay (see Phil. 3:5–6), also offered intellectual resources which were used to express views of the divine-human relationship. Again, we may single out two as most important:

1. Rabbinic Judaism was being developed during Paul's lifetime. It was a way of understanding and expounding the Jewish faith which would, with the fall of Jerusalem and the destruction of the Temple in A.D. 70, become the dominant way to understand the Jewish faith. It has continued to play such a dominant role right down to the present time. This understanding of the Old Testament emphasized the covenant that God had made with Israel on Mount Sinai and the law that accompanied it. If the Jews as God's chosen people fulfilled that law, they could be sure that they were fulfilling God's will for them in all of life's circumstances. Paul of course was much concerned

5

with how God's will was to be discerned and fulfilled, and how that law was to be understood in relation to that problem. Such questions were directly related to the rabbinic concern for interpreting and following the Scriptures which we know as the Old Testament.

2. A second way of interpreting God's relationship to his creation developed from some of the views of the prophets, who emphasized that God was in control of history, shaping events in accordance with his will. After the prophets ceased to appear, some people began to assume that this meant the world was so evil it could only be changed by a radical divine intervention. Acknowledging with the prophets that God's purpose was to lead all of history to the goal he had set for it, they awaited a final judgment on all powers of evil, in which those powers would be completely destroyed. After that divine judgment, God would establish a new heaven and a new earth, within which righteousness would reign and all people would be obedient to him. Because these purposes of God are hidden and can only be known if God reveals them, this way of understanding God's way with his creation came to be called "apocalyptic," which is derived from the Greek word meaning "revealed." This view is an attempt to formulate a universal view of history based on what God has revealed of his purpose in his dealings with Israel. It is clear enough in Paul's letters that he, too, expected such a judgment to occur with the return (the Parousia) of Christ and that therefore he, too, was influenced by such a view.

As we have seen, one can find traces in Paul's letters of all of these ways of understanding reality and God's relationship to it. Recent research, however, has called attention to the fact that from the way Paul expressed his understanding of the Christian faith in his letter to Rome, he appears to have been influenced most strongly by the apocalyptic understanding of the relationship of God to his creation. It was this mode of thinking which Paul found most useful for his own exposition of the Christian faith. Although he was also influenced by and made use of other intellectual resources of his time, those other resources were fitted into a basic structure which understood God's relationship to the world as that of Creator to creature. God is therefore the lord of his creation and, as the culmination of that Lordship, the Creator will finally bring the creation to the point he had envisioned for it from the beginning.

6

The Shape of Paul's Thought

In order to understand the way in which Paul made use of the basic structures of apocalyptic Judaism, it will be helpful to examine how that way of thinking understood the movement of history. We can diagram that understanding in the following way:

DIAGRAM 1

JEWISH APOCALYPTIC VIEW
Two Aeons (Ages)

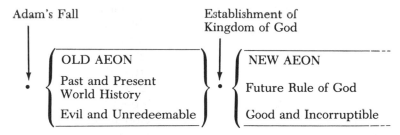

To help us better understand such a view, we may diagram the very different way the Gnostics, drawing on the categories of a popularized Platonism, understood reality.

DIAGRAM 2

GNOSTIC VIEW
(Ontological, not Historical)

The contrast is striking. For apocalyptic Judaism, history is the basic category and everything else is understood in terms of God's plan for his people, now being worked out in the history of the world. For Gnosticism, on the other hand, what is important is the structure of reality. Since historical events have no impact on that structure, history is really not important. Because Gnostics are interested in the shape of reality, not the course of history, their categories are static, not dynamic,

7

and escape from the material world, not its transformation, is the solution they envisage to the problem of evil. If we could term the apocalyptic view "historical," we could term the Gnostic view "ontological" because it is concerned with the structure of Being ("ontos" comes from the Greek word for Being) rather than with the course of history. Salvation lies not in what God finally will do with human history but in learning that human beings share in the bifurcated structure of all Being and hence can cultivate the good spiritual aspects rather than the evil, material ones. According to the Gnostics, God's activity consisted in sending a messenger who tells those who will listen about the structure of Being. Since that is all God does, he is never really involved in the course of history or with people's lives. It is up to the individual to take advantage of that knowledge ("gnostic" comes from the Greek word for "knowledge").

By contrast, the apocalyptic view understands God's activity to consist in a final transformation of reality with the introduction of a new age. Yet for all that, the apocalyptic view did not understand God to be active in present history or in the lives of individuals either. Only when he brings history as we know it to a close and inaugurates a new age will God act decisively to restore his creation. If, then, in Gnosticism God's decisive act lay in the past, with the sending of the messenger, for apocalyptic Judaism it lay in the future, when God would intervene to begin a new age.

It is clear therefore that if Paul took over the basic categories of apocalyptic Judaism rather than the way of understanding reality that was to result in Gnosticism, he also adapted those categories in the light of his conviction that in Jesus of Nazareth God had already begun his final act of the transformation of human history and his creation. We could diagram Paul's basic adaptation of apocalyptic Judaism in this way:

DIAGRAM 3

PAUL'S ADAPTATION OF APOCALYPTIC FRAMEWORK

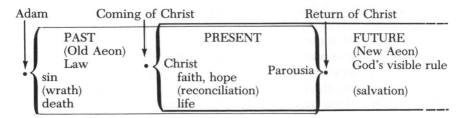

What Paul has done is to collapse the two ages (or *aeons*, the Greek word) into one another because of his conviction that with the death and resurrection of Jesus of Nazareth God has already begun to inaugurate the new age, the full and visible establishment of which will occur when Jesus returns to judge all humankind. That means that while the past (as in Gnosticism) is important for Paul, because it was the period of the Jews as the chosen people and of Jesus as the Messiah, and while the future (as in apocalyptic Judaism) is important, because it will be the period when history finally reaches its goal and the new age will be fully established, the present is also important, because the forces of the new age are already at work within it enabling human beings to align themselves with it or against it. Thus, the present becomes the time of decision—for or against Christ Jesus in whom the new age begins—for which one will have to give account at the final judgment.

There is an implication to be drawn from this structure of Paul's thought as it is exemplified in Romans which is of paramount importance for our understanding of that letter. Because Paul chose that kind of framework within which to work out his understanding of the Christian faith and to give it the exposition he does in Romans, the basic logic of his argument was drawn from the way history has been, and continues to be, guided by God. If, for example, the Jews were God's chosen people, with whom God communicated in a way he had not previously communicated with any other people, that fact will have to be taken into account in any understanding of the way God presently communicates both with the Jews and with non-Jews. If for the most part that chosen people has rejected Jesus as God's Messiah, that too will be of very great importance for understanding both the way God deals with disobedience and the way God keeps his promises. In other words, if Paul's argument in Romans is structured on the logic of history, then the place of the Jews in that history will have to occupy a significant place, as in fact it does.

The alternative would be to view Romans as fundamentally the exposition of a doctrine, enunciating the doctrine as the theme of the letter and then in the succeeding chapters showing how that doctrine applies to various problems and situations. In that case, the logic of the argument in Romans would be doctrinal, and the structure of Romans would reflect the way

9

the understanding and application of that doctrine in one area would affect the way it is understood and applied in other areas. The test of the argument in that case would be its coherence: Does what Paul says about the doctrine in one place lead logically to what he says about it in another place? The structure of Romans would then reflect the attempt at such a coherent exposition of the doctrine.

In fact, many commentators on Romans assume that the letter follows this latter kind of argument, namely that the theme is the doctrine of justification by faith (as announced in Rom. 1:17) and that the remainder of the letter is an exposition of the meaning of that doctrine for the way we understand our faith and practice it in our lives.

It is of course evident that Paul makes much of the idea of justification by faith in Romans, just as it is the case that the fate of the Jews also plays a significant role. Obviously therefore it is not a clear case of an exclusive either/or: *Either* Romans is solely concerned with doctrine to the total exclusion of any concern with history *or* it is concerned solely with the way God has dealt with his rebellious creation in the course of its history with no concern for any reflection about the implication of those acts. It is a question, however, of which of these two ways of thinking provides the underlying structure for Paul's letter to the churches in Rome. That is, is the logic that of the movement of a history God is guiding to its goal, with doctrinal statements and expositions included as a way of making sense of that movement, or is the logic that of a systematic exposition of a doctrine, with historical events cited as illustrations of the way the doctrine is to be understood?

This commentary will proceed on the assumption that the logic of the structure of Romans is more nearly the logic of history than the logic of doctrine, simply because that assumption lets us make more sense of the way Paul's argument proceeds. It is, for example, easier to understand why questions about the Jews as chosen people keep cropping up throughout the letter if the assumption that their central place in the history of God's dealing with humankind makes it imperative to consider that question than it is to understand why their status as chosen people should be so important if the central theme is the doctrine of justification by faith. That is especially true, for example, of Romans 3:1–8 or chapters 9–11; these sections provide difficult problems for any attempt to understand the basic issue in Romans to be that of an exposition of the doctrine of justification by faith. Such a preoccupation with the "Jewish question" must then be seen as tangential to what is thought to be Paul's central concern. Some commentators go so far as to say that when Paul deals with such questions he has lost the thread of his argument and has gotten confused (e.g., C. H. Dodd). Others have asserted that chapters 9—11 represent an "appendix" to the letter, since they are not central to a discussion of justification by faith (e.g., Sanday and Headlam).

The final decision about the correctness of such an approach will therefore have to be whether or not it enables us to make more sense of the way Paul carries on his exposition of the Christian faith in his letter to Rome. A preliminary understanding of the way the structure of Romans can be understood on the assumption that Paul is adapting an apocalyptic framework for his presentation of the faith, and is pursuing an argument predicated on the logic of the history of God's dealing with his rebellious creation rather than on the logic of doctrinal development, is provided by diagram 4 on the following page. In it the various themes that appear in Romans can be located on the larger structure of Paul's adaptation of that apocalyptic framework.

As the diagram illustrates, the sweep of Paul's thought runs from the beginning of humankind in Adam to its final fate at the Parousia (Christ's return in glory). For Paul, the history of humankind prior to Christ is under the power of the sin introduced by Adam and his disobedience (chaps. 1:18—3:20). As all human beings are related to Adam and to his disobedience by their physical birth, so Christians have come to be related to Christ and to his obedience by their new birth, baptism (6: 3–11). Adam and Christ are therefore in a sense each the epitomization of a new direction for humanity: Adam through sin to death and Christ through righteousness to life (5:12–19).

Related to that sweep of human fate is the path of a chosen people. Here the related concepts are *Abraham*, with whom a chosen people begins, a people limited to those who are Israelites by physical birth, and the *church*, open now to all who are children of Abraham by being related to the faith of Abraham, and upon whom the mantle of "chosen people" has fallen after the resurrection of Christ (chap. 4).

11

The fate of Israel is thus important for this sweep of history: first as chosen people; then as those who, in the main, exclude

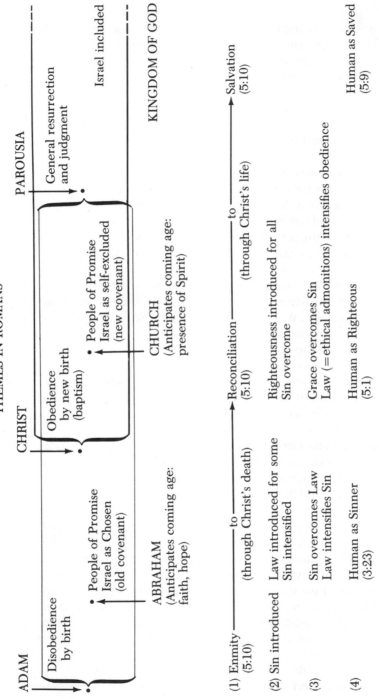

DIAGRAM 4
THEMES IN ROMANS

ADAM

Disobedience
by birth

• People of Promise
Israel as Chosen
(old covenant)

ABRAHAM
(Anticipates coming age:
faith, hope)

CHRIST

Obedience
by new birth
(baptism)

• People of Promise
Israel as self-excluded
(new covenant)

CHURCH
(Anticipates coming age:
presence of Spirit)

PAROUSIA

General resurrection
and judgment

Israel included

KINGDOM OF GOD

(1) Enmity ————— to ————— Reconciliation ————— to ————— Salvation
     (5:10)   (through Christ's death)   (5:10)   (through Christ's life)   (5:10)

(2) Sin introduced   Law introduced for some   Righteousness introduced for all
                     Sin intensified   Sin overcome

(3)   Sin overcomes Law   Grace overcomes Sin
                     Law intensifies Sin   Law (=ethical admonitions) intensifies obedience

(4) Human as Sinner   Human as Righteous   Human as Saved
    (3:23)   (5:1)   (5:9)

Eschatological terms: Righteousness, Salvation, Eternal Life themselves from being members of the renewed chosen people through their rejection of Christ; finally, in Paul's view, to be included once again at the Parousia (chaps. 9—11). Again, as Abraham is characterized by faith and hope and anticipates the reality of the new age inaugurated by Christ (4:19–22), so the church is characterized by the presence of God's Spirit and anticipates the reality of God's final rule (8:18–25).

The numbered lines below the diagram illustrate some of the concepts Paul uses in relation to this sweep of human history, to this overview of the way God has exercised his gracious lordship over his rebellious creatures. In line (1), the enmity brought about by sin has led through Christ's death to human reconciliation and will lead through Christ's (risen) life to salvation in the consummation of the age. Line (2) shows the new element in each of these periods: sin in the time following Adam (3:9); law in the time following Moses (implied in 5:-13–14); righteousness in the time following the coming of Christ (3:21–22). As line (3) indicates, the law, introduced in the period following Abraham, was powerless to counteract the power of sin and served instead as an instrument whereby sin was intensified. Only with the coming of Christ could sin be overcome, now not by the law but by grace. Within the rule of grace, however, the law, which for Paul from the beginning is based on faith (see 3:31; 9:31–32a), now can serve the purposes of obedience to God. The law thus acts in a sense as a catalyst, intensifying the effects of whatever force holds sway over a human being, whether that force be sin or grace. What power it is that holds sway over the human being in this sweep of the history of God's dealing with his creation is shown in line (4): in the period prior to Christ, the human being is under the sway of sin. Only with the coming of Christ does the human being have the possibility of serving something other than sin. It is not until Christ's return, and the consummation of the age, however, that the human being reaches the point where sin has lost the possibility of having all power over him or her.

As the diagram shows, the sweep of Paul's thought in Romans concerns not so much the spelling out of the implications of a doctrine like justification by faith as it concerns the course of the history of God's dealing with his creation, from its rebellion against him to its final redemption. The outline of the first eleven chapters of Romans can be seen from the course of that history between God and his creation. It is the story of God's

13

gracious lordship rejected and restored. The first four chapters deal with the first third of the diagram (the left-hand third), with their discussion of human rebellion and sin (chaps. 1—3) tempered only by the anticipation of Christ's redemptive act (3:21–26) in the trusting response to God by Abraham (3:27—4:25). The next four chapters in Romans (5—8) correspond roughly to the middle third of the diagram, focusing on the contrast between what was brought about by Adam (sin through disobedience) and what was brought about by Christ (righteousness through obedience, chap. 5); how we have been delivered from the former to the latter (by baptism) and what our reaction to that deliverance is to be (chap. 6); what our new situation means about our relationship to the past, which was dominated by sin and the law (chap. 7) and to the future which is dominated by the Spirit (chap. 8). The last three of those chapters (9—11)correspond to the right-hand third of the diagram, with its concentration on the fate of the Jews as chosen people who, although they have rejected Christ (chap. 9) despite the apostolic proclamation (chap. 10) and have thus opened the way for the gentiles to share in their inheritance (11:1–24), will nevertheless be included again in the inheritance at the time of Christ's return (11:25–31). The sweep of those eleven chapters is then summed up in 11:32.

The next four chapters (12—15) apply to the life of the Christian community the insights gained from this account of the sweep of God's redemptive dealing with his rebellious creation. A final chapter contains Paul's personal greetings to Christians he knows in Rome.

In the last analysis, it should not be surprising that Paul should choose the logic of history, the logic of the story of God's dealing with his rebellious creation, as the structure within which to tell the Romans about his understanding of the meaning of that story. That story is the matrix out of which Christian doctrines develop and on which they are intended to comment. Until one has heard the story of Jesus one has no reason to seek to understand him as the Christ or to clarify his relationship to the Creator. It is precisely through reflection on the story of the chosen people as Israel and as the church that one is driven to formulate doctrines to clarify the implications of, and interrelationships within, that story. Because that is the way Paul proceeds, his understanding of righteousness, for example, is rooted in the story of God's gra-

14

cious lordship over creation, both rebellious and redeemed. It is that story, that history, which is Paul's primary mode of reflecting on the relationship between creatures and Creator which is caught up in the term "righteousness." The relationship is without question a key element in Paul's theological reflections, but it is a relationship rooted in the context of the history of that relationship; and it is the grammar of that history which provides the structure for Paul's argument in his letter to the Roman Christians.

It is with a more detailed consideration of that shape and sweep of Paul's argument that the pages of this commentary are concerned. It will be helpful when one reads them if the general outlines of the structure of Paul's discussion in Romans are kept in view.

History as the Relationship Between Creator and Creation

There is another point about which we must be clear, however, if we are to avoid confusion in attempting to follow Paul's arguments and to trace his logic. That point centers on the fact that the kind of history about which Paul is concerned, and with which he is dealing, is history as it illumines and displays the relationship between God and the world or, to use other terminology, between Creator and creation. It is necessary to keep that fact in mind if we are to be clear about why Paul conducts his discussion as he does. The history which shapes the contours of Paul's discussion in his letter to Rome is not a history in which the relationship between God and human beings is a relationship among equals. Nor is it an account of the give and take which characterizes all history as we live it, with some forces relatively greater (Creator) and some relatively weaker (creation). Rather, Paul is speaking of creation and its history under the lordship of God, a lordship to be sure which is expressed in Jesus Christ but a lordship nevertheless. That basic structure of the history with which Paul is dealing—the Creator as Lord in his relationship to his creation—carries with it certain presuppositions which underlie much of what Paul has to say both in Romans and elsewhere. We must look at some of those presuppositions.

At the basis of Paul's understanding of the history between God the Lord and his creation is Paul's conviction that the only way a creature can survive is if that creature enjoys the continuing favor of its Creator. Because God is our Creator, he can in

15

fact dispose over us as he will—Paul makes that abundantly clear in a passage like Romans 9:20–24. God the Lord therefore has every right to judge his creation on the basis of the way it behaves (Rom. 2:6–11), and his wrath toward a disobedient creation is fully justified (1:18–32). It is a measure of the nature of that Creator that the lordship he exercises over his rebellious creatures is characterized more by kindness than by wrath. Nevertheless, it remains true that for a creature to survive, it must enjoy its Creator's continuing favor. Such favor by the Creator is then to be accepted by the creature as the only source of its continuing existence. Such a favorable disposition by the Creator toward his creation Paul calls "grace." Acceptance of that favorable disposition Paul calls "faith" or "trust" (the same word in Greek).

A corollary of such thinking about God the Creator, who as Lord is free to dispose over his creation as he sees fit and who, as human history has shown, has disposed over it not as it deserved but in gracious overlooking of his creatures' rebellion, is the unavoidable fact that human beings, as creatures, are never the rulers of their own destinies. Only the Creator, not the creature, has the power to shape his own destiny. Only the Creator, not the creature, is fit to exercise lordship. That means that as Paul understands human creatures everyone is subject to some lordship, to some power which one is forced to serve. A creature is not free to be its own lord, to dispose over its own life. It was the desire to do just that that led Adam to rebel against his creaturehood, and hence against God, when the tempter told him he could be "like God" (see Gen. 3:5). For Paul, that temptation of the creature to be his or her own lord, to dispose over his or her own destiny, continues; and hence creatures continue in rebellion against their Creator. Because the creature cannot exercise such lordship, yet rebels against it, the creature becomes enslaved to the forces that oppose God. For that reason, Paul is clear that since Adam the power to which creatures are subjected is sin. Because the creature is enslaved to that power, the creature is powerless to effect his or her own deliverance from it. Only a force stronger than sin can deliver the creature from sin.

16

Such a way of understanding the nature of reality and the course of human history has a further corollary for ethical and moral behavior. It will do no good, for example, to urge someone under the power of sin to "try harder." If, as Paul makes clear in chapter 7, for example, a human being "under Adam" is incapable of freeing himself or herself from sin, then all "trying harder" can do is to drive that person further into sin. If every act is under the control of sin, more action will simply mean more sin. Ethical commands therefore are pointless for someone in whom the power of sin has not been broken. That is why the law intensifies sin: It cannot break sin's power, so all it does is encourage acts which remain under the power of sin. Only after the power of sin is broken, and that means only after the lordship of God has been restored—and it has been with Christ's death and our baptism into it—does it make sense to give admonitions on how one is to live so as to avoid sin. It is for that reason that Paul does not begin with his ethical admonitions, he ends with them. Only after God's act in Christ has restored his gracious lordship so that the power of sin is broken in principle and only after our baptism into Christ has restored that lordship so that the power of sin is broken in actuality will it do any good to urge someone to do good and avoid sin.

A further corollary of that human situation concerns the kind of choice faced by the person who hears the good news that God in Christ has acted to restore his gracious lordship and thus to free humanity from the burden and domination of sin. The person confronting the gospel does not occupy some kind of neutral ground, faced with the choice either of being under the power of sin or being free from it. Since Adam, that choice has been made. We belong to a rebellious race, and rebellion which places us under the power of sin is our unavoidable fate. We do not, as it were, stand in a hallway facing two doors, one of which leads to sin, the other of which leads to salvation, with our choice being which of those two doors to enter. In Paul's understanding of our situation, we have already passed through the door marked "sin"; and the choice we face is whether or not we will remain there. Not to choose the gospel is therefore to choose sin. We cannot remain neutral in this conflict between God the Lord and his rebellious creation, since we are already, by our being human, members of the race that shares the corruption of Adam's disobedience. The only choice we face therefore is whether or not we will accept God's gracious lordship and therefore reconciliation with our Creator, thereby ending our rebellion. Failing that choice, as creatures we remain in sin, ruled over by a power beyond our control.

Paul engages in an exposition of those last points in chapter

17

6, and they underlie not only that chapter but the whole of his discussion of our current status in chapters 5—8. It will be necessary to keep that fact in mind when we consider that portion of Paul's argument if we are to make sense of it.

Romans as a Letter

There are many things we would like to know about the circumstances under which Paul's letter to the church or churches in Rome was written. That there may have been more than one church is suggested by Paul's reference in 16:5 to "the church in their house." It may be that there was more than one such "house church." Perhaps if we knew more about the circumstances of the letter, it would make it easier to understand some of the points Paul wants to make. It would be interesting to know, for example, when the letter was written or where Paul was at the time he wrote it. It would also be quite helpful to know how much Paul knew about the situation among the Christians in Rome, that is, was he trying in his letter to deal with some aspects of their internal situation? If we knew the answer to this last question, it might help us in ferreting out the meaning of the discussion in chapters 12—15. Again, it would be interesting to know who founded the church—obviously it cannot have been Paul since he had never been there (see 1:10) —and what influence that founder had on the Roman Christians' subsequent understanding of the faith. Again, it would be interesting to know the composition of the church or churches in Rome, that is, were most of the members converted Jews? or were most of them gentiles? or was the membership about evenly divided between those groups? It might help to clarify certain emphases in Romans if we could answer these questions.

Unfortunately, we have very little to go on in our attempt to find answers to such questions. There have of course been many guesses; one can find a survey of them, and the reasons for them, in any good introduction to the New Testament (e.g., W. G. Kümmel, *Introduction to the New Testament*). We will therefore not repeat them here.

Where it is useful for understanding what Paul has to say, we will, in the pages that follow, discuss how one or another of those questions may be answered. For example, when we discuss Paul's concerns about his impending trip to Jerusalem (15: 25–27, 30–32), we will be able to gain some clues into the reasons that motivated him to write the letter. We can probe further into that motivation when we listen as Paul tells the Roman Christians about his desire to visit them (1:11–13), and to continue his mission in Spain (15:24), now that he had completed his work in the eastern half of the Mediterranean world (15:19–20).

Beyond that, we will content ourselves with noting that the letter appears to have been written toward the close of Paul's career as apostolic preacher, somewhere in the time between A.D. 55–64. According to Acts 19:21 Paul traveled through northern and southern Greece (Macedonia and Achaia) on his way to Jerusalem, so it is a fair guess the letter was written from somewhere in that area. How much Paul knew about the church or churches to which he was writing can only be answered from the content of the letter itself, so again, we will discuss those questions when we come to the appropriate passages (see *"Reflection: Chapter 16 and Paul's Letter to Rome"*). Before we come to the discussion of the individual passages, however, we must discern the larger contours of Paul's argument in his letter to the Christians in Rome; and it is to such a discussion that we must now turn.

The Structure of Romans

The attempt to discern the organizing structure around which Paul composed his letter to the Christians in Rome is often hindered, rather than helped, by the traditional chapter divisions of the letter. Placed as they are they frequently break into the flow of the argument and give the impression that Paul's thinking is considerably more fragmented than is in fact the case. That is true, for example, in the very first chapter division (between chaps. 1 and 2), where the argument Paul has begun in 1:14 does not run its course until he turns directly to address the Jews in 2:17. Again, the first verse of chapter 3 does not introduce a new argument; it grows directly out of the discussion begun in 2:17 and hence the break indicated by the end of chapter 2 is also misleading. Perhaps most misleading of all is the break dictated by the division between chapters 3 and 4. According both to the rhetorical form Paul is using and to the logic of his argument, 4:1 dictates that 3:31 is not the end of a discussion; it is the question to which the discussion of Abraham, initiated in chapter 4, is the answer. If that fact is ignored, it will look as though the discussion of Abraham is unrelated to what

19

went before; and it will be correspondingly difficult to discern why Paul would want to introduce it there.

Similarly, to assume the introduction of a new argument with the advent of chapter 5, the first verse of which by its very structure indicates it is dependent on the discussion of the concluding verses of chapter 4, fragments Paul's flow of thought unnecessarily. The first verses of chapter 5, along with the last verses of chapter 4, sum up the foregoing section and announce the themes which will occupy Paul's discussion in the next four chapters.

A similar disservice to the understanding of Paul's logic occurs if one finds a break at the end of chapter 6. Paul poses three fundamental questions which work with law, sin, and grace in all possible combinations (in 6:1, 15; and 7:7), an arrangement rather effectively obscured if one follows the division between chapters 6 and 7. A similar obscuring of Paul's flow of argument will occur if one attempts to follow the chapter divisions between 9 and 10. Verse 4 of chapter 10 represents the climax of Paul's discussion begun in chapter 9, and the attempt to find the introduction of a new thought in 10:1 simply renders it impossible to see the point Paul is trying to make. The same is true, finally, with the division between chapters 14—15, where the discussion of strong and weak continues unabated from 14:1 until 15:13; and it is only at this latter place (15:14) that Paul introduces the discussion of a new point.

All of this must be taken into account as we seek to trace out the logic of Paul's presentation of his gospel to the Christians in Rome. The Table of Contents to this volume also serves as the broad outline of Paul's argument as we will discuss it; a more detailed outline will be found at the end of this introductory chapter. It represents the attempt to see that argument in terms of the way Paul proceeds, rather than in terms of the traditional chapter divisions. Reading Scripture chapter by chapter, as though each chapter represented a thematic and logical unit, is rarely a good practice; in the case of Romans it can be fatal to an understanding of what Paul is about. Our comments will therefore be organized on a different plan.

The four major divisions of the Table of Contents indicate by their titles that the central subject matter of Paul's apostolic proclamation as it is contained in Romans is God's act of grace in re-establishing his lordship over his rebellious creation. While justification, or righteousness (both translate the same Greek word), by faith is a major topic of discussion, righteousness is the expression of the new relationship the rebellious creature enters into when he or she accepts God's gracious lordship in Christ. Faith, or trust (both translate the same Greek word), is the mode by which that lordship is accepted. The fact that that relationship of gracious lordship between Creator and creation is now based on faith, rather than on race (as it was in the case of the Jews as chosen people), means the relationship has now been universalized to extend beyond the bounds of the Jewish race. Abraham is therefore a key figure for Paul precisely because, although he is the physical ancestor of the chosen people, his response to God's promised grace was faith. He therefore can serve as a model for the universality of the response to God's grace which has appeared in Christ Jesus. It is for that reason that we have chosen to emphasize in the outline the grace of God, expressed in the lordship he exercises in Jesus Christ, a gracious lordship that underlies righteousness by faith and to which righteousness by faith points, rather than treating this latter topic as though it were the major premise of Paul's gospel. Symptomatic of the difficulty of finding in righteousness by faith the central theme in Romans is the need then to point to 1:17 as the statement of that theme and the key to the discussion that follows. Grammatically, 1:17 cannot function in that way, since it is simply one member of a series of members, each of which substantiates the statement that preceded it. Verse 17 functions grammatically to substantiate 1:16 (as 1:16 in turn substantiates 1:15). To find in such a subordinate clause the statement of the theme of the letter is to overload the grammar to the point of ignoring it.

None of that is meant to say that righteousness by faith is not a central concern of Paul's letter to the Christians in Rome or that it is not a central concern for us. It is simply to say that it is not the central theme around which Paul has organized his letter. Righteousness by faith is rather the means by which God's gracious lordship may now be accepted by all, whether Jew or gentile, and hence is the means by which Paul understands the gospel to be universal in extent. Righteousness by faith is also the way the ungodly can come under his gracious lordship—it is the way God makes the ungodly "righteous" (4:5). Yet, as such, it is subordinated to the larger point that such righteousness is now open to all who follow Abraham in trusting God to do what he has promised, namely to make Abraham a blessing to *all* peoples. In the discussion of Abraham in chapter 4 therefore as in the discussion of the power of the gospel in

21

1:15–17, righteousness by faith is understood within the larger context of the universality of God's gracious lordship over his creation exercised in Jesus Christ. Righteousness by faith is therefore of very great importance to Paul's discussion, but it is not the central theme. That central theme, as we will see, is the plan God is pursuing to extend his gracious lordship to all peoples by his act in Christ, a theme stated at the very outset of the letter (1:2–4).

There will also be occasion from time to time to call attention to other problems which have arisen in the attempt to understand Paul's argument, and ways will be proposed to understand them in terms of Paul's broader discussion. Another such problem, for example, is posed by 2:14–16 which, understood as it normally is, seems to assign to gentiles an innate wisdom denied to Jews. Yet another is posed by 3:1–8, often misunderstood as simply a digression; and another by 5:1–5, which can appear, on some attempts to outline the letter, to be again a digression from the main thrust of the argument. A similar problem is posed by chapters 9—11, which have appeared to some to represent a digression rather than a coherent part of Paul's argument, a problem made more acute when justification by faith is taken as the letter's theme and that discussion appears to conclude with the end of chapter 8. In such cases, we will show how an understanding of the underlying logic and an assessment of the structure of Romans can aid us in resolving some of these problems.

We shall attempt, then, to think with Paul as he lays before his Roman readers his understanding of the gospel which he identifies as the power of God which is effective for the salvation of all races (1:16). If we do it well, the light it cast then will continue to be reflected onto the contours of our world, and we too will begin to catch a glimpse of the power of that gospel of Jesus Christ to shape our lives.

The Structure of This Commentary

Some of the characteristics of this commentary, for example, its outline and the way Paul's argument is understood, derive from the nature of Paul's letter to the Romans and have already been discussed. Other characteristics are due to the appearance of this volume as part of the INTERPRETATION series, and the commentary will be more useful if the reader takes note of them.

One such characteristic is the fact that the comments concern paragraphs of Romans rather than individual verses (a practice followed in all INTERPRETATION commentaries). The purpose of the comments is to explicate the line of thought Paul is following both within that paragraph and within the larger argument of Romans. More so perhaps than in any other Pauline letter, the argument in Romans is cumulative. One could read, say, the seventh chapter of First Corinthians by itself and have a pretty good notion of what Paul's argument was about. That is not the case in Romans. Much confusion about Paul's argument in Romans stems from paying too little attention to the context within which the argument appears. For that reason, summaries of Paul's argument have been included, and they appear more frequently and are more extensive as the comments move toward the end of Paul's argument in the letter. Because Paul's argument in Romans is cumulative, one will best understand the letter if one reads it from beginning to end. The same is true of this commentary, but for those for whom that is not possible, the summaries will call attention to the context within which a given passage appears.

A second characteristic of this commentary (also shared by the other volumes in this series) is the fact that it is intended to aid those who see Romans as a part of the Scripture of the church and who seek in it resources for the tasks of preaching and teaching within the church.

To understand Romans in that way, as the Scripture of the church, means to understand it as part of the larger canon. To understand Romans in that larger context means to anticipate that other writings included in that canon will shed light on dimensions of meaning in Romans that would otherwise remain obscure, if not hidden altogether. Christian worship practices have recognized the canonical character of Scripture by including in their lectionary readings passages from both Old and New Testaments, in that way calling attention to the fact that new light is shed on parts of the canonical literature when they are read in connection with other parts of that literature. To call attention to that dimension in the teaching and preaching of the message of Romans, there is frequently included in the discussion of the individual units in this commentary an indication of the light the canonical context can cast on it. Where a given passage from Romans has been regarded by various Christian traditions as appropriate for a particular Sunday in

23

the church year, that fact is often acknowledged, but the comments are not related exclusively to that Sunday, nor to any prescribed lectionary system. The indication of various passages from the Old Testament and the Gospels which give added substance to the points made in Romans is intended rather to serve a paradigmatic purpose, namely to show what it means to understand passages from Romans as part of the canonical Scriptures of the church.

The reader will find comments at the conclusion of each passage divided into reflections appropriate for the preacher and for the teacher. That division is of course not meant to be in any way exclusive. The preacher often faces the task of teaching the faith from the pulpit, and the announcement of the good news contained in Jesus Christ is part of the regular purpose of the effective church school teacher. The division is intended simply to help those engaged in preaching and teaching to begin appropriate reflection on the passage from Romans.

In addition to the comments about Paul's theology in broader scope and the comments on the nature of the argument in this epistle which are contained in this Introduction, four *Reflections* have been included within the body of the commentary. These *Reflections* are self-contained essays on topics which play an important role in Paul's argument. To confine their consideration to one passage would have been less helpful. They have been placed in juxtaposition to those parts of the letter where they are appropriate. References to a given *Reflection* are then made where that topic reappears. Suggestions for further reading are included at the end of each *Reflection.*

In the final analysis, the commentary has been shaped, and the limits of individual passages determined, as much as possible, by the structure and flow of thought in Romans itself. As the outline for the letter, on which the Table of Contents is based, will show, that means in some cases a different division of the letter than that indicated by chapter divisions or that customarily followed by other commentators. That is simply further reason to use this commentary in conjunction with others in order that the contributions of each may be appreciated. The goal, in the end, is to understand what the Apostle to the Gentiles wanted to say to his readers in Rome, and it is to that end that this commentary seeks to make a contribution.

OUTLINE OF ROMANS

INTERPRETATION

PART ONE

God's Lordship and the Problem of the Past: Grace and Wrath

ROMANS 1:1—4:22

If "what's past is prologue," it appears to be nothing other than a prologue to disaster. No sooner does Paul announce that he is writing about the gospel as God's power of salvation for all who trust him (1:14–17) than he turns to a discussion of wrath (1:18). That discussion, which covers the opening section of Paul's letter to the Christians in Rome (1:18—3:20), is a litany of failure and rebellion on the part of all humanity (3:9–18). It is a story of denying the God who is God and choosing instead to put non-gods in his place (1:18–23). It is a story of God's chosen people ignoring the law God gave them to guide their lives and doing instead the very things that law opposed (2:17–24). It is a story which shows clearly enough that the only response a righteous God could make to that past would be wrath and destruction.

Paul includes such a past as part of the proclamation of his *gospel* (1:14–15), because despite the universal spread of sin and rebellion and the inevitable consequences those acts brought after themselves (1:24–32; 2:24), the final story is not a story of destruction but of salvation (3:21–30). If the conclusion of humanity's past is universal sin, the reaction of God is to invite universal trust in him through his Son Jesus Christ.

It is precisely that fact that gives us the clue to understanding how Paul sees the past. Paul is not viewing it from some neutral perspective, taking into account the total sweep of the past and casting up a balance in view of all acts of all people. On the contrary, Paul is viewing the past from a very specific perspective, namely the perspective of Christ. That is why he sees the whole of humanity's past as the story of sin and rebel-

27

lion. That is also why he sees in Abraham the key to understanding the way God reacts to that past (3:31—4:22). God does not leave himself without witnesses to his purposes, and in Abraham we have the clue to the divine solution to universal sin. In Abraham the first intimations of universal faith can be seen (4:2–3, 13–17). Therefore, it is not the whole past of humanity that is the prologue to God's future; but rather a very specific strand in that past, namely, the strand woven by the existence of God's chosen people Israel. But it is not even the whole past of Israel which is the prologue to God's future. Rather it is specifically Abraham, the father of that chosen people, who represents in his response to the God who calls him the solution to the sinful mess into which humanity, including the chosen people, have gotten themselves.

To understand the way in which the past is prologue to present and future therefore is in the first instance to understand the nature of that past as sin which deserved wrath. But more, it is to understand that in the midst of that sin and rebellion the sign appeared that pointed to God's plan to rescue his creation from the disaster it had brought upon itself. Paul's task in this first section of his letter therefore is to outline the nature of that past and to point to Abraham as the clue to understanding Christ as God's way out for a humanity wallowing in its self-inflicted morass.

Introduction and Opening Remarks

ROMANS 1:1–13

The proverb "Make a good beginning, and you're half the way to winning" held true for Paul as he faced the task of writing a letter to some churches he had never visited, and it holds true for us when we attempt to understand what Paul meant to say in that letter. The beginning of Paul's letter to Rome presents us with an interesting mixture of the conventional and the innovative, and an understanding of that mixture will set us off on the right track for understanding his message.

28

Faithful to the letter-writing conventions of his day, Paul begins this letter by identifying himself as sender (1:1–6), greets the receivers (1:7), and expresses a prayer on their behalf (1: 8–10) before he begins his message. Yet in each case he expands on the customary formula for beginning a letter, and those expansions tell us much about him and his message. For that reason, we must look at them carefully.

The first thing to notice is that Romans is a letter from Paul, period. Contrary to his usual practice (in those letters whose authenticity is not disputed), he mentions no one else at the beginning of this letter. Even in his letter to the Galatians, where his apostleship was at issue, he mentioned in addition to himself "all the brethren who are with me" (Gal. 1:2). That makes the omission of any mention of co-senders for this letter all the more significant. To be sure, the naming of co-senders implies that they share with Paul responsibility for the content of the letter. Such a letter should therefore be understood as a formulation of the commonly-held Christian tradition. Omission of co-senders in the letter to Rome may very well be intended to make clear that in this letter we confront what Paul intended to be a statement of his own understanding of the gospel of Christ.

If that is the case, then we have in this epistle a unique insight into Paul's theology. Here we see, in its clearest form, the theology he had developed as he carried out his task of preaching the gospel to the eastern Mediterranean world. Here is the theology for which Paul is willing to take sole responsibility, something he did not do, for whatever reason, in any of his other letters. But why in this letter?

Paul had now completed that task of proclaiming the good news of Jesus Christ in the area in which he had been traveling (15:19, 23*a*), and he was now ready to undertake its proclamation in the western half of that world (15:24). If Rome is to support Paul in this enterprise, as he obviously hopes they will, they need to know more about his understanding of the gospel than they have been able to glean from those of Paul's acquaintance who have settled there. This letter is therefore very likely intended to lay the theological groundwork for Rome's support of his mission to the western part of their world. It is this theology, this understanding of the ways of a righteous and merciful God with his creation that Paul now sets about expounding.

If this letter is different because of the omission of co-

29

senders, it is also different because Paul expands on his normal self-identification as sender. To be sure, Paul normally includes more by way of identification than simply his name, but even that customary "more" is expanded in Romans. Into the midst of this self-identification (1:1, 5–6), Paul has inserted what may well have been a traditional statement about Jesus, which he has then shaped for his own purposes. What results is a sweeping christological statement about the significance of that Jesus. It is just this christological insertion, as we shall see, which sets the tone and the substance of the discussion which follows. In those three verses (1:2–4), we have summarized for us the entire sweep of God's relation to us and to his whole creation: The chosen people, to whom a messiah (Christ) was promised (v. 2), the birth of messiah to that people (v. 3), and the resurrection of that messiah which established messiah as Lord of all the peoples (v. 4; cf. Phil. 2:9–11). It is precisely that sweep which Paul explicates in the remainder of his letter. The "theme" for Paul's letter is thus announced here in its very opening verses.

Although Paul's self-identification as sender of this letter shows a development on the customary Hellenistic form, unique even for the other letters of Paul, his expansion on the greeting is the one he is accustomed to use: "grace" *(charis)*, a word play on the normal Greek greeting *(chairein,* greetings), is combined with "peace" (Heb., shalom), the normal Hebrew greeting. Yet even here there is a symbolism which ought not to be missed, for that combination of greetings signals what is also one of Paul's chief concerns in this letter, as it was in his mission as a whole; namely, the universal applicability of the gospel. As in this greeting, so in the gospel, Hebrew and Greek (i.e., gentile) lose their absolute distinction, and without either disappearing, both are combined in the gospel message of God's caring and redeeming love. Indeed, it is just that universality which, as we will see, is the theme of Romans; and Paul turns to it (v. 14) as soon as the formalities of the customary letter are concluded.

While the "prayer" in the customary Hellenistic letter normally confined itself to a vague sort of wish for the recipient's well-being, Paul usually expanded it to include the concerns which had motivated that particular letter. He does the same thing here. In this instance, his expansion on the prayer of good wishes introduces his apology for neglecting to visit the Christians in Rome. In addition, Paul's respect for the maturity of the

30

faith of the Christians in Rome is evident in the care he takes in stating what his impending visit there will mean: not only what he has to offer to them (vv. 11, 13) but also what they have to offer to him (v. 12). Good preaching is never a one-way street. Only those who listen are also able to preach or teach.

The prayer which stated Paul's concern over his neglect of the churches in Rome and his impending visit there has in its turn moved into the primary concern of his letter, namely, a statement of the gospel as he understands it (beginning with v. 14).

That is the way Paul has made the "good beginning" of his letter to the churches in Rome. If in making that beginning Paul has used a combination of the conventional and the innovative, there is every reason to think he will continue in that vein in the remainder of the letter. There was surely much that the first readers of this letter found conventional, just as there were surely parts they found innovative and startling. The same is true of contemporary readers. Much that we shall find in the pages of this epistle will conform to our normal understanding of the faith, and of Paul's theology. But a careful study of Romans will also show that Paul's innovative power is as strong in our day as it was in his own and many surprises lie in wait. The surprises are both exciting and instructive, and Paul through this letter to the churches in Rome extends to us, as he did to its first readers, the invitation to undertake with him such a voyage of discovery.

There is much in these opening verses which is useful for the proclamation of the gospel and for teaching its significance. Paul's opening verses, which clearly show the Messiah, Jesus, as the fulfillment (vv. 3–4) of God's promise to his chosen people, echoes a theme which is prominent throughout the whole of the Bible. The conviction that God fulfills his promises lies not only at the heart of the story of the chosen people, occuring as fulfillment of God's promise to Abraham (see Gen. 12:1–3), it also underlies the Christian conviction that Jesus is the one promised as fulfillment of the promises of a final redemption made to that chosen people. That Jesus is God's anointed one (Christ means "anointed" in Greek; Messiah means "anointed" in Hebrew) is therefore to be understood against the background of God's history with his chosen people, or it will not be understood at all.

When Paul begins with the announcement that in Jesus

God has fulfilled his promises of redemption, he announces a theme which is also prominent in the Gospels. Matthew, for example, finds the very birth of Jesus (1:18–25) to be the fulfillment of a deliverance promised by God through the prophet Isaiah (7:5–17). That way of beginning the story of Jesus as the fulfillment of God's promises recorded in the Old Testament is also found in the other Gospels.

Yet God's promise was fulfilled in Jesus in a way not wholly expected by that chosen people. As Matthew shows in the use and interpretation of the passage from Isaiah 7, fulfillment is also a new and startling beginning. That is why these passages would be appropriate to Advent: The fulfillment found in Jesus as the Anointed of God is also God's new beginning with his creation. If redemption is the fulfillment of a promise, it is also the announcement of a new stage in God's dealing with his creation. The old taken up, fulfilled, and made new is thus appropriate for Advent, as it was appropriate for the way Paul chose to begin his letter to the Christians in Rome.

The passage from Isaiah which Matthew finds fulfilled in Jesus', birth, when linked to the opening verses of Romans, lets us see the point Paul is making from yet another perspective. The reluctance of Ahaz to accept a sign from God (Isa. 7:10–12), a reluctance which cannot hinder the giving of the sign, points to the fact that that relationship between God and humanity is finally God's doing, and not our earning. That is of course also the point of the birth of Jesus from the virgin: Human activity, whether religious or biological, is finally unable to accomplish the birth of the deliverer. God's grace is based on his mercy, not our merit. That is also the point of Paul's emphasis on our being righteous by faith, rather than by our own accomplishments ("works of the law"). It is because it is God who promises, and God who fulfills in his own time and in his own way, that we have confidence that that promise will in fact be fulfilled. It is God's mercy that is reliable, not our response to it, or our acts in earning it. Finally, Paul's gospel calls us to trust in God, not in ourselves, a call echoed in the sign given to the reluctant Ahaz and in the astonishing birth of Jesus in a way beyond normal expectations.

32

Another perspective on the new element which regularly accompanies God's fulfillment of his promises lies in Paul's emphasis in these opening verses on his own call to win the obedience of the gentiles. The blessing God had promised to his chosen people is, with the resurrection of Christ, extended to the whole of creation. The promised blessing is no longer limited by birth, it is opened by new birth (Paul will discuss that more fully in chap. 6). In what is likely to be an echo of the convictions that came to Paul with his conversion, he tells the Roman Christians that grace is now offered to all in Christ; and he, Paul, has been charged to be the agent of that offering (see II Cor. 5:17–20). The very message of grace is a part of that grace. That is what gives the gospel its power, a point Paul will turn to in the next verses (esp. v. 16). That of course is why Paul feels compelled to visit Rome, lest they be denied some fuller understanding of the power of God's grace given in Jesus Christ.

It is thus the very message of grace to gentiles that shows the newness of what God has done in fulfilling his promise to the chosen people through Jesus. The fulfillment of that promise has opened the gate of "chosen people" to any who accept and trust the news of God's grace. What had been promised to Abraham is therefore now also our heritage, and Abraham is now also our forefather in the faith (Paul will make this explicit in chap. 4). The whole history of the chosen people is thus now to be rethought and appropriated as the personal history of each one who finds in Jesus Christ God's gift of grace to all peoples. We are to appropriate the Old Testament as our own history, we gentiles who have accepted Christ, the seed of David, as God's Son, anointed with power through his rising from the dead.

If this passage is appropriate for Advent, it would also thus be appropriate for Easter. It is precisely through his resurrection that Jesus opens the way to God for all peoples. That is a note to be struck in Advent as well, when sentimentality at the birth of a baby may not be allowed to overcome knowledge of the violent death—death for our sake—awaiting that babe. As the virgin birth marks off the beginning of Jesus' life as having its origin and meaning beyond the normal bounds of human experience and activity, so the resurrection marks the end of Jesus' earthly life as beyond that same activity and experience. Virgin birth and resurrection thus bracket the life of Jesus, reminding us that while Jesus was fully human, his life finds a meaning beyond the realm of normal human possibilities. If it did not, it could not be the source of a power which breaks the hold of sin on that humanity. Jesus Christ, risen from the dead

33

in the full power of God's own mighty Spirit, is the one to whom we look for our redemption, or we look in vain.

These themes, then, expressed and implied in the opening verses of Paul's letter to Roman Christians, will be explored in the following chapters of that letter. In them is contained what Paul understands to be the correct appropriation of God's promised blessing upon humankind. Christ is the key to a new beginning in the history of God with his creation, a new beginning that fulfills and recreates the promise made by the God of grace that he will be a blessing to us all, because in Christ God's gracious lordship, even over his rebellious creation, becomes visible.

The Gospel and God's Wrath

ROMANS 1:14—3:20

Paul begins his discussion of the gospel of God's grace, paradoxically enough, with a discussion of God's wrath. Yet they are, as Paul understands them, but the two sides of the same coin of the faithfulness of God to his promises made to Israel, and through Israel to all of humankind (cf. Gen. 12:3). As human sin preceded God's salvation made known in Christ, so in Romans a discussion of sin (1:18—3:20) precedes the first discussion of that salvation through Christ (3:21—4:22).

Romans 1:14—2:16
Universal Sin and Its Consequences

Although this passage involves an uninterrupted flow of argument—Paul announces the new element in his thought when he turns directly to the Jews in 2:17—it will be convenient to divide this passage, for the sake of discussion, into three component parts: 1:14–23; 1:24–32; and 2:1–16.

34

Creatures' Reaction to Creation: Idolatry (Romans 1:14–23)

Melanchthon once observed that one who was ignorant in matters of grammar was perforce also ignorant in matters of theology *(Ignotus in grammatica est ignotus in theologica)*. Although Melanchthon probably did not have these verses of Romans in mind when he coined that aphorism, they apply as though he had. We need here to pay especial attention to matters of grammar, particularly because the argument of Romans has so often been thought somehow to undergo a major shift in direction with 1:18, after the announcement of what is taken to be the doctrinal "theme" of Romans in 1:17 (i.e., righteousness by faith); see Introduction, pp. 10–14). We will do well therefore to rehearse carefully not only the vocabulary but also the grammar and syntax of what Paul says in these verses.

Grammatically, verse 17 is formed as a subordinate clause to verse 16, as verse 16 in its turn is grammatically subordinate to verse 15. That construction does not end with verse 17, however. Verse 18 is shaped in such a way as to be subordinate to 1:17, 1:19*b* is subordinate to 1:19*a* and 1:20 in its turn is subordinate to 1:19*b*. Such a long chain of subordinate clauses is unusual, to be sure, but if we want to understand what Paul is trying to say in these verses, this grammatical structure will have to be taken into account.

What is the point of this long string of subordinate clauses? They suggest that Paul understands each subordinate clause to give the reason for the statement which has preceded it, that is, the statement in verse 15 is supported by the point Paul makes in verse 16; verse 16 is then in its turn supported by the statement contained in verse 17, and so on down the line. It is immediately apparent, in that case, that the dominant statement of this chain of subordinate clauses is verse 15, for the support of which all the rest have been written. The whole chain of reasoning tells us why Paul is eager to preach the gospel to the Christians in Rome.

The subtlety of Paul's logic is greater than that, however, for we can learn much about his thought by noticing the order in which the subordinate clauses are given. Careful attention to them will give us the clue to the structure of Paul's thinking about his commission to preach the gospel. He is eager to preach the gospel (v. 15) because he is not ashamed of the gospel (v. 16*a*). He is not ashamed of the gospel (v. 16*a*) because

35

it is the power of God for salvation for all (v. 16b) and so on. To show more vividly the logical sequence of thought that moves through these clauses, and the way the sentences are linked to one another, we will, in the following translation, indicate by questions placed within parentheses what element of the preceding statement Paul seeks to explain in the subsequent sentence. In each case in the following translation, the "because" accurately reflects Paul's use of that word (*gar* in Greek), a point which can be easily overlooked when one is intent upon establishing verse 17 as the theme and verse 18 as the beginning of a new discussion. As we will see, Paul's grammar alone all but precludes such a division. Here, then, is the translation:

> [14]Both to Greeks and barbarians, both to wise and foolish, I am under obligation (to preach the gospel; so v. 5). [15]For that reason my purpose also to preach the gospel even to you who are in Rome. (Why even in Rome?) [16]Because I am not ashamed of the gospel. (Why am I not ashamed of it?) Because it is God's power for salvation for everyone who believes, Jew first and also Greek. (Why to everyone who believes?) [17]Because God's righteousness is revealed in it from faith for the purpose of faith, just as Scripture says: "The one who is righteous by faith shall live." (Why is God's righteousness needed in order to live?) [18]Because God's wrath is being revealed from heaven against every impiousness and wickedness of those people who are suppressing the truth by wickedness. (How do we know they are suppressing the truth out of wickedness?) Because what is known of God is plain to them. (Why is it plain to them?) [19]Because God made it plain to them. (But how can it be plain to them?) [20]Because God's unseen attributes, both his eternal power and deity, are seen from the creation of the world, perceived through the things God has done. (But why then the wrath?) [21]Because although they knew God they did not glory in him as God or give thanks to him, but they were made foolish in their reasonings, and their stupid minds were darkened. (What is the result of all that?) [22]Thinking they were wise, they fell into stupidity, [23]and they exchanged the glory of the immortal God for the likeness of the image of mortal humans and birds and animals and reptiles.

Several things are important to observe about the argument contained in those verses. Because Paul had completed his introduction with verse 13, he returns in verse 14 to his statement in verse 5, that he has been set apart to preach the gospel to the gentiles, and in these verses he proceeds to explain what that means. Paul's obligation to *preach* is grounded in the gospel, which alone represents the divine power necessary to effect salvation. His obligation to preach *to the gentiles* is grounded in the fact that, through faith in Christ, that power is now opened to them as well. The fact that that righteousness is to come by faith, rather than by birth, as it came during the period that the Jews alone were the chosen race, is therefore the way that salvation is opened to all humanity. If a human being of whatever race or background can stand before God on the basis of having trusted his purposes in Christ, then such salvation is now open to any who will so trust God.

That is the incredible good news announced in the gospel. That is why the gospel must be brought to all people of every race and every cultural attainment. With God's act in Christ, all former boundaries have been removed, those that had existed between Jews and gentiles as well as those that had stood between sinful humanity and a righteous God. It is therefore no longer our task to remove boundaries or impediments. Our task is to accept the good news that those boundaries have been removed and that our way to a righteous and merciful God is no longer barred by the race into which we have been born or by what we may have done in the past. It is Paul's good news that God has remained true to his promise to provide, through Abraham, a blessing to all humankind. He has done it in Christ, who was the seed of Abraham as he was the seed of David to whom everlasting rule for his seed was promised (see II Sam. 7:12–16). God has therefore remained true and faithful to his covenant word. In that way he has shown himself to be "righteous" (see *"Reflection: Righteousness in Romans"*).

God's faithfulness to his promises, his "righteousness," however, is not something to be trifled with. To abuse God's offer of salvation, to imagine that God is something other than he is, the sovereign Lord and sole Creator of all that exists, brings in its train terrible consequences. If God is faithful to his covenant promises, he is also faithful to his own nature as God; and to refuse to acknowledge him as divine Creator and Lord is to remove oneself from any possibility of fellowship with him. Not to acknowledge him as Creator and Lord is to remove oneself from his lordship, and the results of that are simply terrifying. As Paul makes clear, rejecting the God who is the Father of Jesus Christ as our Lord does not remove us from all lords. All it does is remove us from the benevolent lordship of God and place us under the tyrranical lordship of something completely unworthy of our submission to it. Such lordships are incapable of exercising their lordship in any but the most destructive way.

37

When we exchange lords in that way, Paul claims, we have handed ourselves over to some creature instead of to the Creator. Ignoring the clear evidences of God's lordship, human beings instead chose for themselves other lords. Inevitably, one comes to resemble that to which one gives oneself in devotion. If therefore instead of giving our devotion to a benevolent God and his gracious Son we give our devotion to lords of a bestial nature (Paul names birds and beasts and reptiles), is it to be wondered that we ourselves finally become bestial?

Are we really to take that seriously? People in Paul's day may have worshiped idols in the form of eagles or lizards or lions or whatever, but no one, other than some hidden aborigines, do that in our day. Is this not a clear example of history having outrun any meaning we might find in Paul's writings? Yet worship of things bestial in nature need not be so crude as to kneel before the statue of some animal. Will anyone who reads contemporary newspapers or watches television network news deny that our society shows signs of bestiality? Does that not reflect the "idols" to which we give our devotion? If in our desire to overcome a competitor in whatever area, whether as student or professional, whether as husband or wife, whether as business man or woman, we take as our model the rapacious drive of the beast of prey, sweeping all aside in our desire to overcome, is it any wonder that our society becomes bestial? If our goals are set with no final regard for the will of the true God as expressed in Jesus Christ, is it any wonder that we become less than we as human beings made in God's image ought to be? Do we not in fact come to resemble the "idols" to which we devote our lives?

Yet there is even a more insidious result of rejecting God as our Lord, and that is to take as Lord—ourselves. That we are totally incapable of functioning as our own creator, and hence as our own Lord, does nothing to hinder us. Thus we show our incorrigible ignorance. Substituting the darkness of our own desires for the light of God as Lord of creation, we grope about, lashing out at all who hinder our futile desire to function as our own Lord. Such substitution of creature for Creator, of ourselves as Lord in place of the Father of Jesus Christ, is nothing other than idolatry.

38

That is precisely the point Paul is making here. The root of the human malaise, of human sin, is the substitution of something other than God the Creator and Father of Jesus Christ as lord. It is the temptation to which Adam and Eve succumbed: the temptation to become God, and hence Lord, themselves (see Gen. 3:5); and it is, in Paul's view, the continuing root of our malaise. The good news of the gospel is that we no longer have to take upon ourselves this terrible, destructive necessity of becoming our own lord. We are free in Christ to accept the creator for the Lord he is.

We are to be under no illusions in this matter. It is not a question of whether or not we are to have a lord over us. As creatures, we have no choice in the matter. The only question is, What sort of lordship will it be? Whatever lordship it is—wealth, male chauvinism, feminism, racism—it will claim us as its own and use us to our own destruction in its malevolent purposes.

If the way to salvation lies in accepting the good news that we need no longer be under the lordship of any creation but rather under the lordship of a benevolent Creator, rejecting that good news brings in its wake terrible consequences. What those consequences are and how the wrath of God works itself out in them is the subject of the next segment of Paul's argument.

That there is much here for the preacher to ponder and then proclaim, and for the teacher to understand and then expound, needs hardly to be said. Paul's point that the key to the human malaise is idolatry, which is to be understood as having as lord someone or some thing other than the Father of our Lord Jesus Christ is the key to this passage. Examples of such idolatry will multiply themselves for anyone who contemplates seriously the state of the world. These verses provide a means of analyzing both human society and human nature, and careful reflection on them will enable Paul's message to be presented to our world with considerable force. A modern theologian who understood Paul's point with particular clarity was Reinhold Niebuhr, and careful consideration of his work, even of his shorter books, will enable the preacher and teacher to see how Paul's insight can be used in analyzing our contemporary scene.

Creator's Reaction to Idolatry: Permissiveness (Romans 1:24–32)

The most frightening thing about this passage is the way Paul describes God's punishment for the sin of idolatry. It is frightening simply because, had Paul not told us they were signs of wrath, we could easily have mistaken them for signs of grace! When God visits his wrath in the way described in this passage, there is no divine cataclysm, no fire from on high sent to consume sinful society. Rather, the wrath which God visits on sinful humanity consists in simply letting humanity have its own way. The punishment of sin is therefore simply—sin! God, says Paul, delivers sinful humanity over to its own desires. In a move that our contemporary world shows is perhaps the most terrifying thing God could do, God punishes sin by letting us have control over our own destinies. God's wrath therefore does not mean some divine restraint imposed as punishment on humanity. Rather, that wrath gives us a free hand to do whatever our desires incline us to do. The way God in his wrath delivers humanity over to the just punishment of sin is to become permissive. He withdraws the gracious power of his absolute lordship and allows other lordships to prevail.

God's wrath, in sum, consists in letting humanity carry out the results of its idolatrous rejection of the Creator as Lord. That our present world and our own society begin to resemble ever more closely what Paul describes in verses 24–28 should therefore be seen in this perspective. Freedom for us to do what we want is the punishment of our rebellion against God. A celebration of life freed from the constraints of the Word of God is therefore a celebration of the visitation of God's wrath upon humankind.

Paul shows here a lively sense of what is appropriate in relation to our use of the created world. It is abuse of that world, through idolatry, that leads into sin, just as it is abuse of the created order of male and female, for example, in which the fearful consequences of that sin make themselves felt. "What is more just," Luther asked, "than that those who turn away from the glory of God should be dishonored, not only in their hearts (and this is idolatry) but also in their bodies?" Idolatry is not something left in the spiritual realm. It makes itself felt in the physical realm as well, since both are created by God, are subject to his lordship, and hence are perverted when that lordship is denied.

40

It is clear for Paul that we as creatures have a responsibility to use creation properly, both in the way we live life as individuals and as we live it in relation to others. God is the one who ordered the created world, and any abuse of that created order is an insult to the one who ordered it. Such an insult, Paul makes clear, will not go unpunished.

The violation of the created order in human sexuality is therefore, as Paul understands it, an outgrowth of the violation of the created order, a violation whose root lies in idolatry. For Paul, the kind of life he describes, (vv. 26–27) "women exchanged natural relations for unnatural, . . . men committing shameless acts with men," cannot be understood as an alternate life-style, somehow also acceptable to God. It is, as Paul understands it, a sign of one of the forms God's wrath takes when he allows us free reign to continue in our abuse of creation and in our abuse of one another as creatures. Such conduct may not be celebrated as another expression of God's grace. It is clearly portrayed here as a sign of God's wrath. When the created order is abused in idolatry, in denying the lordship of God, the consequences into which humanity is delivered are the consequences of wrath. On that there is no question for Paul.

The exchange of the truth about God for a lie which brings with it the dishonoring of bodies also brings with it the disordering of society, a point Paul also makes unavoidable. The list of vices Paul gives is not exhaustive, it is illustrative. This is the improper conduct that destroys decent society among God's creatures. Those who are quick to condemn the homosexual and lesbian practices described in verses 26–28 should be careful, lest in the form that that condemnation takes they themselves display the destructiveness of deceit, malignity, or gossip, all of which are equally signs of the rampant permissiveness which characterizes the wrath of God (vv. 29–31). The "evil . . . malice . . . strife" (v. 29) that characterize a racist attitude are therefore as surely a sign of a society under wrath as is homosexuality. The point of the passage is not to find reasons to feel superior in the condemnation of others. It is to repent of sin and to pray desperately for forgiveness for ourselves and our society.

It may strike us as odd that Paul (v. 32) seems to think approving such acts is worse than doing them, but what he is pointing to is the fact that those who do such things not only do them in their own lives but make them a matter of public encouragement for others to follow. Not content to let wrath take its course in their own lives, such people, Paul says, seek

41

to make the measure of their sinful conduct the norm for the conduct of others. It is the desire to make private sin the measure of public conduct that Paul is condemning here.

So here we are, we rebellious peoples, glorying in the freedom we think to be grace, only to be told by Paul it is instead the fearful punishment of sin and a manifestation of God's wrath. The permissiveness we celebrated as a world "come of age" we now find to be nothing more than the permission to fall deeper into sin. When God visits his wrath, he withdraws his restraining hand and lets his rebellious creation do as it pleases. In such a context, God's law is clearly a manifestation of his gracious order, rather than a wrath-filled reaction to our human disorder. Divine discipline is the measure of grace, as divine permissiveness is the measure of wrath. A society in which discipline is disappearing and in which anything is permitted is, in light of this passage, clearly a society suffering under the wrath of God. Grace, it would appear, is God's act of exercising his lordship over his creation in spite of creation's rebellion. Unless that lordship is forthcoming, creation is doomed. We will see that God's lordship, God's "righteousness," was (and is) reestablished in Christ; but Paul has not yet finished with his catalog of the fearsome consequences of rejecting that lordship. The human desire for self-justification continues to operate in all of this—how quick we are to identify those awful other people who do the things deserving of God's wrath, and how loath we are to admit that what we do similarly deserves it. It is to that problem that Paul next turns his attention.

There is obviously much in this passage which bears on the preacher's task of proclaiming the gospel to contemporary society. How strikingly similar are the problems we face in our society to the problems Paul describes as facing his! This passage presents an opportunity to make clear what grace and sin are and to point out that as Paul describes them they tend to be just the opposite of what we normally think. Letting us have our own way is not a measure of God's grace, it is the visitation of his wrath. The discipline which does not let us do whatever comes into our heads is not a form of evil, it is the very essence of grace. In that light it can be seen that to put oneself under the lordship of God is an act that opens us up to grace and protects us from wrath, for it is that lordship whose discipline keeps us from ruining our lives with idolatry, and all the consequences of it Paul has been describing. The gracious dimension

42

of discipline, whether divine, societal, or parental, is a message that needs very much to be heard in many segments of our society. Abusive discipline is of course not gracious, but lack of discipline appears, in light of this passage, to be equally evil. Discipline in family life, within the church fellowship, within other institutions—such as schools and social organizations, as well as within national life—all fall under the purview of this text.

The teacher preparing to base instruction on this text should recall that the human predicament in Paul's view results from idolatry, from rejecting the lordship of the Creator, and from putting in its place the lordship of some creature. Whether idolatry be subjection to an idol shaped in the likeness of some creature or subjection to some ideology shaped by the mind of some creature, the result is the same. Through such an abuse of creation, we become something other than we were intended to be. That is the gist of Paul's exposition in these verses.

There are of course many ways creation can be, and regularly is, abused; and the teacher can aid the class in understanding what Paul is about in this passage by developing some of those ways. Such abuse may take the form of the exploitation of the earth, where land is cultivated in such a way that the land is destroyed, or minerals are extracted in a way that renders the land useless for any further human benefit. While such abuse of creation is implied in what Paul says, and can legitimately be developed in an effort to understand the point of the passage, however, the teacher should also remember that such are not the abuses Paul chooses to discuss. The abuses resulting from the rejection of the lordship of the Creator which Paul singles out all have to do with relationships among human beings, and this ought to be the major point of the lesson.

No One Is Excluded from Judgment (Romans 2:1–16)

There is a popular saying that it is not what one knows but whom one knows that is important. By contrast, the point Paul is making in this passage is that it is not what one knows but what one does that is the important thing. This contrast between knowing and doing is also seen in terms of the contrast between appearance and reality. Whenever one speaks of the difference between appearance and reality, however, one is immediately drawn into the problem of judging which is which, so this passage is also concerned with judgment. Seeing the way

43

Paul weaves these themes together in this passage aids us in understanding Paul's thought in this part of Romans, as it aids us in understanding our part in God's creation. For that reason, the passage deserves careful consideration.

Paul turns in this passage to draw some preliminary conclusions from the argument that the visitation of divine wrath (1:18) takes the form of God's allowing human beings to do whatever they desire (1:24, 26, 28). The point is clear: Since everyone is involved in the self-indulgence brought about by idolatry and made possible by God's withholding divine discipline, no one is in a position to judge others as though the one judging were morally superior.

The logical structure which underlies Paul's movement from 1:32 to 2:1-3 is rather compact, but the structure is nonetheless there and can be discerned. The connection can be laid out in the following way. If, as Paul argued in 1:32, applauding evil (i.e., giving it public recognition) is as bad as doing that evil, can one argue that the converse is equally true? That is, can one argue that condemning evil is as good as not doing it, so that simply by condemning it, one can avoid the consequences for the evil one does do? Paul's answer is a resounding No (2:1-3)! To continue to do evil, under any guise, is wrong; and those who do evil gain nothing by their condemnation of it. The problem here lies in the mistaken impression that God's willingness to let evil go unpunished means there will be no judgment on it at all. That is, however, completely to misunderstand the reason for such a delay. That delay occurs not because God is indifferent to evil. It occurs rather in order to give the evil-doers a chance to repent of previous evil, not give them time in which to do more (v. 4); but that delay is not permanent. There will in fact be a day of reckoning when all will receive their due reward (vv. 5-10).

When that day comes, no one will be able to avoid judgment by pleading special or extenuating circumstances of whatever kind, because in the matter of such judgment, God is impartial (v. 11). He remains the universal God with universal purposes about whom Paul began to speak in this portion of Romans (see the section beginning with 1:14 above). That means that all people, those with the Law (the Jews) as well as those without it (gentiles), will have to give account for what they have done (vv. 12-16).

That line of argument contains within it a problem, how-

44

ever, and it must be considered before we venture further exposition of this passage. The problem lies in 2:14 and centers on the phrase "by nature." The phrase as it is placed in the Greek sentence could be construed either with the phrase "who do not have the law" or with the phrase "do what the law requires." Most translators assume that it goes with the latter phrase, and that, used adverbially, it describes how gentiles accomplish things that the law requires, that is, "naturally" or "by nature." That of course raises the problem: If gentiles know by nature what is good and then do it, they are morally superior to the Jews, who need the law to tell them what is good and how to do it. Such inherent moral superiority of gentiles over Jews not only makes the chosen people morally inferior to all others but it also makes nonsense of Paul's argument, which intends to show that all people are equally under condemnation (see 3:9). In fact, careful attention to the way Paul uses the phrase "by nature" in other places shows that this is not what he meant at all.

In every other instance in Paul's letters, the phrase which conveys the sense of "by nature" is used not adverbially, to describe an action, but adjectivally, to characterize further some group. That would mean, if we want to be consistent with the way Paul normally employs the phrase, we ought to relate the phrase in 2:14, not with "do the law," but rather with "have not the law." Paul is describing gentiles who "by nature" (by birth) do not have the law (are not members of the house of Israel), not gentiles who "by nature" (inherently) do what the law requires (God's will). That in turn results in the following translation: "For when gentiles, who by nature (by birth into a particular people) do not possess the law, do the things the law speaks about, those who do not have the law are a law for themselves" (we will consider the meaning of the second half of the sentence below). Such an understanding of this verse, completely in line with Paul's usual employment of the phrase "by nature," implies no claims about any inherent moral superiority on the part of the gentiles and is consistent with Paul's larger argument. For those reasons, it is most probably what Paul intended the verse to say.

This verse appears in the midst of a group of verses which point to the universal scope of God's judgment, and that group of verses in turn is part of the larger discussion of the universal scope of his salvation, which began with 1:14. This group of

45

verses (vv. 11–16) is designed to show why it is that even the chosen people can expect judgment: The point is that knowing about the good (e.g., having God's law) is not the important thing, it is doing the good that God wants. Again, as in 1:16–23, Paul has constructed a series of sentences, each of which gives the reason for what is stated in the preceding sentence. A rehearsal of his argument, with the assumed questions again within parentheses, will make this clear. Because verses 7–10 spell out the implications of God's impartial judgment announced in verse 6, we will include verses 9–10 in the translation so the connection with verses 11–16 is clear.

> [9]There will be tribulation and anxiety for every human being who brings about evil, for the Jew first and also for the Greek. [10]But there will be glory and honor and peace for everyone who does the good, for the Jew first and also for the Greek. (Why for the gentiles as well as for the Jews, the chosen people?) [11]Because God is no respecter of persons. (How can one say that?) [12]Because as many as sin without the law will perish without the law, and as many as sin with the law God will judge by means of the law. (Why does he judge his chosen people, who, after all, listen to his law?) [13]Because it is not the hearers of the law who are righteous with God, but rather those who do the law are the ones whom God will justify. (But how can the gentiles be justified by doing what the law wants if they don't have that law?) [14]Because when the gentiles, who do not by nature belong to the people of the law, nevertheless do things the law requires, then those who don't have the law show they are a law for themselves. (How can one say they are a law for themselves?) [15]Because they show that things the law requires are written on their hearts, to which their consciences are also a witness, along with the discussions they have with one another, witnesses which accuse, or even excuse them, [16]on that day when God judges the secrets of people, as I preach in my gospel through (the power of) Christ Jesus.

The issue in all of this is appearance as against reality, which to Paul's way of thinking leads directly to the issue of human responsibility. That connection is displayed by the kind of question Paul raises in these verses. Is the appearance of doing what is right enough? That is to say, do we show our solid moral stature when we righteously condemn others for their evil acts (2:1)? Does such condemnation of evil not display the righteous nature of those who carry out the condemnation? No, says Paul, not when those who condemn others are also involved in what they condemn. Indeed, their own moral insensitivity is displayed precisely by that fact: They condemn in

46

others an involvement in evil of which they themselves are also guilty.

God is not fooled by such pretense. He will hold all people responsible for what they do. It is not enough to know about the good if one does not do it. If there is one thing Paul is clear about, it is the unavoidable scope and consequence of human responsibility. God expects his creatures—he expects us—not just to know about the good or to talk about it but to do it. If that holds for Jews as well as non-Jews here, it is clear Paul thinks it holds for Christians as well as non-Christians too (see I Cor. 3:11–15). One may know who God is and who his Son is and therefore what the good is; but if such knowledge does not lead to doing what is good, it is vacuous and of no avail. God's grace does not deliver us from responsibility for what we do. Paul is convinced that we will all finally have to answer to God for what we have made of the life God has given us. That is part of the task laid on all creatures by the Creator.

It is for that reason that the sign of grace to the chosen people was a law, which told them what it was God wanted them to do. It was for that reason that the Jews treasured that law as a manifestation of God's favor, God's grace to them. If God's wrath means letting creatures do what they want (see 1:24–32), then God's grace means giving the creatures a means of discipline so that they do not fall into the trap of following their own desires, which, just because they are creatures, inevitably have evil consequences. If creatures are incapable of serving as their own creators, and hence of doing what is good on their own, then it is a sign of the grace of the Creator to give to such creatures a way to do good rather than evil. To receive God's law was therefore for the chosen people the supreme sign of God's grace. To follow that law is to be responsible before God. To ignore it is to be irresponsible.

Yet by such logic, only the chosen people have any chance of doing what is good; and they alone could then be held responsible for doing what is evil. That point Paul cannot concede, since God is the Creator of all peoples, not just the Jews. God is therefore impartial in his goodness as he is in his judgment. Just as everyone knew enough about God to recognize him as Creator and hence themselves as creatures (1:19–20), so everyone has enough sense of what is good to be able to act responsibly before their Creator (2:14–15). There is therefore no partiality with God either in the matter of grace or in the matter

47

of judgment. Yet if judgment is universal, then so is the offer of the gospel of God's Son, a point Paul made at the very beginning of this part of his argument in Romans (see 1:16).

Finally, Paul's gospel of the power of God is a gospel of grace even when he points to the unavoidable responsibility for doing good laid upon every creature. Indeed, it is a gospel of grace precisely because it is a word of judgment and hence of responsibility. The power of Paul's gospel lies in its ability to shatter our illusion of self-sufficiency, the illusion that we can live under our own lordship. Judgment and grace are thus the same act: in the judgment on our own pretensions as creatures, our propensity to idolatry, to put some created thing in the place of the Creator—in that very judgment God's gracious desire to deliver us from that predicament is evident. That is why Paul can begin his discussion of the grace of God shown in his Son with a discussion of wrath. Wrath is itself finally a servant of the gracious purpose of God to restore his lordship over his rebellious creation.

Paul's gospel is therefore the divine word of power that shatters our illusions with its message of judgment and calls us to responsibility with its message of grace; and because the God who speaks that gracious word of power is the Creator of all, that word of power, of judgment and grace, is universal in its application. It is to further consideration of that universality that Paul turns in the next passage.

Perhaps the most powerful word for the preacher in this passage is its affirmation of the inescapable responsibility laid upon all creatures of God. The message of grace is not a message of indolence or irresponsibility. It is rather a summons to accept responsibility for one's acts and hence to act in a manner for which one is willing to assume responsibility. It is therefore a call to give up pretense and to come to terms with the kind of reality Paul has been describing. Again, it is clear from this passage that God's grace does not eliminate his judgment. Rather, by his grace we are allowed to live in a way that spares us from condemnation in that judgment. The relationship between appearance, idolatry, irresponsibility, on the one hand, and reality, the lordship of God, and responsible action, on the other, provides a further theme which could be profitably developed in a sermon.

The teacher working with this passage will find in it an opportunity both to summarize the course of Paul's argument in Romans to this point and to anticipate the direction the argument will take in the coming passages. In that light, it will be profitable to develop the contrast between appearance and reality and its relationship to grace and judgment. Underlying the whole argument is the universal applicability of all that Paul is saying, a point that comes to the fore in verses 6–12 and which underlies the discussion in verses 13–16. When Paul speaks of "Jew and gentile" he means to describe the whole of humanity, and the appearance of that phrase in this discussion is a further indication of the direction Paul's thought is taking.

Romans 2:17—3:8
The Jews Are Included, Despite the Law

Although these verses from the end of chapter 2 and the beginning of chapter 3 constitute a unity of thought for Paul, it will again be more convenient if we consider the passage in two parts: 2:17–29 and 3:1–8. In this passage, Paul for the first time directly addresses those who call themselves "Jews." Although some commentators have argued that Paul had already turned to address them in 2:1, it seems more likely that he had continued there to address all of humanity as he had been doing since 1:18. Of course the Jews had been included with the gentiles in 1:18—2:16 (see 2:9–10), but the shift to addressing them directly here in 2:17 makes it more likely that up to this point Paul has had both Jew and gentile in mind.

The Law and the Disadvantage of the Jews
(Romans 2:17–29)

Why turn here to address the Jews? Is it because Paul was himself a Jew and therefore preoccupied with the question? Was it because they represented a problem to the Christians in Rome to whom Paul was writing? Why single out the Jews?

Certainly it is true that Paul was himself a Jew, and by the time he was writing this letter the Jews whom the Roman emperor Claudius had expelled from Rome in A.D. 49 had begun to return and perhaps cause difficulties for the Christians. Yet Paul turns to speak of them here not because of any contemporary situation but because of their past relationship with God.

49

Any attempt to explicate the way a gracious God has dealt with his rebellious creatures, such as Paul is undertaking in the letter, must deal with the Jews simply because they have figured so prominently in those dealings between God and humanity. Paul therefore turns to the Jews because in the kind of argument he is following in this letter he cannot avoid it.

Paul here singles out the Jews precisely because their status as chosen people could have tempted one to assume they were exempt from the wrath of God about which Paul has been speaking. After all, their religious law did not prescribe the worship of idols. In fact, it forbade all such worship. As a result, one could assume, they could not have fallen prey to the kind of idolatry Paul described in Romans 1:23. In addition, they had known more, not less, about God than anyone else; and so 1:18-22 would not have applied to them either. That Paul was addressing faults of the gentiles in those verses would be immediately apparent to Paul's readers, since he was drawing on traditions current among the Jews as well when he condemned gentile idolatry and when he associated homosexual practices with gentile society. But Paul had already suggested that what he said applied in fact to Jews as well as to gentiles in 2:9-10, and with verse 17 he makes it unavoidably clear that he intends what he says about the universality of God's wrath to apply equally to the chosen people.

Paul begins by admitting as true everything the chosen people could claim by way of exempting themselves from God's wrath because of their chosen status. The New English Bible has a particularly good translation of this passage, and one would do well to read it carefully.

After conceding that the claims the Jews could make about themselves were true, Paul applies specifically to them what he had already applied to all humanity in 2:1-3, namely, they are guilty of doing precisely what they condemn. One ought not to read verses 21-22 as though Paul thought every Jew did every one of these things. As is always the case in Paul, this list is exemplary rather than exhaustive. The point once again is the contrast between words and deeds, between appearances and reality. That contrast becomes explicit in verses 25-27 and unavoidable in verses 28-29. It is in fact of no benefit at all to belong to the chosen people if what one does is in complete contrast to what one claims for oneself. If such a contradiction between what is claimed and what is done is the case, the result

50

is that God himself, who chose the Jews and gave them the law, is the object of ridicule rather than praise (v. 24). In that situation, there can be no possibility of any claim to exemption from divine wrath. Simply belonging to the chosen people, Paul says, is not enough. One must act the part or the marks of chosenness, law and circumcision, are rendered of no avail. True "chosenness," true "Jewishness," is not a matter of outward marks or appearances; it is a matter of inner reality, a reality perceived not by other people but by God, before whom such reality is honored and where the appearance, however honored by other human beings, is not. Echoing what he had said in 2:14–15, Paul affirms here that even those who do not belong to the chosen people can in fact do things the law requires and hence will act as judges of those who have only the appearance, not the reality, of chosenness (i.e., membership by birth in the chosen people, v. 27).

There is a problem here that has caused some commentators to suggest that the contrast is not so much between Jews and gentiles as between Jews and gentile Christians. After all, it is the Christians who Paul thinks will exercise judgment in the eschatological times (see I Cor. 6:3). Again, to claim that the requirements of God's law are "written on the heart" looks so much like the promised new covenant (Jer. 31: 31–34) that one could only imagine Paul thinking of its fulfillment within Christians. The reference to circumcision of the heart by spirit and not letter recalls II Corinthians 3:12–18 and Philippians 3:3 (see also Col. 2:11).

Yet the fact that Paul makes no reference at all to the new situation in Christ until 3:20, after he concludes his section on universal wrath, and the fact that the context is dominated by the contrast between appearance, or claims, and reality, make it more likely that he does in fact have gentiles, not gentile Christians, in mind. Paul's point is not that the law is written in the hearts of such gentiles. Rather, he is arguing that such gentiles are capable of doing some of the things the law requries, when, for example, they avoid murder or robbery or value truth or honesty in courts of law. What Paul is pointing to is simply the fact that the claim of the Jews to any exclusiveness on the basis of the content of their law must reckon with the fact that many of the virtues commanded in the law are also practiced by other peoples. Since that is the case, it is what one does, not what one has, that is important. Gentiles can no more escape

51

judgment by claiming not to have known either God (so 1:
19–20) or what he wanted of his creatures (so 2:14–15) than can
Jews escape that judgment simply by claiming that they belonged to a people to whom God had shown the grace of revealing his will in the law. Neither Jew nor gentile can escape God's
wrath and his future judgment, whether by reason of ignorance
or knowledge. God will judge impartially on the basis of performance alone (2:6), not on positive or negative claims regarding knowledge of him or of his will. In that context, it would
make no sense to introduce the idea of the fulfillment of the
covenant among the Christians (2:14) or to refer to the Christians' role in the coming judgment (2:27). The context thus
appears to require our understanding the gentiles as just that
and not as gentile Christians.

Paul continues in this section his argument that God's grace
confers with itself responsibility. We saw earlier that God's punishment for sin is the withholding of discipline from the sinners
(see section 1:24–32) and that for that reason the giving of a law
precisely for such discipline is an act of grace. In this section,
Paul is at pains to make clear that the gracious act of conferring
discipline carries with it the responsibility to enact that discipline in one's life. To be shown favor by God does not absolve
one from responsibility; rather it confers responsibility upon
one. There is no reason at all to think that Paul was being ironic
or sarcastic when he listed the claims made by the chosen people on their own behalf in 2:17–20. They relied on God's law
rather than on their own standards, they gloried in the living
God rather than in an idol, they knew God's will through study
of his law and hence could tell what was important from what
was not, all of which gave them the privilege as well as the
responsibility of telling others about this God and his will, to
lead others from darkness and foolishness to a knowledge of the
true God.

Yet if their actions belied such claims, their claims would
become hollow mockeries of the reality they proclaimed. Their
status as chosen of God did not excuse them from realizing
God's will for them in their concrete lives. Quite the contrary,
such knowledge laid upon them the responsibility to create that
reality.

It is clear in all this that the God of that chosen people,
whom we learned in the very first verses is also our God through
Jesus Christ (1:2–4), takes such responsibility on our part very

52

seriously and expects concrete results. Claims of past privileges avail nothing. God remains a God of concrete reality, as he is also the Creator of that reality. That is also true of the reality of grace. Unless the reality of grace, given concrete form in the life, death, and resurrection of Jesus, is also given concrete form in the life of those to whom the grace is given, that grace has not yet become the reality it is intended to become. Grace changes the reality it encounters; and where reality is not changed, grace has been rejected (see Matt. 18:23–35). God intends for his grace to produce concrete results; that is the message of these verses. Where such results do not appear, the reality of grace has not yet been fully realized (see v. 25). God expects us to *do* as well as know or we have made his grace of no avail. Grace, as Paul seeks to make clear, brings with it the responsibility to act on it.

A sermon on this text could well center on the power of grace to change the reality it encounters. Indeed, unless that change occurs, grace has been rejected. Using this passage with Jesus' parable about the servant who refused to grant the pardon to a fellow servant the king had granted him (Matt. 18: 23–35) will enable the preacher to present from the Gospel an illustration of the point Paul is making. Sermons on this passage ought above all to avoid smug contrasts between (presumably) virtuous Christians and (presumably) renegade Jews. Paul's point that even God's chosen people are responsible for their acts indicates that Christians have no grounds for hoping they will be exempt from that responsibility. Sermons on this passage will be sermons of challenge, not self-congratulation.

The passage presents the teacher with an opportunity to discuss the role of the chosen people in the history of God's dealings with rebellious humanity. What role were they to play, if their distinguishing mark, circumcision, depended for its validity on how they handled their responsibilities as chosen people? The idea that God calls to responsibility rather than privilege, to a task rather than to a status, is clear from this passage. That of course would apply equally to one's calling to be a Christian; and while Paul does not make that application here, the larger context of this letter makes it clear that it is not far from his mind. The application of this passage to a contemporary class might be enhanced by having members of the class substitute affirmative claims Christians might make about themselves for those Paul claims for the Jews (vv. 17–20). As in

53

the case of the sermon, however, the passage will be sorely misused if it becomes the occasion either for Christian self-congratulation or for self-righteous denigration of Jews, historical or contemporary.

The Law and the Advantage of the Jews (Romans 3:1–8)

At issue is the significance of God's call. What place does that call occupy in the way God deals with his rebellious creation? Of what use is it for those who are called? As in the preceding passage, the discussion here centers on the Jews.

Paul's argument proceeds with relentless logic. If, as he has said, circumcision has value only as it is put into practice through doing the will of God (2:25), and if those who do God's will are as good as circumcised even if the physical marks are lacking (2:26), then, logically enough, the question of the value of being a Jew in general, and of being circumcised in particular, must arise. If true Jewishness is internal, not external, and if circumcision must be understood spiritually rather than literally, then what is the value in being a circumcised Jew?

Instead of the answer one would expect—no real value—Paul's answer seems surprising: being a member of God's chosen people, the Jews, is in fact of great advantage. The greatest advantage of all is that the chosen people are the ones with whom God communicated and they are therefore the ones who know who God is. Even more, they are the ones to whom God gave the promise of the convenant, first to Abraham and then to David. God made promises to the Jews he made to no other people. That is their great advantage, rooted in their history. Indeed, apart from the act of God in freeing Israel from Egypt and giving it his law on Mount Sinai, there would have been no Israel at all. More than any other people, the Jews owed their existence as a people to God. That is their undeniable advantage, rooted in their very existence as a people.

The general word Paul used to describe such communication between God and Israel (Greek *logia*, oracles) is to be understood in the light of covenant promises, since it is just the issue of such mutual covenantal promises that Paul next raises. In a covenant, each side pledges something to the other: In the case of Israel, she promised to obey God's will (Exod 19:8) and God promised to hold Israel as his own people (Exod 19:7). It is also the case that when one covenant partner breaks the covenant promise the other partner is absolved from keeping his promise.

Now that poses a problem. We have seen that the Jews have not been faithful as a people to their covenant promise. God's wrath is universal, and the Jews have become a source of blasphemy rather than blessing in God's name (2:24). They have not been faithful to their covenant promise. Does that mean God will break his promise, as he has every right? To put it as Paul does, will human faithlessness to the covenant cause God to abandon his covenant promise (3:3)?

A great deal is at stake here. God has promised to Abraham that he and his descendants will be a blessing for all humankind (Gen. 12:1–9). If God now abandons that promise, as Israel has abandoned its promised activity, all of humanity will be affected. From the placement of the story of the promise to Abraham in Genesis 12, it is clear that Abraham represents God's new beginning with rebellious humanity, a rebellion that has dominated the narrative contained in Genesis 3—11. Abraham thus represents not only the beginning of Israel as a people, but through God's promise, Abraham represents the hope of humanity for a way out of its rebellion and resulting condemnation. Abraham is the bearer of God's call to a new way, a way of obedience, for humanity, and if finally God abandons the promises that accompanied the call of Abraham, humanity's last best hope for survival before God is destroyed. As Paul will make clear in chapter 4, it is just that promised blessing to Abraham's descendants that Christ has opened for gentiles as well. What is at stake is therefore the future of humanity itself.

It is Paul's great good news that God will not reply in kind. However faithless humanity may prove to be, God remains faithful to his promises, delivered to Israel and through Israel to all humanity. That faithfulness does not depend on reciprocal human faithfulness. If every human being proves faithless to God, God remains faithful. That is finally Paul's gospel. However God's promises may be tested, he will remain faithful to them (3:4).

Answers have a way of provoking further questions, as solutions often represent new problems. That is also the case here. If God is faithful despite our faithlessness, and thus sets in sharp relief God's unreciprocated faithfulness (v. 4b), ought not God be grateful for that opportunity to show his true nature? Ought he not then indulge those who have given him that opportunity? Put another way, the question asks: Can evil be a sufficient cause of good? The answer is an obvious and sharp No! Evil remains evil and must be rooted out at the final judgment. Humans can receive no credit for the perfidy that throws God's faithfulness into sharp relief.

Paul's choice of words in these two questions (vv. 3–5) are most revealing for understanding what Paul means by "righteousness" or "justice" (as in the RSV; the same Greek word is translated by both English words). Righteousness in verse 5 is paralleled to faithfulness in verse 3. It is therefore when God is faithful to his promises that he is righteous. Righteousness carries with it covenantal overtones in Paul. To be "righteous" is to be faithful to what one has promised and thus to uphold one's covenant promises. To break those promises is to separate oneself from covenantal benefits. It is to "sin" or "transgress." To be "righteous by faith" thus means to trust that despite our faithlessness, our sin, God continues to be faithful to his covenant promise, renewed in Jesus Christ. To trust that we can share in the renewed covenant means to be righteous by faith (trust) in Jesus Christ, that is, to trust that in his Son God opens his covenant anew, this time to all people. We will see how Paul works out that understanding as we continue our examination of Paul's discussion in Romans, but it will help if we keep that framework in mind (see *"Reflection: Righteousness in Romans"*).

The question persists. If God can make good out of the evil I do, why must I still suffer for that evil (v. 7)? In other words, why must I still be held responsible for my evil, rebellious actions if God can take those actions and by his almighty power turn them to his own good purposes? Given Paul's logic to this point, are we not saying that when God remains faithful to his promises, and thus shows his righteousness precisely in our rebellion and sin, we by doing evil have caused good to come? Should we not pursue this and be as logical as Paul? Does this not mean we not only can but should do evil, if in doing that we cause God to turn it to good? Some people had apparently accused Paul of saying just that (v. 8b).

56

Again, the answer is No. We cannot so lightly evade responsibility for what we do. God may transmute our evil intent to his good purposes, thereby demonstrating his omnipotent control over the outcome of the course of history, but we are not thereby absolved of responsibility. The condemnation of evil, and of evil-doers, is in fact just (8*b*). There is a temptation, to which many commentators yield, to see in that last phrase—"Their condemnation is just"—Paul's condemnation of those who are slandering him. Yet that is not the case. Verse 8*b* is not an instance of pique on the part of Paul against those who draw slanderous conclusions from his preaching. The rhetorical structure of the questions in verses 3 and 5 have received answers of a similar form in verses 4 and 6. Paul is following that same structure in verses 7–8, although his parenthetical remark in the midst of verse 8 ("as some people slanderously charge us with saying") interrupts it. Yet the structure is there, and it is into that structure that the final comment in verse 8 fits. Paul is therefore not condemning those who slander him at the end of verse 8. Rather, Paul refers here as he did in verse 6 to the divine condemnation of evil (similar questions, vv. 5 and 7, receive similar answers, vv. 6*b* and 8). He is not yielding to a vengeful curse. He is making his point. Human beings are responsible for what they do. Human evil will face divine judgment. Our inability through our rebellion to thwart God's merciful purposes for humankind does not absolve us of the responsibility for that rebellion. Evil is to be condemned. God's wrath remains in effect, and it remains universal.

Such observations are not finally to be allowed to overshadow the good news these verses contain. We must be clearly aware of the much-needed consolation they contain, as Calvin pointed out: ". . . such is the perversity of men in rejecting and despising God's word, that its truth would be often doubted were not this to come to our minds, that God's verity depends not on man's verity" (p. 116). That is the gospel in this passage of human responsibility and divine judgment. God does not depend on our reciprocal faithfulness to remain faithful to his beneficent purposes. Despite our lies, he remains truthful; despite our perfidy, he remains faithful.

The preacher will find in this passage an excellent basis for a sermon on the faithfulness of God. Indeed, in refusing to yield any ground at all on God's faithfulness, Paul makes as clear a statement as he ever does about the basic fact of the gospel. God's faithfulness, shown in Jesus Christ, is precisely what the gospel is about, and this passage will allow the preacher to make that point from a text which is probably less familiar to his congregation than some others. There is here both the comfort

57

of a God who is faithful to us through thick and thin and the challenge to meet such divine faithfulness with faithfulness of our own. That divine faithfulness is the solid rock upon which the response to the gospel is founded (see Matt. 7:24–27).

Teaching this passage presents the opportunity to develop the fact that any advantage resulting from the call of God resides in God's further faithfulness to that call rather than in the faithfulness of the recipient. Useful examples from the history of Israel may be cited: the call of Abraham, God's promise to David despite his sinful act with Bathsheba, God's continual sending of prophets to recall Israel from her rebellion against him, God's release of Israel from the Babylonian captivity, and finally, of course, God's sending of his Son. Seen in that perspective, the faithfulness of God is more than simply words. It shows itself to be grounded in history. If the God who is the Father of Jesus Christ is also the God of the Jews, as Christians claim, then we can discern how he acts toward his creatures in the history of that Israel.

A lesson based on this passage will therefore have a double opportunity. On the one hand it can show God's continuing faithfulness to his rebellious people, and on the other hand it can show how the Christian understanding of the meaning of God's act in Jesus, that is, his faithfulness, is grounded in the history of God's dealings with Israel found in the Old Testament. That will help the class members understand not only the continuity between what is told in the Old and New Testaments and therefore why the Old Testament is part of our Christian Scripture, but also how the actions of God with Israel and his act in sending his Son are part of his continuing faithfulness to his rebellious creation.

Romans 3:9–20
Conclusion: Universal Sin

The time has come to cast a balance, to reach a conclusion, and that is what Paul is about in these verses. Yet balances, when cast, have a way of proving themselves provisional; and conclusions have a way of pointing beyond themselves, and that, as we shall see, is precisely the case in this passage.

The passage divides itself into three segments: the upshot of the discussion in 3:1–8 (v. 9); a display from Scripture of the universal shortcomings of a humanity in rebellion against its Creator (vv. 10–18); and an announcement of the inadequacy of the law for a right relationship to God (vv. 19–20). Taken together, they sum up the argument Paul has been carrying on about the universality of wrath and sin, and they provide the transition to the next section on God's grace.

The conclusion Paul draws about the advantage of Jewish birth and its sign, circumcision, seems incongruous at first. Having apparently affirmed the advantage of being born an Israelite in verses 3–8, Paul seems to deny such an advantage in verse 9. What Paul is saying, however, is that the historic advantage belonging ineradicably to Israel—it was God's chosen people—does not set Israel free from responsibility to God. On that score, Israel's history gives her no exemption from judgment on how she has acted toward God. In this divine balance, Israel stands on a level with the gentiles. The conclusion is now clear and unavoidable: All humankind, Paul affirms, is separated from a positive relationship to God. All are "under sin."

Lest there be any remnant of an idea that possession of the law confers any exemption from this universal indictment, Paul frames that indictment from the very law that could be thought to provide the exemption. The collection of verses, principally from the psalms, serves to wipe out any claim anyone might advance to be free from the universal indictment on sin. From lack of righteousness (v. 10) to lack of reverence for God (v. 18), the rebellion of God's creatures against him is catalogued. There is no escape. Supposed merit from the past cannot shield from present sin. All are rightly under the wrath of God.

Paul concludes the section with one more assertion of the universality of deserved judgment by God. Once more, possession of historic advantage (the law) will not deliver one from the present predicament: The condemnation just announced, coming from the law, clearly includes those "under the law," that is, Israel. There is no further plea that can be entered. No other claims will be allowed. No one may raise a voice in personal defense.

Verse 20 sheds a whole new light on the law, however, and we must take it very seriously. Up to this point, one could have the impression that the fault lies in lack of compliance. One could conclude that had one done the law, one could have escaped condemnation; verse 20 points in another direction. Even total fulfillment of the law would not have been sufficient. That is not the way to a restored relationship with the Creator. No one has a legitimate excuse to escape judgment and wrath, not even those who could claim to have obeyed the law, because doing the law is not the way to restore the relationship between creature and Creator. That is why "every mouth is stopped." The reason for the inability of the law to accomplish this lies in the close relationship between that law and sin. Although the law makes clear our condemnation (vv. 10–18), it cannot be the means of our salvation because of that close link with sin. Paul will develop this thought in much greater detail in chapter 7, but he has announced here the fundamental flaw in the law: It is not strong enough to resist the power of sin.

If one gets the impression here that forces are in command of our lives over which we have no control, one will begin to understand the dimensions of what Paul sees as the "human predicament." While it is clear that we are responsible for what we do, it is equally clear that we are not, indeed cannot, be saved by what we do. Such a conclusion echoes Jesus' words in Luke 17:10: "So you also, when you have done all that is commanded you, say, 'We are unworthy servants; we have only done what was our duty' " (RSV).

Both preacher and teacher will note that in this passage the terrible contours of sin are becoming evident. Sin is the pit into which we have fallen, but it is too deep for us to escape. It is the quicksand into which we have foolishly blundered but from which we cannot extricate ourselves. It is the death we have entered but from which we cannot restore ourselves to life. "For what will one give in return for one's life?" Jesus asked (Mark 8:37), and the question is as unanswerable now as it was then. We are responsible for our sin, but having allowed it to enter our lives, we are powerless to evict it. Like a criminal we unwittingly allow to enter our house and then have no power to evict, sin, once in control, prevents us from removing it.

Even the law was not strong enough to resist the power of sin. Rather, the law adds to our despair by showing us what we ought to do, while sin, mocking us, uses our law-inspired efforts at escape to bring us more firmly under its control. We have gotten ourselves into a frightening situation, we rebellious creatures, and we cannot get ourselves out of it.

That is where the pride of a rebellious creation has led it.

It has led it into domination by forces opposed to its Creator. That is why that rebellion, that sin, is so frightening: It makes our Creator the one whom we oppose and therefore the one we have to fear. To whom can we go for refuge and help? It is to the answer to that dilemma that Paul turns in the next section of his letter.

REFLECTION:
Righteousness in Romans

The idea of "righteousness" plays a key role in many of Paul's letters, and it is important enough for an understanding of Paul's argument in Romans that we must take time to consider it. Whether or not it is the central theme of Romans, as some have indeed argued (see Introduction), it is surely a central theme in Paul's thought; and a clear notion of what he means by "righteousness" and related terminology is essential if we want to follow his argument.

Some confusion has on occasion been generated by the fact that the Greek noun has been variously translated as "righteousness" or "justice," and the verb as "to justify" or "to make (or pronounce) righteous." The translation chosen already reveals decisions the translator has made about the meaning of this concept. The terminology can be understood in several contexts, each of which throws a different light on the passages in which it occurs.

It can be understood, for example, in the sense of "distributive justice," that is, in the sense that one gets what is coming to one. A sentence in a law court is "just" if the punishment meted out is appropriate to the crime committed. A decision is "just" if it renders to each person involved what that person has coming. A synonym would be "fair." Something is "just" if it is "fair" to all involved. Because that is a use most closely tied to law courts, it is called the "forensic" or "legal" use of the term. One is then "just" or "righteous" if one has conformed to the legal norms in effect in a given society. If that is what the concept means for Paul, then he is using the terminology of the law court to say that we are pronounced "just" by God through our faith in his Son; that is, we are judged not to have broken

61

God's commands. We are thus, by that verdict, freed from the charge and penalties of sin. The difficulty with such an understanding of "righteousness" is that God appears to regard us as something we are not, that is, sinless. Some have wanted to say God regards us "as if" we had no sin, but then God's judgment is based on an untruth, hardly what one would expect from a just and impartial God. The second problem lies in the fact that Paul can say God is "righteous," and one must then wonder who is in a position to pass judgment on God and say that he has conformed to some legal norm. If this is juridical terminology, who has brought God into court to try him, to see whether he can "justify" himself and can then pronounce him righteous?

Because the translation of the Greek words as "justice" and "justify" implies a forensic (legal) context, some scholars have preferred the translation "righteousness" and "make righteous" and have understood it then in the sense of an attribute of God, in a moral sense. God by his very nature cannot do what is morally wrong, and so it is appropriate to call him "righteous." The problem then has to do with what it means that humans are "made righteous." Does it mean they have a new moral nature given to them? Yet it is clear that even those who are "made righteous" by faith are often morally indistinguishable from those who are not so made righteous. Indeed, Paul complains to the Corinthians that some outside their Christian fellowship are more moral than they are (I Cor. 5:1). Again, to say God regards what we do as moral even when it is not is to introduce an element of sham into divine judgment that is quite foreign to Paul. God does not judge by such "appearances" (Rom. 2:11)!

A third way to understand this terminology grows out of the way it is used in the Old Testament, where the words are regularly used in connection with the covenant. To be "just" or "righteous" is to uphold the covenant; to be "unrighteous" is to act in such a way that the covenant is broken. In that context, righteousness is used to describe a relationship. What upholds the relationship is "righteous"; what destroys the relationship is "unrighteous." Similarly, to be "made righteous" then means to be put into, or restored to, a positive relationship with someone, while an "unrighteous" act is one that destroys such a positive relationship. Such an understanding of the terms "make righteous" and "righteousness" allows us to make sense of those places where Paul can speak of God as being righteous or doing

62

what is righteous. It does not mean that God conforms to some norm that is even more important than he is. It means instead that God acts to restore or uphold a covenant, to hold human beings in, or restore them to, a positive relationship to himself. A human being is then "made righteous" when he or she is put in that restored relationship to God. If then sin as unrighteous activity means activity that ruptures our relationship with God, righteousness or being "made righteous" means to have the effects of sin nullified by entering into a restored relationship with God.

Yet that covenant is not an agreement between equals. It is a covenant in which God is Lord, and to break the covenant (sin) means to reject God as Lord and to take upon oneself some other lordship. Thus to be made righteous in this kind of covenantal understanding means to accept the lordship of God, and therefore to seek to do his will rather than the will of some other lord. It means an end to idolatry, which is precisely to make something other than God one's lord.

It becomes increasingly clear as one continues to examine Paul's argument in Romans that he understands "righteousness" and its related terms in this third way. One can see that Paul has equated God's righteousness with his faithfulness (3: 3,5), and one can further see in the next passage (3:21–30) how God's act in Christ is both the sign of God's righteousness and the means of our being made righteous (3:25*b*–26). In other words, Christ shows God's faithfulness to his positive relationship to human beings, as Christ is also the means by which a restored relationship is offered to us. Since Paul has made clear that our ruptured relationship (i.e., sin) with God is something we are responsible for, it is also clear that it is up to God to make the next move, as it were. As the aggrieved party, he can then decide whether to uphold, or end, the relationship with humanity. It is the good news of the gospel that Christ represents God's decision to uphold the relationship and give humanity a new chance to enter into it. But we enter it because God has upheld it, not because we deserve it. Only on such terms can we enter the renewed relationship. Those terms Paul calls "faith."

It is also clear, if this is the way Paul uses the terms for righteousness, that acts that uphold any relationship can be called "righteous." It is just for that reason that Paul can talk about two kinds of righteousness, one which comes from God and the other that comes from the law (see Phil. 3:9; Paul has

63

this in mind in his discussion in Rom. 9:30—10:3). The problem is that the acts which uphold the law are acts which uphold a relationship that was corrupted by sin, and hence, while they can be called "righteous," they are not the kind of righteousness that has any validity before God because they cannot remove us from the lordship of sin. Only God can break that lordship and restore us to a right relationship with himself. That is why "works of the law" do not make us righteous before God, that is, they do not put us into a positive relationship to God.

It is not that one cannot fulfill the law; Paul says as a Pharisee he did just that (Phil 3:6b). It is because even when one does fulfill the law, one does so in terms of one's subjugation to the lordship of sin and thus within a relationship corrupted by sin. For that reason such fulfillment cannot set sin aside. Only when one admits, by trusting God (by faith), that any restoration of one's relationship to God comes at his initiative in freeing us from sin's power, its lordship—only when one admits that, can one enter that positive relationship offered through Christ. Lack of such trust means to reject the lordship of God and remain under the lordship of some other power. That is the problem with any attempt at maintaining a relationship with God based on the law: Because sin has overpowered the law, the law offers no way to freedom from sin's power. Trust in one's ability to come under God's lordship by means of the law is thus an illusion, since it excludes trust in God's act in Christ and thus it has no validity before God (see Rom. 9:30–32).

All of this means "righteousness" is not a "quality" or a conformity to some legal norm. Rather, it is a positive relationship to God growing out of his power to restore through Jesus Christ his gracious lordship over us, a lordship which our idolatrous rebellion had turned into a wrathful lordship. That effect of our idolatrous rebellion, our sin, has been the point Paul has been making in his argument in Romans from 1:18 to 3:20. God's righteousness also represents his power (recall 1:16!) to re-establish his lordship over his creation and in that way to restore his creation to a positive relationship to himself (so 1:17!). Righteousness does not describe something God is therefore so much as it describes something he does. God's righteousness is his power by which he breaks the power of sin and sets aside its corruption, restoring sinners to a positive relationship with himself. It is therefore also God's gift to sinful humanity, given in his Son. It is that gift alone which can rescue humanity

64

from the doleful results of the idolatry into which it has fallen (see 1:18–32).

It is also clear in all of this that Christ is the key to an understanding of both God's righteousness and the possibility of our being "made righteous." Because Christ is that key, Paul in another context can identify him as "our righteousness" (I Cor. 1:30) and can identify the consummation of God's gracious plan with the confession of Christ as Lord (Phil. 2:9–11). Because it is a matter of being broken free from one lordship in order to enter into another, we cannot generate this new relationship, this "righteousness." We can enter it only by accepting God as lord and trusting him to restore and uphold it. That is the only proper response to God's breaking us free from the lordship of sin through the gift of his Son. Only by leaving the now broken lordship of sin and accepting the lordship of God, which we do by trusting that God has in fact restored us to himself in Christ, can this relationship become real for us. If trust is the key to Christ and Christ is the key to our restored relationship to God, then that relationship is "rectified" by our trust in Christ.

That is the reasoning that lies behind the phrase in Paul which is often translated as "justification by faith." It can also, and perhaps more accurately, be translated "rectified by trust"; that is, our relationship to God, ruptured by sin, is once more rectified and our lives are transformed when we now take God as Lord and trust in him rather than in some idol, whatever form it may take, or in our ability to fulfill the law to make us "right" or acceptable to God.

For further information: A good summary of the various views on Paul's understanding of "righteousness by faith" will be found in an article by Ernst Käsemann, "The Righteousness of God in Paul" (pp. 168–82 in *New Testament Questions of Today*). For a much more detailed review of current discussion, see *Righteousness in the New Testament,* by John Reumann; this volume grew out of the Lutheran/Roman Catholic Bilateral Discussions and includes responses by Fr. Joseph A. Fitzmyer and Jerome D. Quinn. In *The Commentary on Romans,* W. Sanday and A. C. Headlam see righteousness as an ethical attribute of God transferred to human beings. Günther Bornkamm, in his book *Paul* presents a forensic understanding of righteousness. Ernst Käsemann's *Commentary on Romans* makes a forceful case for understanding righteousness as God's power to restore his creation to its rightful relationship to him. The arti-

65

cle "Righteousness in the New Testament" in the *Interpreters Dictionary of the Bible* (pp. 91–99, Vol. 4; Abingdon Press, 1962) represents an understanding of righteousness in covenantal terms. The article on the various Greek terms related to the concept of "Righteousness" in Kittel, *Theological Word Book of the New Testament,* presents a summary of the way righteousness may have been understood in Greek culture and the Old Testament, as well as in the rest of the New Testament.

The Gospel and God's Grace

ROMANS 3:21—4:22

The significant shift in the direction the discussion is to take with this passage is signaled by its opening words: "But now . . ." (3:21). For the beleaguered readers of this epistle, the shift comes none too soon. We have learned that we cannot look to our collective past for any kind of comfort or salvific aid. Whatever our ancestry, whether Jewish or gentile, it has distinguished itself principally by its resolute sinfulness and rebellion against God. Our past has left us the inheritance of being unacceptable to God through our separation from him. The root of our problem is the human propensity to put non-gods in the place of God. Such idolatry clearly means the rejection of the Creator for a deity more pliable to our wishes. Basically, idolatry means not trusting God to be the kind of God we can live with. God's reaction to that lack of trust in him has been to allow us to "get away with" our desire to have something other than him for god. Paul has called that abandonment of us by God "God's wrath." The description of a society gone awry (1:24–32) is so contemporary as to send a chill through the most hardened reader.

We face, in short, a problem. How are the results of the rejection of God to which we are heir, and in which as heirs we participate, to be overcome? What hope is there for creatures who have rejected and alienated their Creator? What can we do in that situation? What will God do in that situation?

66

The answer: God can show clearly what kind of God he is, and in such a way that the power of our rebellion is broken. Once that has occurred, we can then finally put away that rebellion and come to trust him. That is why Jesus who is God's solution to the broken relationship with his creatures is also our solution. In Jesus, God proves himself faithful to his creation and invites us to be faithful to him. In Jesus, God shows his willingness to maintain a positive relationship with rebellious humanity and to open the way for such rebels to enter into that relationship by trusting the God who offers it. In short, Paul's answer to our dilemma is Christ Jesus, who is God's demonstration of his righteousness and our hope of receiving righteousness (see 3:25*b*–26).

By framing the discussion in these verses in such terms, Paul is picking up on the language he used in 1:16–17, where our discussion began. Here, as there, having our relationship to God set right by trust ("righteous by faith") is the means by which Paul demonstrates the universal scope of God's act in Christ.

Romans 3:21–30
Christ and the Answer to Universal Sin: Universal Faith

The fact that these verses are placed after the discussion of human rebellion and divine abandonment, and resume themes stated in 1:16–17, is of high importance for understanding what Paul is getting at in these verses. For example, by contrasting (see the "But now" with which this section begins) God's righteousness in Christ with God's abandonment of humanity to sin, Paul makes clear that God's gracious lordship which we ruptured by our idolatry is now to be restored. Thus, God's desire to re-establish a positive relationship with rebellious humanity (his righteousness by grace) is the counter-pole to his wrath visited on human unrighteousness. That helps define righteousness (see *"Reflection: Righteousness in Romans"*) as the opposite of the abandonment of humanity to its own devices. God re-expresses his faithfulness to his creation, thus opening the

67

way for humanity to re-enter a positive relationship with him.

A second theme Paul takes over from 1:16–17, and which indeed has also dominated the discussion since that point, is the universal scope of God's act in Christ. Note the emphasis in 3:22 on *all* who believe and the added emphasis that "there is no distinction" (i.e., between Jews and gentiles) in this matter. Since all have sinned (v. 23), it is clear that all are to be made righteous through Christ. That is true because there is only one God for all peoples, Jews or gentiles (v. 29). Thus, in Christ, the religious distinction between Jew and gentile has been set aside.

It is precisely this universal scope of the good news of the gospel that has occupied Paul in his letter to this point. Indeed, that universal significance of God's act in Christ goes to the heart of Paul's understanding of the gospel. That universal significance means that *no* persons can exempt themselves from the need for God's generous restoration of his gracious lordship in Christ, because no one is worthy of God's kindness: not the Jews, despite their history as chosen people; not the gentiles, despite their undoubted moral accomplishments (see Rom. 2:-14–15). The universal scope of the gospel points to the fact that if *any* one is to have God as friend it will be by sheer grace, nothing else. The universal scope also means that unless we understand ourselves, *whoever* we may be, as sinners who apart from God's grace are unable to cope with ourselves, our world, or our God, we misunderstand ourselves and condemn ourselves to go right on making the same kind of mess of our own lives and of our world in the future as our ancestors have in the past.

That is the point Paul wants to make in Romans. One will have to have a positive relationship to God on his terms or one won't have it at all. Another way to describe this universal scope of the gospel in Paul's understanding of it is to say one is made right with God by grace or one is not made right at all. Admission of that state of affairs and acceptance of God's gift of friendship to us (grace) Paul calls "faith." The universal scope of the gospel therefore means that whoever one is, whatever one's background or one's past accomplishments, one is saved by grace which one accepts in trust or one is not saved at all.

68

It is Paul's understanding of that universal scope of the gospel that also explains his heavy emphasis in this passage on righteousness by *faith*. It is precisely that righteousness by faith which is the instrument for universal participation in the new relationship with God, as compared to the law which had placed racial limits on that relationship. That is explicit in verse 30: What the law does not do—apply equally to all—righteousness by *faith* does. Yet such righteousness by faith is not to be seen in total discontinuity with that law. Indeed, returning to an item announced in the statement of the theme of the entire letter in 1:2–4, Paul now intends to explicate just how Israel, its prophets and its law, all pointed to God's final redemptive act in Christ (3:21*b;* 3:31—4:12).

Perhaps most important of all, we learn here the answer to human idolatry. To find our way to God solely through trusting reliance on Christ means finally to give up our attempt to prove our worth by what we ourselves can accomplish in the matter of creating divinity. By relying solely on Christ, we are delivered from our attempts to make ourselves acceptable to God by creating gods we can make ourselves acceptable to. It is precisely in this kind of idolatry, which is at root self-idolatry (recall Adam's temptation: "You shall be like God" in Gen. 3:5), in which all attempts at making ourselves acceptable by what we do ("salvation by works of the law") end up. To be in Christ means to be out of ourselves, as Calvin put it, and that is precisely what trust in Christ as God's offer of grace to us can mean. That, finally, is what this passage is all about, and since that is also what the Christian faith is all about, this passage is of central importance not only for Paul but for the whole New Testament. If, as Luther observed, Romans is the purest gospel, then our passage is, as it were, purest Romans. We can go even further; the key to 3:21–30 lies in verses 25–26.

There has been some debate about how to construe these two verses. To understand the issues, it is necessary to translate the verses, indicating the logic of their development. Such indications are included in parentheses. Verse 25 explicates Christ Jesus "whom God publicly set forth as a propitiation, through faith, by his death on a cross, (first) as a sign of his righteousness (a sign that was needed) because God passed over sins committed in the past in the time of his patience—(second) as a sign of his righteousness in the present time, in order that he might be righteous and be the One who makes righteous every one that believes in Jesus."

The problem lies in the relationship of the phrases marked (first) and (second). Are they intended to be parallel statements,

69

both pointing to the same reality? In that case, the first part of the statement emphasizes that Christ's death on a cross is the sign that shows that God is righteous, while the second part of the statement emphasizes that Christ's death on a cross shows that by faith in him God also makes us righteous. Or is the contrast to be found in the words "in the past" and "in the present time," in which case the contrast is between Christ's cross as a sign that even in the past when God passed over sins he was righteous and as a sign that by making us righteous by faith in Christ God is also righteous in the present.

While the substance of what Paul intends is not significantly affected by our decision in this matter, we would opt for the first suggestion, namely that "first" and "second" are to be construed as parallel, both together giving the full meaning of what it is of which Christ is the "sign" or, perhaps better, "demonstration." In either case, however, it is clear in verse 26 that Christ represents both God's righteousness, demonstrated in sending him, and our righteousness, opened to us in trusting him. On the one hand, Jesus proves God is righteous because he is God's demonstration of his faithfulness to his sinful creation, which in the end he will not abandon to its own devices. And on the other hand, Jesus makes it possible for us to become righteous by opening the way for us to share in God's grace-filled relationship to his creation. Jesus does this by allowing us to trust in him rather than in ourselves to make us acceptable to God. Jesus Christ is thus both God's righteousness and ours, because through him God restores his gracious lordship over his rebellious creation.

Such an acceptance of the lordship of God through trust reshapes the way we view our world and our fellow human beings by rebuilding our network of trusting relationships. In a profound way, what we are is shaped by the one to whom we give our allegience and trust as lord. The one whose lordship we accept will determine not only what we believe about that lord but also what we believe about ourselves, and therefore it will effect our relationship to others. A new lordship will therefore mean a radical reorientation of those beliefs and therefore a radical reorientation of the core of our being. With that reorientation of our attitude toward our self and toward our world, and our radical re-assessment of what is worthy of trust comes a reorientation of the way we act toward ourselves and others. Since this new lordship means we are no longer forced to prove ourselves worthy of acceptance by a deity, whether that deity be an idol of our own creation or whether it be God himself, we are free to open ourselves to others and to turn our concern toward them.

When therefore God's gracious lordship breaks apart the vicious circle of self-idolatry and the nexus of relationships which that brought in its train, we are freed to enter a new nexus of relationships motivated by gratitude for grace rather than preoccupation with self. Such a breaking out of an old reality and entering into a new one needs God's power to accomplish it, of course, and Paul will turn later on to a discussion of just that (chaps. 5—8). For the present, Paul is content to announce the new turn in events inaugurated by the coming of Jesus Christ.

Because of the content of these verses, it is not surprising that they have been regarded as highly appropriate for the celebration of Reformation Sunday. Combined with such passages as Habakkuk 2:1–4 and John 8:31–36, these verses point to God's faithfulness to all human beings and to the freedom which such faithfulness makes possible for them. Habakkuk 2:1–4 gives God's answer to the question whether he is just and in control of events. God assures Israel that evidence leading to a positive answer is coming and affirms that when it does come those who are faithful to or trust in God rather than in themselves will live by that faithfulness and trust. Those verses thus underline the point of this passage in Romans: God's faithfulness is the only basis on which any positive relationship to him is possible. Otherwise, human pride makes such a relationship impossible.

A passage like the one in John speaks of the freedom-creating power of the truth embodied in Jesus as the Son of God. Knowledge of that truth breaks the enslaving power of sin and sets one into the freedom of a child of God. In that perspective, preaching on Reformation Sunday needs to emphasize the renewing freedom inherent in God's act in Christ, a freedom that needs to be announced ever anew to creatures not yet delivered from the temptation to set their priorities above those of God.

Another emphasis inherent in these verses in Romans centers on their universal applicability. They are addressed to all humanity. No longer is one dependant on the possession of the law or membership in a race to benefit from God's faithfulness

71

to his promises. The promise of life contained in the law, a promise stymied by sin, is now offered to all in Jesus Christ. He is the proof of God's faithfulness and the means of our faithful response to God's grace. The reverence to be accorded to the law, a reverence emphasized in such a passage as Deuteronomy 11:18–21, is thus now to be accorded to God's Son, and the liberating news that in him God is faithful to his promise of life for all humanity. Such news must be kept constantly at the forefront of our attention. It is never to be far from our sight or our touch or our conversation with others. It is the very key to life with God.

That astonishing authority vested in the message about God's faithfulness manifested in Jesus Christ is matched by the astonishing authority possessed by Jesus himself. That authority is remarked in such passages as Mark 1:27–28 or Matthew 7:28–29, and they show that the Gospel accounts of Jesus intend also to make evident that only through this man and his words can one find a relationship with God freed from the destructive power of sin.

In such a context, our passage from Romans gives the content of the Word of God by which we are to shape our lives, namely trust in God's faithful goodness to us as his creatures. These are the words that are ever to be before our eyes and minds, and they are the authority on which we may rest our lives: In Christ Jesus, God has shown his willingness to forgive our sins, whoever we are, and to welcome us back into fellowship with him. Trust in that kind of God allows a life to survive the worst storms it may encounter.

The teacher will find here an excellent opportunity to aid the class in understanding both the meaning of the term "righteousness" as Paul uses it in this letter and the universal scope of the gospel as Paul understands it. The first half of the passage (vv. 21–26) will lend itself to the former development, the second half of the passage (vv. 27–30) to the latter. Because of that double emphasis, the teacher may want to devote more than one class session to it. Yet however the discussion is handled, the class must understand that the two topics are intimately related, that it is precisely the fact that righteousness comes to us through our trusting acceptance of God's lordship in Jesus Christ that makes such righteousness open to all people of all times and races. Since the gospel is thus open to all, acceptance of that gospel puts one under the obligation of spreading the

72

good news to everyone, since everyone is intended to hear and accept it. The universal scope of the gospel of God's righteousness by faith in Jesus Christ is thus both a gift and an obligation. It is a gift open to all, and it lays upon all the obligation to tell it abroad.

If teaching this passage occurs in the context of a larger study of Romans, the teacher should also take the opportunity to point out the relationship between this discussion of righteousness through trust and the ensuing discussion of Abraham. Paul in the course of these verses has been intent on emphasizing that our relationship to God must come via trust in Jesus rather than trust in what we can do by following the law. That makes it look very much as though the law stood, and stands, in opposition to faith. It also seems to throw "works of the law" into a purely negative light. Is the law in fact the opposite of faith, since, as verse 30 affirms, the new relationship to God is open only to those who trust in Christ, whether they are under the law (the circumcised, Jews) or outside the law (the uncircumcised, gentiles)? Is the law thus thrown out by faith? In the light of 3:21-30, the answer may seem surprising: an emphatic No! The reason why that is the case Paul will discuss in the next passage.

REFLECTION:

Paul's Dialogical Mode of Argument

More so in Romans than in any of his other letters, Paul carries out his discussion in the form of question and answer. One can see that form in the discussion in chapter 2, and it is especially clear in 3:1-8. Paul continued that rhetorical format in the concluding verses of chapter 3 and the beginning verses of chapter 4. That same format is found in chapters 6 and 7, in the closing verses of chapter 8, and in the discussion contained in chapters 9—11. What lies behind that method of argumentation?

Scholars pursuing this question have discovered similar forms of discussion in the secular writings of the ancient Mediterranean world. Perhaps the earliest form is found in the dialogues Plato wrote to celebrate the form of teaching pursued by

73

For further information: Rudolph Bultmann wrote his doctoral dissertation on this topic in the early years of this century; and with its publication, it became the standard work for many decades. It has never been translated. In recent years, renewed research has produced new insights and interesting results. Some of the discussion can be found in *The Romans Debate*, K.P. Donfried editor, especially his article "False Presuppositions in the Study of Romans (pp. 120–48). The best and most thorough study has been done by Stanley Kent Stowers, *The Diatribe and Paul's Letter to the Romans.* Chapter two, "Address to the Imaginary Interlocutor" is especially pertinent, but a careful study of the whole book will prove rewarding.

Romans 3:31—4:22
Abraham and Intimations of Faith

We have much to learn from Abraham, our father in the faith. We learn from him the kind of faith which now, through Christ, is open to all, Jews and gentiles alike. Because we learn from Abraham the true nature of faith, we can also learn from him the true nature of the law. The clue to that is found in Abraham's historical career, where his faithful obedience preceded the law, and indeed anything that could be interpreted as related to the law. We learn from Abraham therefore that the basis and intention of the law is just what faith requires: obedience to God as Lord. As in the Old Testament, so here, Abraham's response to God points the way out of the morass in which humanity had placed itself through the rebellion of idolatry. Abraham, for Paul, is both the climax of this first part of his letter to the Roman Christians and the sign of the direction Paul's further discussion will take. We must now see how that works itself out.

It has been clear since 3:21–22 that Paul is summing up the first major part of his argument in Romans. In those verses, Paul repeated the thought of the first statement of the theme of his letter, found in 1:2–4, in order to show how in fact Christ was anticipated in the career of Israel. Already at that point, the way is being prepared for the discussion of Abraham, the progenitor of Israel. In 3:21–26, Paul resumed a discussion of points he had

enunciated in 1:16–17, where this first major part of his argument began. But where faith is mentioned in Paul, there the
law is never far away, and his discussion of law and faith in
3:27–30 has brought him in verse 31 to his discussion of
Abraham.

Law and Faith (Romans 3:31—4:12)

As before, Paul's argument proceeds on the basis of clear
and forceful logic. If we as sinful people can only be saved by
the grace manifested in Christ and accepted by faith (3:21–26),
then it is clear that we have nothing to brag about in respect
to our salvation. We have been saved, as it were, in spite of
ourselves, not because of anything we have done. Since salvation is thus based on grace received in faith, it does not come
from any credit we might have gained with God by doing what
the law required. That fact has also made it impossible for us to
boast about our salvation as though it were our accomplishment
(3:27–28). The mention of the universal significance of God—he
is the God not of Israel alone but of all people (v. 29)—shows
that Paul understands salvation to be based on faith rather than
law, because the law was the possession of only one people and
hence were salvation based on that law it would be limited to
that people alone. Since, however, God is the God of all people,
not just those who had the law (Israel), his salvation is offered
in such a way (through faith) that all people may respond (3:
29–30; cf. 1:16–17). There are, of course, other problems with
the attempt to find salvation through works of the law; and Paul
will deal with them in the course of his discussion of Abraham.

The line of argument Paul has thus far pursued could quite
logically lead to the conclusion that since faith, not law, is the
way of salvation, those two stand in total opposition to one
another. If our rectified relationship with God comes through
trust in him apart from any works of the law (3:28), is it not clear
that faith and law have nothing to do with one another? The
conclusion seems clear: Law and faith stand in opposition to one
another in God's plan for the redemption of his rebellious creation; when we have to do with faith, we have necessarily ceased
to have anything to do with law. Yet that is not the conclusion
that Paul wishes to draw. Rather, says Paul, what has happened
in this discussion of faith is that now for the first time we can
really see what the true basis of the law is (3:31). It is to explain
how that is so that Paul turns to the figure of Abraham.

77

When Paul turns to Abraham as a key figure in God's plan of salvation, he is following a line of thought familiar to his Jewish contemporaries. Even the language Paul uses shows he is entering into an area already long debated and familiar to all who had concerned themselves with God's redemptive activity. Abraham was regularly cited as a person who was regarded as righteous before God. Paul's strange use of the verb "find" in 4:1 reflects such discussions (cf. Wisd. Sir. 44:19; I Macc. 2:52). Paul wants to make a different point in his discussion of Abraham here, however. Unlike the view held by his contemporaries, which stressed that Abraham's faithfulness in trial and his keeping the covenant led God to count him as righteous, Paul wants to assert that God regarded Abraham as righteous (Gen. 15:6) before Abraham had been either tested (Gen. 22) or circumcised (Gen. 17:10; see Gal. 3:17–18). For that reason, Abraham had nothing to boast about before God (Rom. 4:2b) as though he had gotten his righteousness as payment for something good he had done (Rom. 4:4). Here the New English Bible makes Paul's intention clearer than the Revised Standard Version (especially in v. 2). The point is if Abraham was righteous because of something he did he would have some reason to boast; but since he was given righteousness before he had done anything deserving of it, he has no such grounds for boasting before God.

This is an important point for Paul, because it underlies his argument that the law rests on and points to faith. The reason as we saw is simply that, as is clear from the history of Abraham, he trusted God and so was reckoned righteous before he had demonstrated his obedience through accepting circumcision (Gen. 17:10) or his faithfulness in being tested (Gen. 22), acts that God might have considered worthy of reward (Rom. 4: 9–10). On the contrary, because Abraham was reckoned righteous before such acts (Gen. 15:6), his righteousness is based on faith rather than works of obedience. And that is why Paul says faith does not destroy the law, but rather for the first time shows what the law is really all about. As Abraham was righteous by faith before the law came, so the law itself is preceded by faith and rests on it. Abraham is thus the key to understanding the true significance and place of God's law.

Abraham is of great significance for another reason: He is the bearer of God's promised blessing to all peoples (4:11–12); and that simply means that if we, now, want a share of that promised blessing, we are going to have to get it through Abraham or we will not get it at all (see Gen. 12:2–3). Paul is quite serious about that point. In fact, Paul argues, it was precisely to make it possible for Abraham to be our father in the faith that God made Abraham righteous on the basis of Abraham's trust (4:11*b*). Unless we share Abraham's trust therefore we are not his descendants; and unless we are his descendants, we cannot share the blessing promised to those descendants. But one becomes a descendant of Abraham, in Paul's view, only by sharing his trust, not his genes. Verses 11–12 make that unavoidably clear: One shares Abraham's patrimony by sharing his faith or one does not share the patrimony at all. Paul began this passage (4:1) referring to Abraham as "our father according to the flesh" and ends it with a reference (v. 11) to Abraham as "father of all who believe." That clearly shows the movement of Paul's discussion in these verses.

There is a further implication to be drawn from the fact that Abraham was blessed before he had done anything worthy of it, and it is that God in fact "justifies the ungodly (v. 5; the purpose of v. 6 and the quotation from Ps. 32:1–2 in v. 7 is to reinforce that point). On the face of it, that is an unlikely proposition. One's reaction could easily parallel that of Proverbs 24: 24: "A judge who pronounces a guilty man innocent is cursed by all nations, all peoples execrate him" (NEB). Yet in its best moments, Israel knew that it had been chosen not because of its worth but because of God's grace; Deuteronomy 7:7–8 makes that clear enough. What Paul is doing in these verses therefore is returning to the roots of Israel's faith, to show that Christ in fact has fulfilled not only the letter but also the spirit of the law as he fulfills the promise to Abraham. Paul returns here to an element he stated in the theme of the letter in 1:2–4: Christ fulfills what "had been promised beforehand" (1:2) in the Old Testament.

All of this is of profound significance for our grasping the way Paul understands the law. In itself, the law is not evil; Paul will make that explicit in his later discussions (see 7:12, among other similar statements). Within the framework of faith, the law is God's gift of order and, hence, a gift of grace. The problem with the law, in Paul's view, does not rest with the law but with sin and what sin does through the law. We will see in great detail how Paul works that out in chapters 6—7. Basically the problem is that sin uses the law to make us think we do not need

79

to rely on mercy but can, somehow, make it under our own power, as it were. It lets us think we can, somehow, establish our worth in such a way that we do not need God's mercy. We want that "boast before God" that not even Abraham could muster. We want our salvation as wages, not mercy. In short, we want to do what only God can do: Furnish the grounds for our being declared righteous and hence acceptable to God. Clearly, the fundamental sin of idolatry is again at work. It was not accidental that Paul identified that as the root of all sin in 1:23. Idolatry is at work wherever we assert our worthiness to be saved or deny the firm hold sin has on all our human virtues. It is idolatry because, in doing that, we show we want a god different from the God we know in Jesus Christ.

The teacher will find in this passage an excellent illustration of the way Paul makes use of the Old Testament in his exposition of the Christian faith. It would be instructive to have the class study carefully the story of Abraham in the Old Testament, and particularly the passages from which Paul quotes (Gen. 15:5–6; 17:4–18; 18:11; 22:17–18 cf. also Ps. 32:1–2). In the Old Testament, Abraham is the new beginning God makes after the baleful account of one human sin after another (chaps. 3—11). In Romans, Abraham is similarly the first ray of hope in the midst of Paul's discussion of the frightful consequences of God's wrath which his creation, through its rebellious idolatry, has brought upon itself. Apparently a discussion within the biblical perspective of God's plan for the salvation of his distorted and rebellious creation must find great significance in Abraham, and a class session devoted to the reason why Abraham is important, both in the Old Testament and in Paul's writings, would be useful.

The preacher will find here an opportunity to discuss the problem with any attempt to find salvation in works of the law. To want to depend on such works means to want to depend on ourselves, rather than on God. Put another way, the problem with the law is the problem of our unwillingness to receive the generosity of God. We would rather, we think, be paid what we deserve than to be given something we have not earned. Jesus had a parable that made the same point about some workers who resented mercy and expected high wages (Matt. 20:1–16). Like the laborers, we begrudge generosity to others; but carrying it a step further, we begrudge it to ourselves as well. The reason is clear: If we are acceptable to God only because of his mercy, not because of our own value, then in the final analysis we must not be worth much at all. It is just that confession that is so hard for any self-sufficient modern person to make. Yet directly athwart all our assertions of our religious worth before God there lies Paul's judgment on that Israelite paragon of virtue, Abraham: If Abraham was justified by works, he has a reason to boast; but he was not justified by works but by grace, and so he has no such boast before God (4:2). We have indeed much to learn from Abraham, our father in the faith.

Promise and Faith (Romans 4:13–22)

Lines of grace converge in Abraham. He is the origin of God's promise of grace to humankind, God's answer to the ravages of human evil outlined in Genesis 3—11. In Abraham, God undertakes a new beginning, calling Abraham out of his familiar and secure surroundings to begin a pilgrimage founded on trust in the God who led him out. Abraham is the new beginning because in him God's purpose of calling sinful humanity back to trust in him becomes evident. Abraham's response to the God who called him forth as well as his trust that God could give him an heir display the faithfulness appropriate to God, a faithfulness that responds to his faithfulness to sinful, rebellious humanity. Because Abraham received the promise of blessing to all humankind, he also reveals the true basis of God's law when it came, a law based on God's gracious decision to instruct his chosen people in the proper ways for God's people to act. Finally, it was from the seed of Abraham that the Redeemer came, a Redeemer who died to deliver us from sin and who rose from the dead as the reality of a renewed relationship with God. All of those lines converge in Abraham. Small wonder then that Paul finds in him a key to understanding the meaning of God's faithful grace and our appropriate response.

In the preceding verses in Romans (3:31—4:12) we learned *that* Abraham is our father in the faith. In these verses (4:13–25) we learn *how* he is our father in such faithfulness. Our passage begins by citing the reason why Abraham, who trusted God and who had that trust counted as the means of getting right with God, could be reckoned as the father of all humanity, Jews and gentiles alike (v. 12). The reason: The promise to Abraham came as a word of grace, not as a demand of law (v. 13; see v. 16). If it had come as a demand of law, and had thus depended on Abraham's ability to keep it, it would have perished, since

81

the law cannot keep out sin, that is, the law does not have the power to uphold the relationship it presumes if its demands are to be met (v. 15). Such unmet demands rightly bring punishment (wrath) in their wake. Only if the relationship God promised to establish and maintain with Abraham, and hence with us as Abraham's descendants in the faith, is framed in such a way that human sin has no chance to rupture it will that promise have any chance of fulfillment.

To guarantee the fulfillment of the promise therefore God bases it on grace (v. 16a), a grace that includes all who share Abraham's trust in that God. The story of Abraham amply demonstrates why such trust in God is not misplaced. It is demonstrated in the birth of Isaac, born to an impossibly old father and mother (v. 19). That simply proves that God can create whatever he may need in order to fulfill his promises, even if that means creating something where before nothing at all had existed (v. 17). Hope that such a God will fulfill his promises can therefore never prove unfounded, even when all appearances go against it (v. 18).

We have therefore in Abraham an example of how trust in God's faithfulness is to be exercised, another reason Paul has chosen to deal with him at this point in his letter to the Roman Christians. As Abraham makes clear (vv. 16–21), such trust means never waivering in the conviction that what God has promised he will in fact accomplish (vv. 19–20). It means not to waiver in that trust even when the whole of visible reality seems to point to the foolishness of such trust. It means trusting in God's good purposes even when the newspapers daily scream their evidence that sin rules the world, and evil rages unchecked (v. 18). Perhaps above all, it means to give God room to work, to fulfill his promises. One sometimes has the impression that while God's enemies respect his power even in seeking to circumvent it, God's "friends" show their distrust in his power and faithfulness by trying to accomplish for God what, so they seem to think, he is incapable himself of accomplishing. Why do so many works of good intention end up with the very opposite results? Why do such works result where Abraham's impatient attempt to take into his own hands the matter of providing an heir results, namely in the birth of an Ishmael, a "wild ass of a man" whose life would be lived out at odds with "all his kinsmen" (Gen. 16:11–12)? Is it not because those who attempt to do those "good works" refuse to trust that the God

82

who has given his promise of grace will fulfill that promise in Jesus Christ?

The trust, the faith which Abraham otherwise displays, on the contrary, allows God room to work (Gen. 17:22). Such trust is confident that the God who gives his promise is also powerful enough to fulfill it, even if in ways and times of his own choosing (Rom. 3:20–21). As chapters 12—15 will make clear, that is not a call to Christian quietism, as though followers of Christ were to undertake no useful activities. But it is a call to do those good things within the framework of trust in the God who bases his promises on grace, and fulfills them in the same way in Jesus Christ. It is that kind of trust, Paul concludes, that put Abraham on the right track with God (v. 22).

It is that kind of trust that God had looked for in Israel, and which, as the prophets announce, he did not find. Israel's rejection of the God who loved her and was faithful to her is poignantly portrayed by the prophet Hosea. Trust in God is not only rejected in overt acts but also in the form of words that have no reality to back them up. Despite Israel's affirmations of trust in God's mercy which can be relied on as one relies on spring rain (Hos. 6:3), the reality of trust is absent. Reciting the commonplaces of the religious tradition (vv. 1–2) will not suffice when what is needed is true and hearty trust. Indeed the kind of trust Israel displays is about as permanent as the morning mist or nighttime's dew (v. 4). What is needed is the kind of trust Israel had displayed during its times in the desert, when according to Hosea, its response to God was unqualified and its obedience to God's will was total. The absence of such trust in the Israel of Hosea's time provides a counterpoint to the kind of trust Paul finds exemplified in Abraham. The need for that trust on the part of God's people is as strong now (Rom. 4:23–25) as it was in Paul's time or in Hosea's.

A similar call for trust in deed as well as word characterized the career of Jesus. The conditions of discipleship in Mark 8: 31–38 display the lengths to which such trust must be willing to go to be genuine trust. The opposition of religious authorities to Jesus, and his call to trust in God, shows how hard it is to bring such trust to reality. In fact, many who opposed Jesus did so precisely because they did not trust God's promise of grace to those they deemed unworthy of it. As in the passage in Hosea, Matthew 9:9–13 provides an account of a lack of that hearty trust in the merciful God which Abraham in Romans 4 displays

83

in such exemplary fashion. In the Matthean context, desiring mercy rather than sacrifice is interpreted to mean the need to have mercy precisely on those who need it most, that is, sinners. Such an interpretation is an almost exact equivalent of Paul's statement about God's setting right the ungodly (Rom. 3:22b–23a) and points to the same reality Paul deals with in our passage (v. 17), that is, God shows mercy where no mercy is deserved, and that is one way he calls into being what before did not exist.

Another reason why the story of Abraham is so appropriate for understanding the Christian faith lies in the fact that when God creates a new relationship based on grace he calls into existence a fellowship which before did not exist. Just as God, from the unlikeliest source—the aged bodies of Abraham and Sarah—created what before had not existed—an heir to the promise given to Abraham—so God, from the unlikeliest source —his rebelliously idolatrous creatures—creates what before did not exist—"righteousness," that is, a positive relationship with his creatures under his lordship. In both instances, what God did was done through sheer grace; and in both instances, the only proper response is gratitude displaying itself in trust.

The teacher who undertakes an exposition of this passage will do well to read the passage in the New English Bible, which is superior on virtually all counts to the Revised Standard Version in catching up into English the nuances of Paul's Greek sentences. The Good News Translation of the American Bible Society has a particularly good translation of verse 25. Teaching the passage will be best if Abraham is taken seriously as an example for Christians even in the present time, as Paul makes clear in verses 23–24. Here, as in the case of 3:31—4:12, the placement of the story of Abraham in Genesis—where Abraham represents God's new beginning with humanity after the catalog of sinful action contained in Genesis 3—11—gives the teacher a good way of pointing to the importance of Abraham in the Old Testament, an importance which Paul continues to reflect in his discussion in these verses as well. An exposition of Abraham in Romans would be best if it began where Paul began, with 3:31, and continued through chapter 4.

Otherwise the train of Paul's argument can easily be lost. The fact that most of the key themes in Romans are found in this passage—the anticipation of Christ in the Old Testament story of Israel; righteousness by faith; God as a God of mercy; the priority of grace over law; the significance of promise—makes this a particularly good place to get at Paul's understanding of the Christian faith.

With verse 22 Paul concludes the point with which he began in 3:31, namely to show that one only then truly understands the law when one understands it in the context of the priority of faith. The point of the law which was given to Israel was to enable it to uphold a relationship established with them by God. The Israelites to whom it had been given were descendants of Abraham. Yet the relationship to which the law pointed had been established with Abraham on the basis of faith, rather than law. Therefore the prior relationship to which the law pointed was a relationship predicated on Abraham's trusting reliance on the God of mercy. For that reason, Paul argues that only an understanding of faith allows one to understand the true reality that underlies the law. That is why the law is not annulled but is rather established by the reality of faith (3:31). That point made, Paul can now turn from the past to the present, a change in perspective which he announces in 4:23. It is in light of this new perspective that he will frame the discussion contained in the next four chapters.

PART TWO

God's Lordship and the Problem of the Present: Grace and Law

ROMANS 4:23—8:39

Unless there is some way our knowledge of the past can influence our lives in the present, the study of the past is of no more than antiquarian interest. The second part of Paul's letter to the Christians in Rome makes clear that what Paul has described in the first four chapters has not been the result of any antiquarian interest on his part. Rather, Paul has had his eye on the present from the beginning.

The past, as we have seen, has been a time of idolatrous rebellion and sin on the part of humankind (1:18—3:20). Yet that past also contained the coming of Jesus (3:21–30), which had itself been the completion of God's reconciling way with humankind in Abraham (3:31—4:22). Between those two events—the call of Abraham and the coming of Jesus Christ—another religious event of profound significance occurred, namely the giving of the law; and it is to the problems posed by that event for humankind that Paul turns in this second part of his letter.

The reason for the problems associated with the law, as Paul understands it, lies not in the law as such, but in the law's inability to protect itself or the human beings who follow it from falling into the power of sin. Paul therefore begins this part of his letter with a review of that problem, cast in terms of Adam, who disobeyed, and Christ, who obeyed. Until Christ breaks us free, we are uncontrollably dominated by the results of that primal sin of disobedience, which Paul told his readers in Part I was idolatry.

The effect on the law of the relationship between the disobedience of Adam, the source of sin, and the obedience of

Christ, the source of grace, Paul then examines in the next two chapters (6—7). Looking at these three realities, sin, grace, and law, in all three possible combinations, Paul shows how the law, in itself good, has been unable to keep its observers free from imprisonment under the power of sin. He argues that baptism into the death and resurrection of Jesus Christ is the only way that God's act which broke the power of sin may become reality in the individual's life (6:1–14). Apart from baptism, the enslavement that is the lot of the creature will dominate that creature's life (6:15—7:6), an enslavement the law is powerless to remove (7:7–25).

It is the Spirit of God, rather than the law, that is the agency of the divine power which in Christ has broken the stranglehold of sin on God's creation. Only by that Spirit will a human being be able to enjoy in the present a foretaste of the freedom that will one day characterize all of creation. If it is Paul's purpose in chapter 7 to describe the past (dominated by law) from the Christian perspective, in chapter 8 it is his purpose to describe the present (dominated by God's Spirit) from the Christian perspective. Only from that kind of perspective on both past and present will the reader be able to understand how the religious problem posed by the law is solved.

As in the first part of his letter, Paul has again cast his argument in historic rather than in doctrinal terms. Part Two is therefore not so much a systematic exposition of the meaning of righteousness by faith as it is an account of the way the coming of Christ has overcome the problem of the past—the law—and opened the way to a future freed from that domination by sin which the law was powerless to prevent. That these chapters have profound implications for the doctrinal formulations of the Christian faith, however, will become manifest as we examine the content of Paul's discussion.

Sin and Grace:
Adam and Christ
ROMANS 4:23—5:21

God's Son died, long ago—how interesting! God raised him from the dead, long ago—how nice! But what does that have to do with me, now, here? It is exactly that question that Paul sets out to answer in his discussion of sin and grace, as they are expressed in Adam and Christ. Paul makes his new perspective —the present in which he and his readers live—apparent in 4:23. What Paul has been talking about has present as well as past significance. What was said to Abraham about how one is to be related to God was said to the readers of Romans as well, Paul assures them, and there is no reason for us contemporary readers to exclude ourselves from among them.

In turning from past to present in 4:23, Paul makes the shift in his argument there rather than at 5:1, as many commentators have assumed. As those commentators have discovered, however, to find that transition at 5:1 almost inevitably makes the first eleven verses of chapter 5 seem a random collection of pious thoughts, unrelated to their context or even to one another. A transition at 4:23, on the other hand, allows us to understand 5:1–11 as part of a larger argument with its own internal coherence. It is thus to an exposition of how Paul organizes his thoughts in that larger context of 4:23—5:11 that we must turn first.

Romans 4:23—5:11
Present Grace and Reconciliation

The structure of the passage consists in the statement of three themes, with their subsequent exposition. The three themes are given in 4:23–25; they are righteousness (vv. 23–24), Christ's death for sins (v. 25*a*), and Christ's resurrection for

89

righteousness (v. 25*b*). The structure can be described as A—B —A, a structure Paul then follows in 5:1–11 and which may be outlined in the following way:

First theme: Righteousness (cf. 4:23–24)
    Development: 5:1–5—The righteousness we have in Christ provides hope based on the love that comes through the Holy Spirit; *hence*
    Confidence is appropriate
    Implied question: What is the source of love through the Spirit?

Second theme: Christ's death for sins (cf. 4:25*a*)
    Development: 5:6–8—Christ died for sinners, and is therefore the source of that love (v. 8).

Third theme: Christ's resurrection for righteousness (cf. 4:25*b*)
    Development: 5:9–11—Salvation is certain by Christ's resurrection because he died for us sinners and is therefore the source of the Spirit (see further development in chap. 8); *hence*
    Confidence is appropriate

As the outline makes clear, verses 1–11 (chap. 5) are intimately bound up with 4:23–25. Unless that is realized, the opening verses of chapter 5 appear as a somewhat disconnected series of reflections on various themes appropriate to Christian faith and life but somehow unrelated to their immediate context.

An examination of the exposition in 5:1–11 of the three themes announced in 4:23–25 shows further the care with which Paul has constructed his discussion. Paul begins his discussion (vv. 1–2) with the statement (an inference from 4:25) that we have peace (v. 1) and hence we may be confident (v. 2). He ends his discussion (v. 11) with the statement that we may be confident (v. 11*a*) since we have reconciliation (peace; v. 11 *b*). Verses 1–2 and 11 thus display a chiastic structure (chiastic means x-shaped) which is formed as A (v. 1), B (v. 2), B' (v. 11*a*), A' (v. 11*b*). The fact that the two parts of the chiasm begin and end the discussion in verses 1–11 means they form an "inclusio" (enclosure), a regular form in the literature of Paul's time which was intended to show where a discussion begins and where it ends. In addition to the parallelism found in the opening and closing verses, there is an additional parallelism between verses 6 and 8, which open and close the discussion of the second theme: Christ's death.

The point of this rather detailed literary examination is simply to show that Paul is not setting down some random ideas

on Christian virtues. Quite the contrary, he has carefully organized what he says, using literary devices familiar to his readers,
all in the service of introducing the second major portion of his
letter: the significance of human sin and God's grace for the
present.

The careful literary structure is matched by a careful, logical progression, and by following that progression we will be
able to see how Paul's argument proceeds. That argument runs
as follows:

Now that we have been set right with God through the
death and resurrection of Jesus Christ (v. 25) and hence are at
peace with God through that same Jesus Christ (v. 1), we may,
in addition to having peace, have confidence in our hope for the
future (2). But more, our present status in God's grace is such
that we can even maintain that confidence in the face of adverse reality (cf. Abraham's "hoping against hope" in 4:18!).
Indeed, God's grace is so powerful that even things that work
against such confidence and hope only serve to strengthen it,
since those who know God's grace also know that such adversity
brings out patience (v. 3) and that such patience shows we can
meet the test of adversity and meeting the test simply reinforces our hope (v. 4). The reason such hope is able to meet the
test of adversity lies in the fact that the hope is grounded in
God's love with which he has filled our lives, a love that comes
to us through his Holy Spirit (v. 5). In its turn, that love given
to us through the Holy Spirit is made possible by Christ's death
for sinners (v. 6). Imagine, dying for sinners! It is unusual
enough to die for someone who is good (v. 7). Yet it is precisely
Christ's death for sinners which is the proof of God's love (v. 8).

Since that is the case, we have nothing more to fear from
future judgment (v. 9). If Christ's death means God made peace
with us even though we were his enemies, surely Christ's resurrection means God will save us now that we are his friends (v.
10)! It is just that friendship, that love, that reconciliation which
we have because of Christ, that is the basis for the confidence
we have in God (v. 11).

In addition to making it clear that we are set right with God
only through our trust in him and what he accomplished for us
in the death and resurrection of Jesus Christ (and in that way
showing our kinship with Abraham who was set right on the
basis of his trust in God), this passage adds a new dimension to
our understanding of God's "righteousness," that is, his act of

91

upholding his relationship with sinful humanity (see *"Reflection: Righteousness in Romans"*). We saw (3:3, 5) that one dimension of this righteousness was God's faithfulness to his promises despite the faithlessness of those who received the promise. Here we learn that another dimension in God's upholding of that relationship is reconciliation, turning former enemies into friends. If God shows his faithfulness in upholding the relationship through Christ (cf. 3:25–26), he also, in that same act, shows his friendship. If we saw before that God is faithful, we now see that he is our friend. That shows that to be set right with God means to have him as a faithful friend. Small wonder that Paul can have confidence in such a God and his plans for humanity!

In light of the theological riches contained in this passage, it is not surprising that it has regularly been included among the appointed readings for Christian worship. One finds here themes that are rooted deep in the soil of the biblical faith, and they address perennial concerns of the people of God. Those concerns are also addressed in various seasons of the church year, and one can find appropriate topics for those seasons in this passage.

There is in this passage the theme of suffering and disappointment (vv. 3–5). Those two realities, singly or together, are all too familiar in the life of the Christian. Do they not call into question the validity of faith, or at least its redemptive power? Such questions surface not only in the midst of those experiences but also in times of self-examination when introspection lays bare the weakness of one's faith.

Such questions thus suggest a lenten mood, and it would be appropriate to address them in that season of the church year. Easy answers tend to increase rather than mitigate suffering and disappointment. Yet who can give anything but easy answers? Who has the authority to interpret the problem of suffering and disappointment? Such was the problem addressed by Job, with the wholly unsatisfactory answers of his three friends. Job 6 reflects the suffering Job undergoes at the hands even of those who would help him. To whom is one to turn for such an authoritative word, when well-meaning friends prove so wholly inadequate? Peter poses that poignant question to Jesus in the context of a confession seemingly born of despair yet redolent of truth (John 6:66–69). To whom do we turn in times of perplexity, in times when personal examination leads us to the edge of despair? Our text, particularly verses 1–5 with their message of peace, grace, hope, and confidence, helps us to move through that problem and to find the answer in a hope born of the assurance of the divine love shown in Christ. The deliverance from death Christ received in his resurrection is the assurance of our certain deliverance by the same God, who will defeat our sin and death as well.

Holy Week raises many of the same issues, with its concentration on the betrayal and death of Jesus. Can one discern anything of God's guiding, redemptive purpose in such events? A passage like Luke 22:1–16 suggests that in the midst of those events, God's guiding hand is to be seen, leading them to the end he has planned. If those events culminate in the tragedy of the cross, they find their fulfillment in the joy of Christ's salvific resurrection. An Old Testament passage such as Ezekiel 37: 21–28 also sounds the theme of redemption as the ultimate goal of Israel's bitter and painful exile. Christ, in his death and resurrection, thus recapitulates in more triumphant form the exile and restoration of Israel. In this passage in Romans, Paul, reflecting on those events, draws out their consequences for the present life of the Christian.

Again, the impossibility of reconciliation and salvation apart from the death of Christ, given such emphatic expression in Romans 5:6–11, is echoed in the Suffering Servant of whom Isaiah wrote. Yet such redemption through innocent suffering is again recapitulated in more triumphant form in the passion of Christ. Indeed, what Ezekiel and Isaiah could only promise, Christ has brought to reality, and with that reality the promise of a yet brighter future. When the Synoptic Gospels link Jesus' death to the celebration of Passover (e.g., Mark 14:12; Luke 22:7; Matt. 26:17), it is because Christ has become the paschal lamb by whose death deliverance is announced (see I Cor. 5:7). These verses from Romans 5 thus serve as a theological commentary on the meaning for us of the events enacted so long ago on Calvary.

For the Trinity (Pentecost) season of the church year, when the community of faith reflects on the significance of Christ for the life of that community in its relationship to itself and the world, the emphasis of this passage on the prior saving act of God for sinners especially verses 6, 8, and 10, carries special weight, because they point to that prior saving act in Christ as the source for the life of faith. Again, the origin of the Christian community parallels the origin of the community of Israel,

93

which similarly experienced deliverance from Egypt prior to any response it made to God. A passage like Exodus 19:2–6 makes that point with compelling clarity, a point echoed and re-echoed in the repeated acts of mercy God showered upon his people in the desert (food: see Exod. 16:1–26; water: see Exod. 17:3–7). That prior grace is also exhibited in those healings by Jesus and his followers where that healing comes as a grace–filled surprise. The healing of the paralytic in John 5, for example, or of the cripple in Acts 3:1–10, shows a healing grace that far exceeds the expectations of the one who benefited from it.

Thus the wisdom of God, celebrated in Old Testament (see Prov. 8:22–31) and New Testament (see Matt. 11:25–27; I Cor. 1:18–31; Rom. 11:33–36) and identified by Jesus with God's Spirit (see John 16:12–15) is expounded in this passage from Romans. Knowing human weakness, a weakness exacerbated by rebellion against him, God acted to redeem that humanity before any real awareness that such deliverance was either possible or necessary. Seen within the larger biblical perspective, these verses in Romans 4:23—5:11 display to all who will see the redemptive strategy of the Father of our Lord Jesus Christ: Victory in the midst of tragedy, yet even more, victory by means of what would otherwise be tragedy, were it not transformed by the redemptive power of an almighty God. It is there that our verses from Romans 5 invite us to put our confidence.

The teacher who essays a lesson on Romans 5:1–11 will do well to emphasize the internal coherence of the passage and its relationship to its prior context in 4:23–25. The arbitrariness of chapter divisions, introduced more than a millennium after the text was written, can be pointed out. As a result, such chapter divisions should not be construed as guides to the internal structure of the argument. The logic of verses 8–10—sin, reconciliation, salvation, corresponding to past, present, and future—corresponds in a rough way to the structure of the letter itself (see The Structure of Romans in the Introduction) and hence represents a key passage for entering the thought of Romans. The parallel use of reconciliation and righteousness will also provide an opportunity to add a dimension to the understanding Paul has of those terms. In a way that goes to the heart of the mystery of the Christian faith, the death and resurrection of Christ are understood as the key events in the breaking down of human enmity against God. Those events also point to the totally unmerited nature of God's grace to us which breaks the power of sin and opens the way back to him.

That totally unmerited nature of God's grace in Christ, so strongly emphasized in these verses, is perhaps itself the strongest theological justification for infant baptism: The infant who has done nothing at all to deserve anything at God's hands is nevertheless shown grace in baptism into Christ. As such, the baptism of infants presents a striking metaphor for the way God's grace comes to all: It comes before they have undertaken anything to deserve it. That of course, for Paul, is the meaning of God's act in Christ: He redeems the ungodly. In that context the teacher can undertake a discussion on the nature of baptism as a sacrament that conveys God's grace to human beings.

The whole point of this passage, however, raises a further question. We are told here that, by his death and resurrection, Christ has altered our relationship to God by setting aside the barrier to that relationship erected by sin. That leaves one with some questions: How is the death of Christ able to accomplish that? What was there in his sacrifice on the cross that had the power so to alter reality? It is to an answer to such questions that Paul turns in the verses that follow.

Romans 5:12–21
Adam and Christ: Disobedience and Obedience

One of the problems in a large modern airport is knowing where to get the flight that will take one to one's destination. The choice of which plane to board is of utmost importance to where one will end up! Where one begins determines where one will end. That is also true for our fate as human beings, only here the choices are not nearly so numerous as in an airport. Here the choices are two: Belong to the humanity whose destination is determined by Adam or belong to the humanity whose destination is determined by Christ. The second half of Romans 5 deals with the reality of that choice. Adam and Christ, in Paul's mind each an individual, have nevertheless final impact on the fate of humanity.

95

This is also the passage in Paul's writings upon which Augustine, and many after him, called when they spoke of "original sin." Through some involved reasoning, they came to the conclusion that such sin was born into every human being at the time of the (sinful) sex act by which that individual was procreated. Such a view of the act of human procreation has more to do with medieval problems relative to human sexuality than it does with Paul; but however one may want to understand its origin, there is no question that, for Paul, to be human is to be corrupted by sin. Paul has affirmed that (e.g., 3:9, 10–18, 23); indeed that was the burden of his opening argument (1:18 —3:20). What "original sin" really concerns is the power and therefore the nature of sin. If there were a period in our lives when we were not under the power of sin, then perhaps with a little luck we could avoid it altogether; or, if we did stumble into it, perhaps we could get out simply by undoing the act that got us in. Sin would then be something like a bank overdraft: A little foresight would let us avoid it altogether, but if we did fall into it, a deposit of like amount would get us back out of that situation.

That, for Paul, has nothing to do with the kind of sin with which he is concerned. Sin that easy to avoid, or escape, would hardly need God's Son to die in order to break its power. As Paul's argument advances in the following chapters, we will learn much more about the terrible power of sin. Here we learn of the reason for its universality: Adam, the one in whom all humans find their common ancestor, and who, individual or not, represents for Paul the whole of humanity, fallen under the power of sin. The melancholy fact is, as Paul was at pains to show in his earlier argument (1:18–23), humans as a race repeat the sin of their original "ancestor": They seek to establish themselves as gods (see Gen. 3:5). If then Adam is our "original" human, then his sin is the "original" sin, and those who belong to the race Adam began (all of us) fall under sin's power. Finally the only way to escape it is to escape to another kind of humanity. The possibility of that escape is the burden of Paul's argument in these verses.

In order to grasp what Paul is affirming, we will need to pay careful attention to what he does—and does not!—say in these verses. The New English Bible has a particularly good translation of these verses and helps make the sequence of Paul's ideas easier to follow.

What Paul wants to do in these verses is to tell how it is possible that we could be turned from enemies to friends of God by the death of his Son. What circumstances could make such a situation possible? Paul's answer: Christ got us out of the mess Adam got us into. What Adam did, Christ undid; where Adam failed, Christ succeeded. The stories of the temptation and fall of Adam (Gen. 2:5—3:24), and of the temptation and triumph of Jesus (Matt. 4:1–11; Luke 4:1–13) lurk in the background of Paul's discussion and keeping them in mind will aid us in understanding the kind of logic Paul follows here. A look at them at this point, along with the New English Bible text of our verses before us, will aid us in following Paul's argument.

Verse 12 is in a sense the thesis for what follows: As through one man sin came into the world, and following sin, death, so death passed to all humans because all humans sinned. That is, if death is the result of sin, and all humans die, then it shows all humans are infected by sin. In a sense, the universality of human mortality is Paul's empirical proof of the universality of human sin. It is as useless here to speculate on the biological origins of sin (e.g., in the act of procreation) as it is to speculate on whether apart from sin humans would be immortal. In the present time, to be human for Paul means to be involved in the pain and loss of death, a pain and loss that will be eliminated in the new age (e.g., 8:23; more fully in I Cor. 15:51–57). As long as death remains, therefore, sin continues to exercise power in God's creation.

But Adam's sin was to disobey God. He had a command ("Do not eat the fruit of that tree") and he disobeyed it. That means, does it not, that for sin to happen there must be a command to break? What then of those who had no command they could break? Must not one then say that they could not have shared Adam's sin and therefore that sin is in fact not universal?

That is the implied question Paul answers (vv. 13–14). His answer: Understanding God's command to Adam as "law" does not mean there is no sin where there is no law. Even if sin cannot be recognized or counted as sin (breaking a command, as in Adam's case), it is nevertheless there. The reign of death proves that (remember the logic of v. 12). Adam's sin is destined to be repeated even by those who lived before there was a law (Moses brought the law; that is why he is named in v. 14). It was thus the universal consequences of Adam's disobedience which

97

anticipated the universal consequences of Christ's obedience. It is because of those universal consequences that Paul calls Adam a "prototype of Christ."

The parallelism implied in that anticipation by Adam of Christ is not entirely balanced, however, because trespass and grace are not equivalent (v. 15). Paul explains why in the following verses (16–17). The reasons are twofold: one implied, one stated. The implied reason is that it takes much more power to overcome (by obedience) the effects of sin once that power has been let loose than it took originally (by disobedience) to allow sin to enter. The stated reason is that an act which brings life is greater than an act which brings death.

If trespass and grace are not equivalent, then neither are sin and grace (= free gift) equivalent. The reason: If, on the one hand, the judgment coming after one sin leads to condemnation, on the other hand, the grace coming after many trespasses leads to righteousness. This imbalance between sin and grace, by which grace is the greater because it can undo the power and effects of sin, is thus made clear in the contrast of the results of the acts of Adam and Christ (v. 17).

Having made clear the imbalance in favor of grace over sin, Paul is now ready to draw his conclusions about Adam and Christ, this time in a clear parallelism of grammatical structure which reflects the parallelism of the thought (vv. 18–19). One should not be misled by Paul's use of "many" in verse 19 instead of "all." The use of "all" in verse 18, to which verse 19 is parallel, makes it clear that Paul also means to include all humanity in what he says in verse 19. The same is true of the use of "many" meaning "all" in verse 15.

The discussion has not taken into account one element introduced into the discussion in verse 13: the law. In fact, the discussion of the next two chapters will concern the interrelationship of the elements making up the discussion here: law, sin, and grace. We have been introduced to the parts played by sin (Adam) and by grace (Christ). What role does law play in all of this? Paul's provisional answer (v. 20) points out that even the addition of the law, with its effect of increasing the trespass—probably by making it recognizable for what it really is (see v. 13)—cannot tip the balance in favor of disobedience and sin. Grace simply out-increases sin, demonstrating its superiority not only in quantity but in result: As grace overcomes sin, it also overcomes sin's result, namely death. Thus has Christ's obedience made it possible for humanity to have a new goal: life because of grace instead of death because of sin. It is this act of setting humanity off in a new direction that makes Christ the second originator, the "second Adam." By undoing, through obedience, what Adam did by disobedience, Christ turns humanity in a new direction, toward a new goal.

That new goal will not become evident, however, until the end of the present age and the beginning of the new age, when God's lordship will be visible and universally recognized. Paul develops his thought about the relationship of Adam and Christ to the fate of humanity within the apocalyptic framework of his thought, and that must be kept in mind as well if these verses are to be understood. The final victory over death occurs for Paul in the new age, not in the present. That is why Jesus' resurrection is the announcement of the reality of the new age, but is its promise, not its final fulfillment. The new goal given to humanity by Christ will therefore not become visible and total reality until the full inauguration of the new age. Until that time, one cannot see the difference between those who belong to the humanity of Adam and those who belong to the humanity of Christ. Until the transformation of reality at the beginning of the new age, it remains a matter of trust in God that the new goal in Christ is sure. Until that time, Paul knows, we walk by faith and not by sight.

The teacher who undertakes a lesson based on this passage has in its verses what many commentators have recognized as one of the key passages in Romans. It is here that past, present, and future, discussed in 5:9–10, are joined in the figures of Adam and Christ. The entire Old Testament story of Adam, in its turn the story of each of us as well as of humanity writ large, is embodied in this passage from Romans. The idea that Christ by his obedience has overcome what Adam did by his disobedience provides one of the major clues to the unity of Old and New Testaments. The larger dimension of Paul's thought also becomes visible here, with Adam and Christ pointing to the two possible fates of humanity—sin leading to death and grace leading to life. The problem of physical death as the result of sin is a major problem in the passage for the modern person. The reason lies in the fact that we are simply not accustomed to thinking of sin as a power capable of altering the structure of reality. Seeing death as the result of sin points to the profound effects of sin—in Genesis 3 Adam's rebellion affects even the

99

productivity of the soil (Gen. 3:17–19). To an age trained to think of "sins" as moral peccadillos, this dimension of sin will seem all but incomprehensible. Yet reflecting seriously on it will help us understand the seriousness of sin. God's Son hardly needed to die to alter the effects of moral slips. Paul is involved here in a discussion of the ontological aspect of sin (i.e., its power to alter reality), a point to which he will return in 8: 19–21. Whether or not Paul speculated on Adam's possible immortality prior to the Fall, it is clear his understanding of the effects of human sin included repercussions far beyond its deleterious effects on personal life and human society. For Paul, those effects reach all the way to an adverse effect on the very structure of reality. Such an understanding of sin makes clear why Paul took it seriously and why the death of God's Son is needed to overcome those effects. This passage is a good framework within which to make that point.

The preacher will find in this passage a summary of the whole broad sweep of God's redemptive dealing with his rebellious creation. In broad strokes, Paul outlines the effects of Christ's redemptive death for a humanity mired in sinful rebellion against its Creator, an outline which he will flesh out in the chapters that follow (6—8). Reflection on these verses in the light of other passages from both Old and New Testaments will aid in gaining some purchase on this material.

The two passages mentioned earlier, the stories of the temptation and fall of Adam and Eve in Genesis 2—3 and of Jesus' temptation and triumph in Matthew 4 and Luke 4, will aid in that reflection. In the context of those two passages, the full import of Romans comes clear: the disobedience which brings upon human beings the curse of sin and the obedience of the one who effects our deliverance. Viewed from the perspective of self-examination, which is the traditional emphasis of the Lenten season, these passages provide the opportunity to make clear the larger dimensions of the sin that imprisons us. Feeling guilty for personal shortcomings is not our deeper problem. That deeper problem consists in being caught in the effects of a rebellion against God which we simply cannot overcome. Only if self-examination is conducted in the light of the gracious deliverance by Christ can it face that reality, just as Lent has meaning only when it is seen in light of Easter. Lenten self-examination must lead as much to praise of God's grace as to feelings of sorrow and resolutions to "try harder." When sinners

100

"try harder," they only produce more sin. The deeper element of self-examination is the need to repent of the feeling that by "trying harder" we can effect reconciliation with God. That is simply another form of the temptation to "be like God" that was the downfall of Eve and then Adam. To realize finally we cannot deliver ourselves, no matter how sorry we may feel for past wrongs and how hard we may try to overcome them in the future, is ultimately the point of Lenten self-examination.

Grace thus throws the light that lets us see ourselves for what we are: incurably prone to the idolatry of regarding ourselves rather than God as the final hope of our redemption. It is in that way that grace leads us to the only repentance that matters: placing our trust finally and totally in God, not ourselves.

That same point is made in the account of the temptation of Jesus. The Greek of both the Matthean and Lukan accounts makes abundantly clear that the temptation is not for Jesus to prove, to himself or anybody else, that he is God's Son. Rather, the temptation is to serve himself ("you are hungry, eat!") which is in the end to worship Satan, not God ("fall down and worship me"—Matt. 4:9). When Christ resists that temptation, Satan's hold over him is broken (vv. 10–11), and the long road toward death upon which Adam began has finally been reversed. What Adam (read "human beings") could not accomplish, God in Christ has accomplished: He can save us even from ourselves and our proneness to serve Satan rather than God.

The theological movement in these verses of Romans—sin to death (vv. 12–14) to grace (v. 15)—can be thrown into heightened perspective when it is combined with other passages which show how certain it is that what God proposes will be accomplished. Such an Old Testament passage as Isaiah 55:6–13 combines that certainty (vv. 10–11) with the assurance of God's grace (vv. 12–13) even for the wicked who turn to him (vv. 7–8). Jeremiah 20:10–13 is another passage that speaks of the sure purposes of God. Those verses in Jeremiah voice that prophet's assurance that God can overcome any opposition the prophet faces, as God may be counted on to rescue the poor from oppression. God's will triumphs, whatever the opposition.

If that will of God remains hidden to all but the prophets in the Old Testament, that hidden will of God is made known in Christ, as a passage like Matthew 10:26–33 makes clear. Jesus there combines an assurance that he reveals God's will (vv.

101

26–27) with a second assurance of God's faithfulness, a faithfulness that embraces sparrows and then much more, human beings (vv. 29–31). It is that faithfulness of God which is correspondingly displayed in Jesus faithfulness to those who trust him (v. 32). God is thus the only protection against the power of evil, a power which can destroy us totally (v. 28). The ability of God, displayed in Romans 5:12–15, to overcome the power of sin and its effects by his more powerful grace, is thus thrown into sharp relief by this gospel message of God's faithfulness in Jesus to those who trust in him.

Thus does grace triumph over evil, by burying evil in an avalanche of grace. If there is abundant evil, there is more abundant grace: That is the heart of the gospel. In our perverted minds, we could then conclude that since God takes care of evil, we do not have to concern ourselves with it any more. If our evil is buried by God's grace, what difference if we do evil? Indeed, if more sin brings more grace, maybe we can serve grace by sinning! It is to a consideration of that sort of stupidity that Paul turns in the next passage.

Sin, Grace, and Law

ROMANS 6:1—7:25

Paul undertakes, in this passage, to discuss the three elements he introduced at the end of his discussion about Christ and Adam: sin, grace, and law (see 5:20, where all three are mentioned). He introduces each of the three parts of his discussion with a formulaic question, repeated in 6:1, 6:15, and 7:7. The formula consists of three parts: It begins with the question (1) "what then (shall we say)?", followed by a possible inference (2), which is then emphatically denied (3), "of course not!" In each of the three parts of his discussion, Paul deals with some combination of sin, law, and grace: (6:1) "Shall we remain in *sin*, in order that *grace* may abound?" (6:15) "Shall we sin because we are not under *law* but under *grace*?" (7:7) "Is the *law sin*?"

Paul deals with these three elements because they figured

102

prominently in the discussion he carried on in 4:23—5:21. It should therefore not be surprising to learn that the discussion in chapters 6—7 also carries forward other issues raised in that earlier passage. It will help us follow Paul's argument if we are alert to that continuity and understand that in the entire argument one discussion flows logically from what has preceded it. If, on the contrary, we were to assume that with each new topic Paul broaches he has somehow forgotten what he said before, and hence we were to understand that new topic as unrelated to its larger context, we would simply lose sight of the larger coherence of Paul's thought. Since Paul proves himself, in these chapters, to be preeminently a coherent thinker, we must honor that fact if we are to understand what he has to say.

Romans 6:1-14
Sin and Grace (Baptism)

Does Paul's gospel encourage doing evil rather than good? The question was apparently familiar enough to Paul. He had already mentioned it in an earlier discussion (3:8). The logic is easy enough to understand. If *A* brings *B*, and *B* is good, then why not do more of *A?* If, moreover, *B* is a great good, is it not one's moral duty to increase it by doing *A?* Well and good, but in the matter of sin and grace, we have a case where reality outruns logic. It may please the self-indulgent to feel they can aid God by providing him, with their sin, more opportunity to be gracious; but to play fast and loose with rebellion against the Creator in that way is akin to playing with fire—eternal fire, at that!

Paul's response to such logic gone awry is surprising, however. Instead of the lecture on the awfulness of sin and the danger of presuming on God's goodness (see 2:4!) we might expect, Paul answers the question with a counter-question: Can people who are dead to sin go on sinning?

The response to that is as obvious as it is conclusive: Who is dead? Paul's answer is even more stunning: You are, dear Christian readers! And the justification of that answer takes us back to the discussion of Adam and Christ and forward to an understanding of the meaning of Christian baptism.

103

First, the look back to Adam and Christ. We saw in 5:12–21 that what Adam did by disobedience—introduce sin—Christ undid by obedience—overcome sin (5:18–19). We also saw in 5:6–11 that the undoing of sin and the overcoming of its consequent broken relationship between God and humans required the death of Christ (5:8–10). Clearly, the obedience by which Christ undid the disobedience of Adam involved Christ's death. Any serious discussion of human sin and God's reaction to it therefore must include Christ's reconciling death. In fact, Paul is clear that death itself pays the price of sin. The one who has died no longer has to answer for that sin. Its penalty has been paid. Paul says just that in 6:7, and that is the key to his argument. Obviously if one is dead, one is free of sin. The dead, among other things, are no longer in any position to rebel against God. But how can that help the living? If one has to die to be free of the power of sin, that does not help us much before we have died. And once we have died, it does not make much difference one way or the other! Only if one could die and then come back and live would it be of any help. And that of course is exactly what Paul is affirming in our passage.

The key is baptism. The Christian, in baptism, has shared in the death of Christ. Therefore, as far as sin is concerned, the baptized one is dead to its power. Sin no longer has absolute rule over us (v. 6). Having been buried with Christ in baptism (vv. 4a, 5a, 8a), we are now, Paul says, to regard ourselves as in fact dead, as far as the power of sin is concerned (11a).

That is of course only half the story. Christ died to be sure, but he also rose from the dead. So by dying, Christ conquered sin; and by rising he conquered death. If by baptism we share in that death, do we not also share in that overcoming of death? We do—but not yet! The careful reader of this passage will have noticed that while our participation in Christ's death is described in the past tense, our participation in the resurrection is described exclusively in the future tense (5b, 8b). Until that future, we have, it would seem, no life of our own, only the life of Christ. We will take possession of our new life at the final resurrection (see I Cor. 15:23, 53); but until that time, the new life we have (v. 4b), we have by reason of Christ (v. 10b).

104

This is especially noteworthy since if, as seems likely, the descent into the water symbolized entering the grave, then the coming up out of the water would clearly symbolize rising from that grave. Yet obvious as that parallel was, Paul refused to draw it. For him, our participation in the resurrection, of which Christ was the first example, involves a total transformation of reality, including the transformation of our bodies of flesh into bodies of spirit (cf. 8:21, 23; I Cor. 15:42–44, 49). For that reason, Paul is clear that we do not yet share in Christ's resurrection the way we share in his death.

If we do not yet share the glory of Christ's resurrection, however, the share in his death is enough for now: It has broken the enslaving power of sin over us. Because of Christ, we have, for the first time, a real choice: For the first time, we can choose not to sin! For the first time, it is possible that exhortations to good can be followed. That is why, of course, we now, for the very first time, find moral exhortations in Paul's letter to Rome! Verses 12–14 show us the fruit of our freedom: We now have the possibility not to yield our acts and lives to sin! Freed from the awful enslavement to sin, we can now turn from it to serve another master. We are dead, by baptism into Christ's death, to the enslaving power of sin—Paul means that literally. After our baptism, we have for the first time the chance not to sin. That is the glorious reality we do have as a result of our baptism. If the full benefits of that baptism are not yet ours, if we do not yet share fully Christ's risen life, we at least share fully his redemptive death. The enslaving power of sin no longer rules us. Now if we sin, it is something we could have avoided. If we rebel once more against God, it is not because, belonging only to the race of Adam, we had no other possibility. The death Adam willed us as his heirs we have undergone in our baptism into Christ's death.

If, by freeing us from the domination of sin bequeathed us as heirs of Adam (read "humanity gone astray"), baptism alters our past, it also alters our future. A future leading no longer to death but to life; and a new relationship with God, through Christ's resurrection, is ours. We are members of a new race, whose goal for the first time can be something other than rebellion against God and ensuing death. What a joyful situation! We can now hear, and obey, injunctions not to sin, not to rebel against God, not to establish ourselves as gods in his place. What a joyful sound it is to hear such words of moral admonition! They are the proof that we are now members of a new race, begun with Christ's death and resurrection. In that way, what Paul had discussed as past event in 5:12–19 has become present reality for us.

105

INTERPRETATION

All of this, if it is to be understood, must be seen within the apocalyptic framework within which Paul writes. The realities of which he speaks—dying with Christ in baptism, being freed from enslavement to sin—are certainly realities in this present age, thanks to the death and resurrection of Christ which has introduced the beginning of the new age into the present. Yet the full significance of those realities will not become apparent until the full inauguration of that new age. That one is freed in baptism from the inescapable consequences of human rebellion against God will not become evident until that new age has fully come. The freedom baptism brings from enslavement to sin and the resulting death will not become wholly apparent until that future time. Only with its reality will the full significance of those events become manifest and visible. The new age is beginning to make its reality felt, but that happens in the midst of the present age, and hence its reality is obscured and difficult to identify.

That does not mean that slavery to sin has not in fact been broken, nor that the baptized person does not now in fact enjoy that new relationship with God the Creator. Nor does it mean that the results of that freedom from sin will not become visible in the person's actions. Of course they will. Not doing what they once did, regularly got newly baptized Christians into trouble with their former friends in the Hellenistic world, just as Christian behavior in the present world can at times seem contrary to conventionally accepted behavior. But the final reality of which those acts are the first results will not be visible until the transformation of the ages. Only at that point will the reality of the death died in baptism, affecting as it does the future fate of that person, finally become apparent. Until that time, only the eyes of faith can see the full meaning of those realities.

The person teaching this passage will need to deal with the question of baptism. Just as the symbolism of grace coming to those who had done nothing to deserve it (Rom. 5:6–10) provides the theological understanding of the baptism of infants, so the symbolism of descending into the grave with Christ provides the symbolism for the baptism of adults by immersion (6:4). Neither method is without its theological significance, just as neither is without its theological dangers. Infant baptism runs the danger of assuming God's grace requires no personal response. Adult baptism, particularly if some confession of faith is required before it is administered, runs the danger of assuming we must in that way make ourselves "worthy" of this gift of grace.

106

There is a second problem involved in Paul's understanding of baptism. It is clear from this passage that one takes part in Christ's death, which breaks the power of sin, by baptism into Christ. In baptism we have died with Christ to sin—Paul will make the same point in 7:1–4. Baptism is the way, then, one appropriates the benefits of Christ's death to sin. Earlier, however, Paul had said we are set right with God, and put into a new relationship to him, by faith (trust) in Christ (3:21–27). How are we to combine these statements? Do we die to sin by faith or by baptism? It is clear enough that Paul nowhere suggests that baptism is effective only if the one baptized has faith. It is just as clear that unless there is faith that God has changed our fate in Christ there would not be much point in being baptized. Thus the very act of baptism into Christ's death presumes the trust that in Christ God means well with us. The act of performing a baptism is an expression of the faith that in Christ God has come to us; it is an expression of the trust that in Christ God has opened for us a way out of enslavement to sin. That does not mean baptism could be valid only if the recipient first confessed such faith, as we have already seen. It does mean, however, that apart from that faith baptism would be a meaningless gesture. If the Christ to whom baptism links us is not in some way special, then baptism into his death would hardly be thought to be important. Thus unless faith were present baptism would hardly occur. Where faith in Christ is unknown, or rejected, people do not undertake to baptize other people, whether infant or adult, into Christ's death! Baptism is therefore itself an expression of the trust that in Christ new possibilities have been opened up for us, in our relationship to God and therefore to one another.

The preacher will give added dimension to this passage by combining with it a Gospel passage like Matthew 10:34–42 or Mark 10:28–30, either of which illumine the cost of the new life baptism brings. Jesus' saying that to find one's life, one must lose it for the sake of Christ (Matt. 10:39), and Peter's recounting of the cost of his discipleship (Mark 10:28–29) represent a Gospel commentary on the point that Paul is making. The combination therefore of Romans 6:1–11 with such passages from the Gospels throws emphasis on the potential cost of the alignment with Christ which is undertaken in baptism: It may cost one all other treasured relationships! The promise of new life which baptism brings may well call into question treasured parts of the life to which one has now died (Matt. 10:34–39). Yet the prom-

107

ised sharing in Christ's resurrection means that whatever the cost, the result is sure and worth that cost (Matt. 10:40–42; Mark 10:30). Combined with such Gospel passages, therefore, the passage from Romans shows both the costliness and the surety of the promise contained in our baptism into Christ's death.

A similar account of the cost and reward of entering a new life is nicely illustrated in the account of Jacob at the Jabbok river (Gen. 32:22–32). Facing the consequences of his past sins in the just wrath of his brother Esau, Jacob is given the promise of new life, yet not without pain accompanying the transition. Entering the new existence made real by his receiving a new name, Israel, Jacob is forced to limp into his glorious future. The painful confrontation with God by means of which Jacob entered into his new life is precisely the pain we do not need to bear, because it was borne for us by Christ. Entry into new life is thus never without pain, but the pain of our new birth has been borne by Christ on the cross. It is just that pain that makes baptism the serious matter that it is.

Freed from sin, we are also freed from another entity sin had enslaved, namely the law (see 5:20, where the close relationship of sin and law are touched on). Does that mean, since we are no longer under the law, and since where there is no law, sin is not counted (5:13), that we are now free to sin, knowing it will not be counted and that grace will be more than enough to cover it (5:21)? Is the Christian faith thus covertly at least an invitation to use one's new freedom as freedom to sin? If sin's power is broken, can we not just forget about it and do as we please? Paul turns in the next verses to deal with just such questions.

Romans 6:15—7:6
Law and Grace
(Enslavement, Good and Bad)

The first verse in this section introduces the second of the three questions Paul poses in his discussion of sin, grace, and law (6:1—7:25). Here the major contrast is between law and grace, the second of the three opportunities Paul takes to deal with these three topics in all possible combinations: sin-grace (6:1), law-grace (6:15), and law-sin (7:7).

While the discussion begun with 6:15 continues through 7:6, 6:23 provides a conclusion to the first part of the discussion; and respecting that, we will divide our consideration of the passage into two parts: 6:15–23 and 7:1–6.

Grace, Sin, and Bondage (Romans 6:15–23)

Paul is clear: "The devil made me do it" will no longer work as an excuse. The power of sin has been broken. The Christian is no longer enslaved to it. After dying with Christ in baptism, the Christians are free from the lordship of sin. For the first time, they can do something other than sin. What a heady freedom! What a joyful turn of events! Christians are free! Free to do what is good, not what sin forces them to do. They are now free to do what God wants them to do.

And right there is the problem. As human creatures, Christians are free only within the framework of some lordship, either of God or of sin. There is for the human being, whether baptized into Christ or not, no neutral ground. Human beings are creatures, not gods. It was precisely the search for that "neutral ground," that search to be gods for themselves, that got human beings into enslavement to sin in the first place. So the choice is not slavery or freedom in some absolute sense. The choice is, rather, slavery to which lord, to which ruling power? That is the burden of this portion of Paul's discussion.

The situation is rather like that of one who is newly released from prison. One has shed an old regime (prison), but one has taken on a new one (society). The lack of freedom represented by the old regime has been replaced by freedom from those constraints. But one is not at that point somehow free from all constraints, as though at the moment of release one stood on some level apart both from prison and society. Such a stance does not exist. One passes from one regime and immediately enters another. One is therefore always under responsibility, whether forced to obey (prison) or free to obey (society).

But that new state of freedom is not absolute. It has its limits as well. It is possible to slip back into the old ways that got one into prison in the first place, and in that case that is just where one will end up. Paul is explicit on that. Christians

109

are now free for a new master, but it is still possible to fall back under the lordship of the old one, sin. That is the point Paul is arguing in verses 16–19. In fact, Paul is so intent on emphasizing that our new situation still entails obedience, though this time obedience to a new Lord, that he can formulate a sentence which conveys the sense that one becomes an "obedient slave" to "obedience" (v. 16). One of the dangers for Christians in their new situation is that, thinking themselves free of all lordships, they may fall back unwittingly under the old lordship of sin.

Like the prisoner newly set free, the Christian's new status can foster confusion. The prisoner who had become accustomed to prison life, who had shaped his life to its routines, now has to shift to a whole new way of approaching life and its requirements. Old patterns will no longer work. New patterns are demanded, and the danger is that the Christian, like the newly freed prisoner, is so accustomed to the old that he or she cannot change.

As a college student, I had some small fish in a little round bowl; and they swam around and around in it, limited by the glass perimeter. One day I got a much larger aquarium and, after preparing it, I put the little fish in it. Yet for a time, even in the freedom of the new, uncrowded environment, they continued to swim around and around, tracing the now imaginary boundaries to which they were accustomed. That is the danger of the new freedom; so accustomed to old ways, Christians run the danger of ignoring their new freedom, as though the old lordship still ruled them.

There is another danger. Facing the new situation, with its new requirements of obedience, Christians may so romanticize the old situation that they think back on it with longing. Maybe it was not so bad after all. Paul is aware of that danger as well. Only think back on what that life led to, Paul tells his readers. All that obedience to sin could accomplish was death. Granted, when you were under the lordship of sin, you were free of the requirements that the renewed relationship to God now imposes on you (v. 20); but what good did that "freedom" do? Its final freedom is freedom from God, and from life! Freedom from sin and willing acceptance of the lordship of God, on the other hand, mean freedom for life. Under the old bondage, the only wages one could draw were death. Under the new freedom from bondage to sin, which God graciously gives us in his

110

Son, we have also been given the kind of life God has promised for the new age (v. 23). What kind of fool would trade such life for death? What kind of fool would prefer the old ways to the new, the lordship of sin and its handmaiden, the law, to the loving lordship of a benevolent Christ? Freed from understanding our relationship to God in terms of law, which does not have the power to break sin's bondage—all it can do is tell us as sinners to "try harder" which leads to more sin—we can now accept, in baptism, Christ's death to sin (6:6–7) and to the law (7:4,6). It is to that new lordship that Christians must now give themselves (v. 19).

But how did the law get involved in all of this? It seems to be a peripheral matter—Paul mentions it in the question that introduces this section (6:15) and then says no more about it in the ensuing discussion (vv. 16–23). Is the relationship of law to sin therefore a matter of secondary importance? It is not, and Paul considers that relationship in 7:1–6, the second half of his discussion of this topic.

Some readers will be sensitive to a problem lurking in this discussion about freedom from sin. If, prior to Christ's baptism, one is enslaved to sin, how can one choose to accept baptism? If one was baptized as an infant, of course, the choice to have it occur rested with the parents, and for the parents with their parents, and so on back. But at some point, some one had to make the decision to accept baptism into Christ, and hence into freedom from sin. How can we account for that decision by one enslaved to sin? Does not enslavement under sin include the enslavement of the will as well?

Paul's answer, for some, is surprising: No, sin does not prevent one from willing the good. Paul says that, in so many words, in 7:18*b*. The problem does not lie in willing the good. The problem lies in doing it. That is what slavery to sin prevents. Such enslavement keeps people from accomplishing their good intentions. Sin takes what one does in order to accomplish the good and turns it to evil. That is the problem with enslavement to sin.

That is why preaching, such as Paul carried out, is possible, with its call to the listeners to make a change in their lives by accepting Christ in faith and accepting the baptism which is part of that faith. To will to do such a good thing is quite possible, even for one enslaved to sin. The difference lies in the fact that with that decision for the good there now comes the power

111

also to carry it through. Thus to refuse to accept Christ, or to fall back into the enslavement of sin, cannot be blamed on God. If "the devil made me do it" will no longer work as an excuse for the believer, "God made me do it" will not work as an excuse for one who refuses to believe. What is new, with the advent of Christ and the breaking of the power of sin, is that now the good that one wills can in fact be accomplished. It is now possible to "try harder" and accomplish something! That is the new situation of which Paul speaks. That is what the lordship of Christ brings. That is why those baptized into Christ's death to sin share in a new reality; and that is why the worst thing imaginable is to fall back into the old ways, the old reality, the old futility.

The balance in this passage between the reality of our situation as creatures, and the joyful freedom under the lordship of God rather than slavery under the lordship of sin, makes it useful for both teaching and preaching. On the one hand, by emphasizing that one is now free for such obedience to God, it guards against a kind of negativism that cuts the nerve of obedient action. On the other hand, it guards against the idea that we as creatures somehow can occupy a place where we can choose to avoid both enslavement to sin and enslavement to God, to live out a neutral third possibility, as it were. Such a choice is not open to us. As creatures we are not our own lords. We will either be enslaved as God's enemies, under sin, or as his friends, in the new relationship Christ opens for us. Realization of our true state of affairs may help avoid the false and trouble-inducing pride that we can somehow escape both sin and God. We cannot, and knowledge of that fact can have a wholesome, sobering effect on our pretensions, as it can have a liberating effect on a tendency to have too low an estimate of our worth in God's eyes, or our abilities when we are obedient to him.

The preacher will find that a Gospel passage such as Luke 11:24–26 provides a good example of what Paul is speaking of when he broaches the problem of falling back under the power of sin. The demon who returns with seven friends to make the man worse off than at the beginning is the problem with falling back under sin. The whole passage in Luke, beginning with verse 14 deals with the question of lordships, and verse 23, with its severe alternatives—for me or against me—poses the problem in a nutshell. A sermon on these passages could consider the problem of nostalgia for freedom from the demands of the Christian life, which in fact is a yearning to return to slavery of the worst kind.

A sermon on these passages could also consider the problem of wanting some neutral stance where one need not be under any lordship. To act on such a desire is in fact to be in rebellion against God and hence enslaved to sin, as creatures apart from God inevitably are. Like the Israelites at Shechem (Josh. 24:14–28), we are challenged to make our choice. Refusal to choose God in Christ is to remain under bondage to false gods. Only by choosing God in Christ and rejecting our former life in sin can we finally be freed from our fear-filled and imprisoning past.

The teacher has in this passage the opportunity to inaugurate a class discussion on the meaning for our lives of the fact that as creatures we inevitably must fall under some lordship. What are some lordships under which people fall in current society? Domination by drugs or by a circle of friends who dominate what one does or by some ideology which takes over one's life and dictates one's reactions to other people are current secular lordships which can enslave one under the guise of bringing freedom.

The need for Christian discipline as a necessary protection against re-enslavement by such secular lordships is a further consequence of the discussion contained in these verses and could also lead to a profitable discussion by a class. Types of Christian discipline—for example, regular prayer life, attendance at public worship, regular reading of the Bible, following the commands of Jesus—could be catalogued and their particular benefits discussed. The place of the law, freed from the domination of sin, is also a source of knowledge of Christian discipline; and its place in the life of the follower of Christ could be discussed. What parts of it are particularly helpful for people struggling to know God's will for them as his people, and struggling as well to do it?

Law, Grace, and Bondage (Romans 7:1–6)

Secret Agent James Bond had a double-zero in front of his identifying number, signifying, we are told, that he had a license to kill. Do Christians have a similar double-digit in front of their identifying numbers, signifying they have a license to sin? No, of course not. Being under grace and not under the law

113

is not a license to sin—that much is already clear from Paul's discussion of such a question (6:15–23). Paul has also told his readers that the Christian is freed from the domination of sin by baptism into Christ's death, which Christ died to sin (6:1–14). How did it come about then that Christians were freed from the law? Christ's death freed them from sin by their share in baptism. Did it also deliver the Christian from the law? Paul's implied answer has been Yes. But *how* did Christ's death free the Christian from the law? That is the question Paul seeks to answer in 7:1–6.

We need to pay careful attention at this point. Paul's question is not, Will my death put me beyond the power of the law? The answer to that is obvious: Of course it will! Paul's question is rather, How can the death of *another* person affect *my* relationship to the law? That is the question the example drawn from the law (vv. 2–4) is intended to answer. It is an example, as Paul explicitly says (v. 1), that is intended for those who know something about that law. In other words, Paul will answer this question about the law from the law itself. Yet that would seem to imply that the law continues to have some kind of validity, if only to answer questions about itself. That has implications about Paul's view of the law which we will need to explore below.

The example Paul gives (vv. 2–4) may appear to be complex or even muddled, but in fact it is quite straightforward. A marriage relationship, which is binding on husband and wife (v. 2), is dissolved at the death of one of the partners, so that what is forbidden to both as long as both are alive (v. 3*a*) is in fact permitted the surviving spouse when death takes one of the marriage partners (v. 3*b*). Using the analogy of a new relationship permitted the surviving spouse, Paul says we, like that spouse, are now free to take a new partner, namely Christ. His death affected our relationship to our former master, the law; in that way, the death of another has in fact affected our relationship to that law. But more, his resurrection made it possible for us to find in him a new master. The point is identical to the one Paul made in 4:25: Christ died for our transgressions (law) and rose for our righteousness (new relationship to him).

114　　Paul has, in these verses, simply applied the logic of Christ's death, and the Christian's baptism into it, to our servitude under the law and reached the same kind of conclusion as he did when he applied that logic to our servitude under sin. What

Paul has done, in that way, is reveal the close relationship between law and sin (v. 5). The law is the means by which sin is able to get at us and induce us to follow the promptings of sin, promptings which inevitably lead to death. Freed from domination by sin and its captive, the law, the Christian can now lead a life led by Spirit, not law (v. 6). Those two topics, namely the relationship of sin and law and freedom from sin-dominated law in the Spirit, are precisely the topics to which Paul turns in the remainder of chapter 7 and in chapter 8.

There are three points to be considered which grow out of the flow of Paul's argument as it moves through these verses. They are points which play a key role in this part of Romans; and an understanding of them will aid those who seek to interpret this passage, whether in the context of teaching or preaching. Those points concern the meaning of "flesh," the contrast between "letter" and "spirit," and the nature of the law. These points are interrelated, and we will need to consider each one carefully.

First, the meaning of "flesh" (Greek, *sarx*). As verse 5 makes clear, to live "in the flesh" means to live a life under the baleful influence of sin, which finds in the law a powerful instrument to use for its evil ends. "Flesh" or "in the flesh" is therefore descriptive of a way of carrying on our life. Of course, Paul can also use the word "flesh" simply to describe our physical existence, and when he uses it that way it has a neutral rather than a negative sense. Examples of that neutral use can be found in 1:3; 4:1; and 9:5. Such a neutral use of the word is less common, however, than its use to describe our life under the domination of sin and law, as it is used here in our passage and as it is used in 7:18, 25; and 8:3–4. "Flesh" in that sense means for Paul our total existence as members of the race of Adam, sold under domination by sin and death because of the human propensity toward idolatry, indeed, self-idolatry. "In the flesh" describes the situation we are in as a result of our attempt to be gods for ourselves, and set our own course of action and our own values, rather than letting the One who created us be God. It is precisely from such a "life in the flesh" that baptism delivers Christians and makes possible for them a new life, no longer dominated by rebellion against God but by willing service to him. All of that is, of course, the burden of the discussion in chapter 6.

Because that is what "flesh" means for Paul, it is unfortu-

115

nate that the New English Bible translates it with the phrase
"our lower nature" in 7:5, as though in addition to "flesh" we
had some kind of "higher nature" which we are being summoned to follow. In fact, "flesh" describes our total nature for
Paul, lived under domination to sin. There is nothing in our
nature, high or low, to which we can turn to get us out of our
predicament when we are ruled by sin. Only participation in
Christ's death through baptism delivers us from "life in the
flesh" and opens up for us the possibility of a new relationship
to God. "Flesh" can thus describe human existence as a whole,
when it is dominated by sin and thus broken away from God.
Which meaning we are to assign to "flesh"—whether neutral,
to designate our physical bodies, or negative, to designate our
life as rebellious creatures—will be clear from the context in
which it is used. In 7:5, plainly enough, it means the latter, as
it will throughout the rest of chapter 7 and in 8.

The counter-weight to life in the "flesh" is life in the
"spirit," and that contrast is the second point to be considered.
Paul can also describe this contrast between flesh and spirit as
ways of life in terms of the contrast between "letter" and
"spirit," something he does in verse 6 of our passage. Paul has
already mentioned this contrast between letter and spirit in
2:29, and it is clear both there and in our passage that "letter"
describes the law when it is controlled by sin, and is thus an
instrument for sin's mischief.

There is another dimension involved in this contrast in
ways of orienting our lives which is at work when Paul describes
that contrast in terms of "letter" and "spirit," however. That
dimension is made clear by the way Paul uses this same contrast
in II Corinthians 3:6. In that passage, Paul identifies this contrast with a contrast in covenantal relationships. The "new covenant" is the relationship to God empowered by the Spirit,
which leads to life, rather than the old covenant, based on
"letter" (law overpowered by sin), which led only to death.

The contrast to life in the "flesh" or life under the "letter,"
that is, life in the old relationship of rebellion against God and
obedience to sin, is therefore life in the "spirit," that is, life in
the new relationship of rebellion against law and sin and obedi-
116   ence to God. Knowing that "flesh" and "spirit" refer not to two
parts of our nature but rather to two ways of carrying out our
total existence, and knowing that the contrast between "letter"
and "Spirit" points to two kinds of relationship to God, will help

us in understanding the way Paul carries on his discussion in the remainder of chapter 7 and in 8.

The third point, perhaps most paradoxical of all, concerns Paul's thoroughly positive estimate of the law. Paul is completely unwilling to say the law is evil or to equate it with sin. On the contrary, he explicitly affirms its goodness (7:12) and denies that the law itself is sinful (7:7). It is that attitude that has allowed Paul to draw points from the law all through his argument in Romans (3:11–19; most recently, 7:1–3). If the law has a close relationship to sin, which has taken it captive, it also has a close relationship to faith, upon which it is based (3:31) and to which it is intended to point (9:30–32). Because the law, like human beings, was made captive to sin, the law, like human beings, can be set free from sin by Christ's death. In itself the law is neutral. That neutrality is the strength and the weakness of the law. It is the law's weakness because when the law is dominated by sin (when it is "letter"), it serves evil ends, persuading people they can save themselves from sin by following the law. It is its strength because when the power of sin is broken the law can then serve God and point people to the correct way to act toward him and toward their fellow human beings.

Yet for all that, the law remains a danger, because its weakness can allow sin to regain a foothold and tempt people away from total trust in God for their goodness and their redemption. But finally, Paul knows the law was given by God and is thus unwilling to identify it with sin or to condemn it as evil. That point too must be kept in mind if we are to understand what Paul is, and is not, saying in the remainder of chapter 7.

The teacher will find in this passage an opportunity to discuss sin and law, in contrast to grace and Christ, as pointing to contrasting ways of existing in relationship to God. The contrast between letter and spirit, particularly as that is illumined by Paul's use of it in II Corinthians 3:6, will provide the key to such an interpretation of this passage. The students' general understanding of Paul will be aided by an emphasis on the fact that "flesh" and "spirit" in Paul refer not so much to parts of ourselves as they do to ways of orienting our lives. "Flesh" in that sense means the kind of life Paul described in 1:18—3:20, while "spirit" is the kind of life he describes in 3:21–30 and these chapters in the second part of his letter.

Preaching from this passage provides an opportunity to

117

illumine the meaning of the death of Christ. Coupled with such a passage as Mark 10:45 or John 10:7–11, these verses can make clear that Jesus' death was not the result of his own miscalculation, or a bitter accident of history, but was rather the means by which our freedom from the power of sin was broken. Being baptized into Christ means the power of his death to break sin is now a reality in Christians. But it is a reality which drives to new kinds of actions, in conformity with those shown by Jesus, as a passage such as Mark 8:34–38 makes clear. Such a sermon will touch on the heart of the mystery of God's redemptive ways and should avoid superficial treatment of the death of Christ on the cross. Paul confesses in Romans 11:33–35 his inability fully to understand that mystery, and a similar spirit ought to inform the sermon on such a topic. That is not to say one ought not try to understand the meaning of Christ's death. It is simply to say one ought not give the impression that one has exhausted its meaning in one sermon.

Romans 7:7–25
Law and Sin
(From the Perspective of Grace)

In light of all Paul has to say about the close relation of law and sin, would it not be logical to conclude that the law is sin (v. 7)? After all, it was the effects of sin leading to death that came through that very law. Is that not pretty convincing evidence that law and sin are one and the same?

Paul will have none of it. Despite that close relationship between sin and the law, it remains sin that is the evil, not the law. The law's fault is that it is weak. It cannot resist the power of sin, and hence, like us humans, it was enslaved by sin. Like the hand puppet that is controlled by the hand that gives it motion, so the law is controlled by sin that takes it over and uses it for its own purposes. If a puppet makes obscene gestures, one would hardly condemn the puppet. It is the controlling hand that caused such gestures. In a similar way, Paul understands that if the law results in evil acts, one is not to condemn the law but rather the controlling power that causes such results.

That is the point of verses 7–11 and explains what seems to be the startling conclusion of verse 12. It is *sin* that is the cause of the evil the law brings about—note the repetition in verses 8 and 11: It is *sin* that has taken the initiative and used the commands of the law to work its evil in me. It is *sin* that reversed the intent of the law and caused it to work death rather than life (vv. 9–10). One can no more condemn the law for that evil than one would condemn the puppet for its naughty gestures. In other hands, the puppet is capable of good and decent gestures. If sin corrupted the good law, does that make the law itself evil? Of course not; and that is why, for Paul, emphasis on what the law does when it is mastered by sin does not allow us to identify the two, sin and law. That is why Paul can conclude (v. 12) that the law and its commands are not evil but are, rather, holy and just and good. The law still tells us what God wants us to do, despite the fact it is used by sin to bring about the opposite effects: to lead us to depend on ourselves and our moral achievements rather than on God and his grace. It is in fact precisely because the law *is* good that it can show sin to be as evil as it really is: Sin has used not something evil but something good to work its evil intent. What a terrible power of corruption sin is thus shown to be (v. 13)! Indeed, what it does to the law it also does to human beings: It takes them, good creatures of God that they are, and enslaves them to its own evil purposes. Taking the good law it has corrupted, sin uses it in turn to corrupt God's good creation, so that that good creation can no longer do the good it wants to do, and knows it should. That is the burden of the discussion in the remainder of chapter 7.

So far, so good. But one does not have to read very far into this passage before one is aware that Paul is writing this in the first person. Indeed, he does that with the opening verse. Who is this "I"? Perhaps the most obvious suggestion would be that it is of course Paul himself, speaking of his past here as he did, for example, in Galatians 1:11—2:21. If that is the case here, then what we would have would be Paul's account of how, in the first innocence of youth, unaware of the law and its requirements, he was "alive" (v. 8). When he matured however, and at about age thirteen became a "Son of the Commandment" and assumed responsibility before the law, sin reared its ugly head and the result was his innocent self died (vv. 9–10, 7).

The further discussion in verses 13–25 would then be a

119

continuation of Paul's autobiographical account as he matured and attempted to fulfill God's will by fulfilling the law. Failing in that attempt, he was driven to despair and was finally rescued from his dilemma at the time of his conversion. The present tense which begins in verse 14 would thus be the "historical present," used here to make vivid for his readers an experience Paul so vividly remembered.

The problem with such an understanding is that there is no reference anywhere in Paul's letters that he felt any sense of despair at an inability to fulfill the law when he was a Pharisee. His only reference to the law at that time in his life is found in Philippians 3:6b, where he confesses himself to have been without fault in his observance of the law! If Paul could say that of his career as a Pharisee, then his despair at failing to do what the law requires cannot be the point of these verses. Nor, for that matter, can such supposed despair under the law have driven him to become a Christian (see *"Reflection: The Law and Paul's Conversion"*).

If this is not a reference to the moral quandary Paul felt prior to his conversion, perhaps we ought to take more seriously the change from past to present tense in verse 14 and understand these verses to be Paul's description of his current existence as a Christian, with the obvious corollary that it would then be applicable to all Christian existence, ours as well. The moral dilemma thus described in verses 14–25 would find reflection in our own striving and losing. Luther understood these verses in that way. Indeed, such an understanding goes back to Saint Augustine and has dominated the interpretation of these verses through the Middle Ages and the Reformation right down to the present. Luther wrote: "Indeed, it is a great consolation to us to learn that such a great apostle was involved in the same grievings and afflictions in which we find ourselves when we wish to be obedient to God."

Such a way of understanding this passage has its problems, however, as both Luther and Calvin demonstrated in their attempts to interpret these verses in such a way. Luther was forced to say that what verse 16 ("I do what I do not want") really meant was that Paul "does not do the good as often and to such an extent and as readily as he would like." Calvin, commenting on verse 17 ("It is no longer I that do it but sin that dwells in me") must argue it means just the opposite of what it says. Calvin wrote: "Paul here denies that he is wholly possessed

120

by sin; nay he declares himself to be exempt from its bondage."
Obviously, given what Paul has said about the state of the baptized Christian in chapter 6, he could not say what he says in
7:17 about the same Christian, as Calvin was quite aware. In
order to reconcile that contradiction, Calvin had to force the
verse to mean the opposite of what it quite obviously does
mean.

What that in turn shows is that, given the context within
which these verses appear in Romans, they in fact cannot refer
to Christian life. If we assume Paul meant what he said in
chapter 6, and what he went on to say in chapter 8, and if we
assume he did not forget those points, or disregard them when
he wrote chapter 7, then it is quite apparent that the description of Christian life in chapters 6 and 8 means that chapter 7
simply cannot be a description of that same life.

It is useful to recall some of the things Paul wrote in chapter
6 about the present relationship of the Christian to sin: Verse
2: "How can we who died to sin still live in it?" Verse 6: "We
know that our old self was crucified with him so that the sinful
body might be destroyed, and we might no longer be enslaved
to sin." Verse 7: "For he who has died to sin is freed from sin."
Verse 11: "So you also must consider yourselves dead to sin."
Verse 17: "You who were once slaves of sin have become obedient from the heart." Verse 18: "You have been set free from sin
and have become slaves of righteousness." Verse 22: "But now
you have been set free from sin and have become slaves of
God." The same point is made in 7:6: "But now we are discharged from the law, dead to that which held us captive (i.e.,
the law)."

If that is the state of the baptized Christian, dead to sin and
freed from the law, then Paul can hardly be describing the same
existence when he says in verse 14: "I am carnal, sold under
sin." Can those Christians who have been set free from the law
by Christ's death (the point of 7:1–6) now suddenly be described
as being dominated by the law, and therefore by sin (7:23, 25)?
Unless one believes Paul freely contradicts himself, 7:13–25
simply cannot describe the existence of the same persons described in 6:1—7:6.

Again, the point of these verses in chapter 7 is really not
moral failure but the total power of sin. The subject under
discussion is not the moral dilemma of the redeemed but the
problem inherent in the fact that although sin has used the law

121

the law may not be called evil (see vv. 7, 13). It is well to note in this regard that the problem is not the paralysis of the good will or the crippling of the ability to discern what is good. Both of those are described as not only possible, but actual: Verse 18*b:* "I can will what is right." Verse 21*a:* "I want to do what is right." The problem is not with the will, the problem is the inability to do what one knows to be good and therefore wants to do because one is no longer under one's own control. It is sin that is *totally* in control (vv. 17, 20). And if sin is totally in control, and uses the law as it uses the person, then neither the person nor the law are evil. Rather, sin is the evil that controls the law and, through the law, the person here under discussion. Therefore it is sin, not the law, that is evil. That is the point of these verses, because that is the question (see vv. 7, 13) they intend to answer.

These verses therefore do not speak of the moral dilemma of the Christian. The way out of a moral dilemma is "Learn better to know the good" and "Try harder." Yet neither of those apply here. If "I" do not do the evil and hence am out of control (vv. 17, 20), then "I" cannot stop doing evil either. Only a power stronger than the sin which rules through the law, good though it be, can rescue the "I" from such enslavement. The passage therefore speaks of an absolute imprisonment, precisely the imprisonment from which the Christian has been freed by baptism into Christ's death. The passage does not speak of intentions and, therefore subjectively, about what a person feels. Rather, it speaks about actions and, therefore objectively, about what a person does.

But who then is this "I" if it is not Paul the Christian or any other Christian? Verses 9–11 would apply to Adam! His disobedience of God's command did in fact cause him to go from a life apart from law (and sin!) to a life cursed by death. The serpent did in fact tempt him in terms of the very command God had given him about the Tree of Life. But Adam, as we saw in 5:12–20, is the figure for all of us. Could Paul be speaking of humanity at large in these verses?

If that is likely to be the case, what Paul describes in this passage is not what sensitive non-Christians feel about life apart from Christ. It is not a subjective account in that way. Rather what it represents is non-Christian life under the law seen from a Christian perspective. While it is in that sense an objective description from Christian perspective of the life of anyone who finds in the law of Moses the final declaration of God's will, Paul is probably drawing to some extent at least on his own life as a Pharisee in this discussion. But these verses describe that life, not as it looked to Paul the Pharisee then, but as it looks to Paul the Christian now. The situation Paul faced prior to his conversion was that he knew the law embodied God's will, and he knew God's will was good, and he wanted to do it, and he tried to do it by following the law. The problem was, sin's control over him through the law led him to oppose, rather than accept, God's will as expressed in Christ.

But when did Paul the Pharisee, who did what the law required (recall Phil. 3:6*b*), ever oppose God's will? When he rejected Christ, the final embodiment of God's will, and as a result persecuted Christ's followers! Reflecting from his present Christian perspective on his life as that Pharisaic rejecter of Christ, Paul can see that while as a Pharisee he wanted to do the good (i.e., follow God's will), his devotion to the law led him to do just the opposite of that, since his understanding of the law led him to oppose God's will in Christ. In seeking to do God's will, he persecuted the followers of Christ, so that his very intention to do good then resulted in what he now knows to have been evil. Sin had so taken over the law that it used the law to oppose God! That is what Paul the Christian now knows to have been the life of Paul the Pharisee then! It was that dilemma, a dilemma unknown to him until he became a Christian, from which he was freed when he finally recognized in Christ God's true will for humankind. That is why he can say of his former life, speaking as if from within it: "As a result, I find with respect to the law that when I intend to do good, evil lies right there" (v. 21). That is why he now knows what he did not know as a Pharisee, that such a life is miserable because the very intention to do good and follow God's will had led him to do evil and oppose God's will when he persecuted Christ.

Paul carries on this same kind of evaluation of his earlier life as a Pharisee, and his later life as a Christian, in Philippians 3:7–10. There too he reflects on the change of values brought about when he became a follower of Christ: What once was gain he now knows to have been just the opposite. Paul displays the same understanding of the uselessness of the law for performing the true will of God in Romans 9:30—10:4. There, too, pursuit of the law led to the opposite result of what was intended. There, too, followers of the law stumbled over Christ, whom

123

they opposed in the name of the law, yet who was himself the very goal and end of that law.

But if Paul's Christian reflection on the objective dilemma of his life prior to his conversion informs this discussion, it is also a discussion of the dilemma of all who live apart from Christ. Paul the Pharisee was not the only one whom sin, using the law, had led astray. The law had the same effect on every person who understood it to mean that faithfulness to the law meant opposition to Christ. Yet using a creature (the law) to oppose the Creator is precisely the sin of idolatry which Paul sees as the root of all human sin (recall 1:20–23). What Paul describes in these verses therefore is the dilemma of all human beings who seek to follow God's will apart from Christ. Knowing they ought to do good, human beings nevertheless stumble under the power of sin into the very evil they seek to avoid. Trying to do the good, they in fact oppose the good until that point at which they recognize it in Christ.

That is what Paul is talking about in these verses. Apart from Christ, and his power to break the hold of sin on humanity, humanity will only continue to bring about evil precisely through its intention to do good. Humanity apart from Christ, which is to say humanity of the race of Adam, will continue to be the unwilling servants of sin until a greater power breaks them loose from that power of sin and sets them free to serve God in Christ.

Is the law then sin? Not at all. It is good and comes from God. Can the law then protect us from sin? Not at all, because it cannot even protect itself from sin. Yet it is only from the perspective of Christ that one finally comes to realize the utter futility of life, even a life seeking to do the good, apart from Christ. Only Christ has broken the power of sin. Only Christ can free us from that power. Only Christ can deliver us to a new life in which the Spirit of God can work his will. Paul turns in chapter 8 to a discussion of that happy state.

Those who seek to preach or teach this passage face the problem of overcoming the weight of a long history of interpretation which has distorted Paul's intention in these verses. It will seem at first as though we are robbed of the comfort of knowing that Paul shared the problems we feel as we try to live out our Christian life. To be sure, Paul knows of the continual struggle the Christian faces in resisting the temptation to fall back into the old ways of serving sin. He refers to that problem in 6:12–14. Yet that struggle is not what this passage is about.

124

This passage does not describe the problems we have in trying to do the good, and to try to make it say that means we will miss what the passage really does have to tell us. The problem the passage does discuss is the problem of those who can do nothing but evil, since the power of sin over them remains unbroken. In the first instance, then, this passage should lead us to reflect on our gratitude to God for delivering us from such enslavement through his Son. That is of course exactly the way Paul ends the discussion (vv. 24–25a), and it represents a counterpart to the kind of words of comfort remembered from Jesus (for example, Matt. 11:28–30). What Jesus had promised in the passage in Matthew is exactly what Paul experienced in his delivery by Jesus from slavery to the law.

The passage also serves as a warning against any kind of yearning for what at times may appear to be the freedom from moral restraint enjoyed by those who have not taken on the yoke of Christ. What seems to be freedom to them is in fact unbroken bondage to sin. Part of that bondage is an unawareness of it! Paul the Pharisee actually thought, in the very moment he was opposing God's will by persecuting Christ's followers, that he was obeying God's will! The problem is not only enslavement by sin, it is unawareness that that is even one's condition! There is no freedom there, only blind, unknowing enslavement to sin.

The same is true of those who reject the low estimate of the worth of their own good deeds which is implied when they confess that apart from Christ they only do sin's bidding. Perhaps that is where the power of sin working through the law is at its most insidious. We human beings are constantly tempted to think that, somehow, what we do must have intrinsic worth in God's eyes, that God must have to reckon our acts as worthy as long as we intend them to be good. Yet it is precisely the inability to bring such intentions to reality that shows the power of sin. Thus, good intentions are quite possible even for those still under that power; and there is therefore nothing in those intentions for God to reward. Only when our rebellion against God has been broken by the power of God himself can we be freed from sin's power to turn all we do to serve ourselves rather than God. Wanting reward from God for our goodness betrays an attitude that opens the door once more for the power of sin to enter our lives.

125

Finally, if this passage does not give us the comfort of knowing Paul is describing the problems of our Christian life which are so familiar to us, it does serve as a warning of the state awaiting the Christian who decides the old ways were better or who seeks to take at least some credit for the goodness of his or her Christian life. Baptized Christians are no longer necessarily the slaves of sin, yet, as Paul made clear in chapter 6, the danger of falling back into that enslavement remains. Clearly enough, the Christian is not totally under the dominion of sin as is the "I" Paul has described in these verses. The Christian now has the chance to follow God's will expressed in Christ. But vigilance is necessary, lest we yield ourselves once more to the old bondage (see 6:12–14, 16). Christians have been set free. These verses in chapter 7 can serve as a warning of what awaits them if they reject that freedom.

REFLECTION:
The Law and Paul's Conversion

The events surrounding Paul's conversion to Christianity, both inward and outward, have been the subject of intense interest and speculation for centuries. Although Paul refers on occasion to his conversion (e.g., Gal 1:15–16; perhaps II Cor. 12:1–6), and to his life prior to that event (e.g., Gal. 1:13–14; I Cor. 15:9b; Phil. 3:5b–6; cf. Acts 8:3; 9:1–2), he does not describe it in any detail nor does he inform us specifically about his mental and emotional state prior to his becoming convinced that Jesus was God's Messiah, God's Christ. The earliest detailed accounts of Paul's conversion we do have are found in the Acts of the Apostles (9:1–18; 22:6–16; 26:12–18), but unfortunately they do not agree with one another on details (cf. 9:7 with 22:9; or 9:17 and 22:14 with 26:15–18), or with Paul on the order of events subsequent to his conversion (cf. Acts 9:19b–22 with Gal. 1:15–18 as an example).

Although Paul does not tell us that what he describes in Romans 7:13–23 reflects that pre-conversion state, some scholars thought these verses were an expression of the despair Paul felt in his attempts as a Pharisee to fulfill the law, a despair which finally drove him to embrace Christ as his only hope of deliverance from the quandary in which he found himself. Luther's own quest for a gracious God and his despair at satisfying God by his own good works led him to conclude that Paul had

126

undergone a similar struggle. Such an understanding of Paul's pre-Christian life was then widely accepted, especially by Protestants. The fact that it seemed to give psychological motivation for the drastic shift in life-style represented by Paul's conversion added to its apparent validity.

The difficulty is, as scholars have since noted, there is no evidence, when Paul does mention his life as a Pharisee, that the law drove him to despair. In fact, quite the opposite is the case. Paul claims that far from being in despair at his supposed inability to fulfill the law, he was in fact quite convinced he had fulfilled it (Phil. 3:6*b;* see also Gal. 1:14). That insight, along with the realization that Romans 7:13–23, as its context makes evident enough, does not represent such a conscious internal struggle in Paul the Pharisee, reopens the question of Paul's pre-conversion attitudes, especially toward the law.

While we have no direct statements from Paul about what drove him to embrace Christ as God's redemptive act for humankind, it is possible, from some of the things Paul says about the law, to find clues to his pre-Christian attitudes. Perhaps the most surprising discovery is the one to which we alluded above, namely that Paul was quite sure that the law could be fulfilled. He surely implies that he had done just that as a Pharisee (Phil. 3:6). Under that law, he was "blameless." The problem, as Paul saw it after his conversion, was not that the law could not be fulfilled. The problem was, that even when it was fulfilled, it did no good so far as doing God's will was concerned. That is the clear implication of the discussion that follows Paul's claim to legal blamelessness in Philippians 3. There it is quite clear that all the "gain" Paul thought he had from fulfilling the law turned out to be loss when viewed from a Christian perspective. What was different now was that Paul saw that the righteousness that came from the law had no value. It was, to use Paul's rather strong language, religious ofal (3:8). What counted was not righteousness gained from keeping the law, but rather righteousness gained from trusting Christ to rectify his relationship to God (3:9).

The problem with the law therefore was not that it could not be fulfilled, no matter how hard one tried, and hence led one to despair. Rather, as the discussion in Philippians makes clear, the problem with the law was precisely that it *could* be fulfilled and thus led to a false confidence that one had thereby achieved a valid relationship with God. Paul's conversion can in that sense be understood as a shift from thinking that one could

127

uphold a right relationship with God by fulfilling the law to an understanding that only by trusting in Christ can one's relationship to God be rectified, even if one does fulfill the law.

It is clear therefore that Paul's shift in attitude toward the law was not motivated by despair at his inability to fulfill the law. There is no foothold in Paul's thinking for the notion that Paul, having tried and failed at the harder way to righteousness —fulfilling the law—then fell back onto the easier way of grace. The contrast for Paul is not the (impossible) hard (via law) over against the (possible) easy (relying on grace), as though having failed in his attempt to climb the ladder of the law Paul then resorted to the elevator of grace. Rather, the contrast is between the possible but useless fulfilling of the law and the possible and useful trust in Christ.

It is also clear that such a shift in viewpoint toward the law involved an equally significant shift in attitude toward Christ. What it was that caused Paul to undergo such a shift in attitude he never tells us. He simply says that once God "was pleased to reveal his Son to me" (Gal. 1:16), he set out on his apostolic career. Paul's great emphasis on the cross of Christ as a positive rather than a negative factor in Christ's relationship to God's purposes would tend to indicate that at the time of his conversion Paul realized that Christ's death on the cross did not represent God's curse on Christ (Deut. 21:23; see Gal. 3:13) but rather God's way of reconciling sinful and rebellious humanity to himself (see Rom. 5:8).

If that was true of Christ's death, then his rising from the dead was not just some fluke of nature, or some kind of trick, but was in fact due to God's own act (see Rom. 10:9b). And that, in turn, would mean that with Christ the new eschatological age had begun. It was precisely with such a resurrection from the dead that the apocalyptic viewpoint held that the new age would begin. It may well be the case that Paul had not been particularly favorable to such an apocalyptic viewpoint as a Pharisee, prior to his conversion. Paul could as easily have come to regard the apocalyptic viewpoint as the correct one when he realized it was God who had raised Christ from the dead, as he could have come to the Christian faith with an apocalyptic orientation which he then imposed on his new beliefs. In any case, if in fact Christ was the first of many to rise from the dead, his resurrection was the signal that the new age was already beginning, an apocalyptic interpretation of the events which the Christian Paul obviously shared (see I Cor. 15:20, 49, 54–55).

128

If Jesus is therefore God's Messiah, whose death reconciles from sin and whose resurrection opens the way to the new age (see Rom. 4:25; 5:9–10), then clearly the law is not the way to salvation. It has been superceded. It is clear that Christ, not the law, is the way to a right relationship with God. And that of course is exactly what Paul says he came to understand (Phil. 3:7–11).

Yet if reconciliation cost the death of God's own son, then clearly the law was not only incapable of restoring a right relationship with God, it had in fact been powerless to stop the kind of sin and rebellion that had brought humanity to the place where such reconciliation was necessary. Indeed, as Paul's own experience as a Pharisee had demonstrated, the law was precisely the instrument sin used to keep him from doing God's will. That in turn meant the law was powerless to stop sin. But more, it became the unwitting instrument of sin which spread sin's control over humanity. That of course is the burden of Paul's discussion in Romans 7:13–23.

Yet the law was given by God. Could it have been God's intention for the law to promote sin? To that question Paul gives two answers. On the one hand, he answers it positively: One of the functions of law is to reveal the terribleness of sin, not only by revealing it (see Rom. 7:7*b*), but by causing it to increase (see Rom. 5:20*a;* 7:11). On the other hand, Paul makes clear that from the beginning the law was intended to point to trust in God (see Rom. 3:31). The problem with the law was that it came to be regarded not as pointing beyond itself to the trust in God which rectifies our relationship to him, but rather it was regarded as itself the instrument, through its fulfillment, for rectifying that relationship (see Rom. 9:30–32).

Seen in that light, the course of humanity clearly shows itself under the domination of sin from the very beginning. It was a sin so terrible that only the death of God's own Son could set that course off in a new direction. Until that new direction is brought to its fulfillment with the return of Christ in glory, however, sin, abetted by its unwilling instrument, the law, remains a danger to the follower of Christ. That danger is evident not only from Paul's warnings in Romans 6:12–13, but from his letter to the churches in Galatia, where the full import of sin's ability to dominate the law, and use it for its own purposes, is made clear. Although the law is intended to point to faith (Rom. 9:32), it can, under sin's domination, achieve just the opposite and point away from faith to the idea that we accomplish our

129

right relationship with God through our ability to fulfill it (see Gal. 3:10–12). That is the danger of the law, and it was Paul's conversion that let him see such a danger all too clearly.

In large measure, all of Paul's letters, but particularly Romans, can be understood as the working out of the implications of Paul's conversion from a persecutor of the followers of Christ to an apostle of the good news about Jesus Christ. A study of his letters makes clear those wide-ranging implications and provides us clues to the shift in his views, but they also warn us against trying to make some emotional crisis the basis of that shift in views. Of such emotions—despair in the law or pangs of conscience at the victims of his persecutions—Paul gives no hint whatever. In such circumstances, it would probably be best to be content with such indications as we have and forego further speculations.

For further information: Discussion about the impossibility of Romans 7:13–23 representing Paul's despair as a Pharisee in attempting to fulfill the law will be found in two essays by Krister Stendahl, "The Apostle Paul and the Introspective Conscience of the West" and "Call Rather Than Conversion"; both are included in his book *Paul Among Jews and Gentiles.* A ground-breaking discussion of the general attitude toward the law among Jews of Paul's time and its relationship to Paul's Christian view of the law can be found in Ed. P. Sanders, *Paul and Palestinian Judaism.* For a careful survey of Pauline theology, including Paul's view of the law, see J. Christiaan Beker, *Paul the Apostle.*

The Spirit and the Surety of Grace

ROMANS 8:1–39

This chapter concludes the second major section of Paul's letter to the Christians in Rome. In these verses Paul turns from the problem of the law and its servitude to sin to the power which saves the Christian from law and sin, and which represents the promise of God's final victory over the powers of evil.

That power is God's Spirit. In its immediate context, this chapter represents Paul's view of the present from Christian perspective, as chapter 7 represented his view of the past from Christian perspective. As the presence of God's Spirit given the Christian by Christ (see comments on Rom. 5:1–5) brought about the kind of reevaluation of the past Paul carried out in chapter 7, so that presence brings about the necessity of a total reevaluation of the present. It is that reevaluation to which Paul turns in chapter 8.

Growing directly out of the dilemma expressed at the end of chapter 7, chapter 8 affirms that by his Spirit God has done what the law could not do, namely condemn sin in the flesh through his incarnate Son and thus allow the law to be fulfilled by the power of the Spirit (vv. 1–4). That this is possible is shown by a contrast between flesh and Spirit as powers (vv. 5–9). The Spirit is by much the more powerful and will, at the last, even be able to save our mortal bodies (vv. 10–11). That Spirit by which we are saved means adoption as God's children (vv. 12–17) which now brings suffering (vv. 18–20) but in the future will bring the final redemption of our mortal bodies (vv. 21–23), a redemption we now share in hope (vv. 24–25) and in the prayers inspired by that same Spirit (vv. 26–27). Therefore, whatever comes will result in good for those empowered by the Spirit (v. 28), because God is for them (vv. 29–32) and hence nothing can condemn (vv. 33–34) or harm them because nothing can separate them from that God (vv. 35–39).

It is this reevaluation of the present that we examine when we look at the material contained in chapter 8.

Romans 8:1–17
The Spirit and the Flesh

The first passage to be considered centers on the contrast between the flesh Paul has been discussing prior to this passage and the Spirit. It is helpful to remember in this discussion that Paul uses the words "flesh" and "spirit" not to designate two parts of human nature but rather to represent two ways of living. Life pursued according to flesh is the life influenced by rebellion and idolatry, in which the entire perspective of the

131

human being is turned in on himself or herself and the person becomes the center of all values. Life in the flesh is essentialy life carried on under the lordship of the sinful self. It is a life of self-idolatry.

Life in the Spirit, on the other hand, is life set free from bondage to self and sin, and therefore also law. It is life in bondage to the Creator, which freely acknowledges his lordship in his son Jesus Christ. The power of that lordship has broken the enslaving power of self-idolatry and sin and sets the person free to enjoy a new relationship with the Creator, the relationship of child rather than rebel. In this way of life, even the law has been set free from the domination of sin; and it can now serve the way of redemption rather than the way of rebellion (v. 2). This passage describes the reality that led Paul to exclaim to the Corinthians: "If anyone is in Christ, he is a new creation. Old things have passed away; behold, the new has come" (II Cor. 5:17).

Flesh and Spirit: Law and Life (Romans 8:1–11)

One of the joys of summer is the celebration of the Fourth of July. Parades, picnics, fireworks, and family gatherings all make the observance of our independence as a nation a time of delight. If those who celebrate at times forget that the occasion for such celebration is our national freedom, it is nevertheless that very freedom that allows them to enjoy themselves on the Fourth as they deem suitable. Appropriately enough, therefore, the celebration of the anniversary of the declaration of the national independence of the United States is a time of great joy.

When Paul, in these verses, describes the Christian's freedom from the bondage to sin and its servant, the law, he is similarly in a celebrative mood. In contrast to the despair of bondage which had characterized chapter 7, Paul now writes in the joy of freedom, the freedom of a creation whose rebellion and enmity to its God he has now overcome.

If we are to understand this passage, however, we need first to understand what Paul means when he uses the word "body" (Greek: *soma*). We must be clear on one point at the outset: Paul cannot imagine any form of human life without the body. Whether Paul is speaking of our mortal life or our transformed existence in the new age, he always assumes we will have a body (see as examples I Cor. 15:42–44, 49, 51; II Cor. 5:2–5; Rom. 8:23). "Body" is thus the possibility of our existence as individuals in relation to others. It represents our possibility of communicating with others and with our "world," whatever the constitution of that world may be. If that world is dominated by rebellion against God and hence death, then our communication with it will also result in rebellion and death. In that case, Paul can refer to our existence as the "body of death" (as he does in Rom. 7:24). It is that determination of the self by rebellion against God that Paul terms "flesh." If, on the other hand, our world is dominated by God's Spirit, and hence by life in a rectified relationship to God, then our communication with it will also result in obedience to God and in righteousness. Then Paul can refer to our body as a "member of Christ" (I Cor 6:15) and look forward to its final redemption (as he does in Rom. 8:23). It is that determination of the self by a positive relationship to God that Paul terms "spirit."

Christ's appearance therefore, for Paul, results not only in the transformation of individuals but also in the transformation of the world to which they belong. Leander Keck, in a lecture, describes "world" as it functions in Romans 8, in this way:

> "World" or cosmos here stands for the total environment in which we live; it refers to that which we believe to be real. This "world" is a social construct which humanity has built up for millenia. It includes institutions like marriage and family, or law and government; it includes assumptions like fate and progress, or the perfectibility of humanity. "World" is the reality into which we socialize the young, so that we not only live in this world but it also lives in us ("The Integrity of God").

This is the "world" to which we are related by our "body" for Paul. Prior to the final transformation of that world, with the coming of the new age, that world can undergo a proleptic (anticipatory) transformation when people shape their world in accordance with God's Spirit. That of course is the function of the church, namely to be the place where such a transformed "world" is available to the Christian. There is therefore, for Paul, always a social dimension to the redemption of our "body," namely our relationship to a new "world."

If we keep in mind that meaning of "body," and remember as well that, for Paul, "flesh" means not exclusively, or even primarily, our physical bodies, but rather an orientation to our world which is dominated by rebellion and sin, we will have made a good start in our effort to understand what Paul is saying in chapter 8.

There is a second point in addition to the meaning Paul

133

attaches to the word "body" that we need to keep in mind as we consider the significance of this passage, and that is the fact that when Paul in these verses emphasizes that transforming power of the Spirit, and the assurance of God's favor its presence reveals, he is drawing on a prophetic insight which similarly identified the presence of the Spirit as the mark of the presence of God with his people after the new covenant had been made. That insight came from the prophet Ezekiel.

When Ezekiel wanted to describe the reality of the new covenant between God and his people, he described it in terms of a "new spirit" which God would give them (11:19; 36:26–27). It is Paul's insight that that "new spirit" is in fact the Spirit of God which is now given through God's Son. If Ezekiel is clear that that new spirit would mean that God's people could finally keep God's commandment with true trust and obedience, Paul is equally clear that the presence of God's Spirit will enable them to keep his law as well. In fact, it is precisely the transformation brought about by God's Spirit that now enables God's people to fulfill "the righteous requirement of the law" (v. 4a), something they formerly could not do because they were imprisoned by sin (v. 4b). Delivered from their enmity to God, which is what "flesh" describes in these verses, and their inability to obey his law (vv. 7–8), God's people are now free to pursue God's will as it is manifested in Christ, after his Spirit has freed them from the law with its servitude to sin (v. 2). Sin is no longer able to bring about condemnation for those who live by God's Spirit (v. 1), since God in his Son has broken the power of sin, something the law could not do because sin had so thoroughly taken it captive (v. 3). Only when the power of sin, that is, only when life in the orientation of "flesh," has been overcome by the greater power of God's Spirit, working through his Son, can people trapped in that life be free to pursue another kind of life. Until the power of sin is broken, it continues to dominate life, a life which is then diametrically opposed to a life pleasing to God (vv. 5, 8). But once the Spirit, working through Christ, has broken that power, a new world is born and a new life is possible (vv. 9, 11a).

It is the presence of the Spirit therefore that marks those who belong to Christ (v. 9b); and where that Spirit is present, there the promise of new life in the age to come is also present (v. 11; note the future tense: "will give life"). Indeed, that promise is so real that, even though we continue to be involved in a world marked by rebellion and death, the presence of the

Spirit assures us of life through our rectified relationship to God (v. 10; in its context, it ought to be translated: "When Christ is in your midst, although the body means death because of sin, the Spirit means life because of righteousness"). Thus the new life we now share in the Spirit is precisely that life which we will have in full at the final re-creation of reality when our total being will be transformed in God's new world (v. 11*b*). That is the life we now share because of the presence of God's Spirit among us (v. 9*a*).

The teacher will find in this passage significant opportunities to engage a class in discussion on the way Paul understands the Christian's new life in Christ. One aspect that could be fruitfully explored would be the freedom Christ gives the Christian to stop brooding about a wicked past and to turn his or her attention to the present life with its opportunities for good. Preoccupation with how bad one might have been in the past, and unwillingness to let it go, is a form of resistance against God's freeing Spirit. If God forgives sin through Christ, why should the Christian insist on cherishing its memory? Forgiveness is real. It should be taken seriously.

In another vein, the class could explore the significance of the fact that Paul uses the insights of an Old Testament prophet to explain the bright new reality of a life under the benevolent power of God's Spirit. The significance of that fact for the continuity between Israel and the Christian church could be explored. Again, a careful reading of passages like Ezekiel 11:19–20 and 36:26–27 in their broader context will show that the renewing Spirit, as an integral part of that renewing, creates a new people. Renewal is therefore not simply an individual affair. In fact it is not primarily an individual affair at all. It is a matter of renewal through membership in a new community. Serious discussion of that fact will open the class to an understanding of the important place the church as the "body of Christ" plays for Paul.

Yet a third approach would be to aid the class in understanding what Paul means by such concepts as "flesh," "body," and "world." Clarity with respect to those concepts will keep the student of Romans from thinking Paul is speaking here about some kind of permanent duality in human nature, called "flesh" and "spirit," with our task being to exert ourselves to follow the higher rather than the lower part of our nature. As has been obvious from the outset, Paul understands human nature as totally under the dominion either of sin or of God. It

135

will be useful to emphasize in these verses that the transformation not only of ourselves as individuals, but also the transformation of our orientation to the "world" in which we conduct our individual lives, is brought about by the presence of God's Spirit. That transforming Spirit is God's gift to us through his Son, not a part of our own nature we ought to follow.

The preacher will also want to ponder the significance of the fulfillment of Ezekiel's prophecy about the people of the new covenant represented in this passage and what that says about the relationship between the community of Israel and the community of Christians. The further insight that both Ezekiel and Paul spoke primarily of a renewed community rather than renewed individuals will also need to inform reflection on this passage as the sermon is prepared.

The power of God to preserve life by the power of his Spirit, indeed to overcome death, is a theme that the preacher can also exploit to good advantage. Freeing from the fatal power of sin is the same kind of action that lets God create something from nothing, give life to the dead (Rom. 4:17) and bring the ungodly back into relationship with himself (4:5). It is that same power, of course, by which God raised Christ from the dead.

One of the surest signs therefore that Jesus works by the power of God is the demonstration that he too can restore life to the dead. The story of the raising of Lazarus in the Gospel of John (11:1–44) is thus the climax of Jesus' public career; he has now demonstrated that he bears God's own power of life over death. In that context, the verses in Romans 8 display God's Spirit, given through his Son, as having the power to sow life in the midst of death.

Yet that creative power of God to bring life from death is shown with equal persuasiveness in his ability to create a new people for himself. While we share God's defeat of death only in anticipation of the final resurrection at the return of Christ, we do already share in the life-giving power at work in God's own people. For that reason, an emphasis on that point will have more immediate meaning for a congregation. While the story of the exodus of Israel from Egypt is a demonstration of that power (Exod. 14), the account of the restoration of the dry bones in Ezekiel 37:1–14 shows it in clearer perspective. In that passage, God tells Ezekiel the meaning of the prophet's vision of a plain covered with bones, numberless and "very dry" (Ezek. 37:2): God will re-create his people in a way that can only be compared to calling them back from the dead. It is clear from that passage that the power of God to restore life and to create, or re-create a people for himself, is the same power.

Presented in that kind of context (John, Ezek.), these verses in Romans 8 can be seen as the evidence that the presence of the Spirit is at the same time the presence of Christ with his people, a presence that can convey the power of life displayed in culminating fashion in the resurrection of Jesus himself. For that reason a message derived from such a context would be appropriate for Lent. To a people engaged in somber Lenten self–examination, these passages show us that if even the dead are not beyond the pale of God's vivifying power, then neither are we. Spiritual sickness, even if it is a sickness unto death, cannot separate us from God's power. The very existence of a Christian community involved in such self-examination is proof of God's grace and power!

The sound of victory implied in that context can be made more explicit by combining these verses from Romans 8 with passages that make that victory more obvious. A passage like Zechariah 9:9–17 sounds the note of God's coming victory, and when echoes of that passage are found in the account of Jesus' triumphal entry (Matt. 21:1–11), it is clear that that entry is to be understood in terms of his coming victory of the cross and resurrection. In that context, we hear with Zechariah the sounds of God the victorious warrior, and in Romans the echo of the defeat of flesh and sin. With Matthew we hear the sounds of one who comes in peace, who will nevertheless conquor sin and death by his cross, and in Romans the echo of the rectification of sin-distorted life. In all three passages, we recognize the accomplishments of the all-conquering Spirit of God.

God's Spirit and God's Family (Romans 8:12–17)

"They treated us just like family" is a way of expressing how warmly one has been received by others as a guest. To be a member of a family confers upon a person certain privileges and responsibilities toward other members of that family that are among the closest of any human ties. To be a member of a family means one shares with others a common life shared in mutual interdependence. God through the Spirit not only treats us "just like family," but actually unites us into his family. It is that change in the Christian's status that Paul discusses in these verses.

As the phrase that introduces verse 12 shows, Paul is draw-

137

ing the logical inference of his discussion in verses 1–11, just as that same phrase in verse 1 showed those verses to be the logical inference of his discussion in 7:13–25. The upshot of the transformation of ourselves and our relationship to our world brought about by the Spirit is simply that any obligation we may have had to a world dominated by "flesh," rebellion against God, has been annulled. Our obligation is not to that world but to the new world into which the Spirit has put us. To honor that new obligation means life, as following the ways of the flesh means death (Paul uses "body" in the sense of "flesh" in v. 13).

The Spirit has brought about a second transformation, however, and that is the transformation from "slave" to "child." God's Spirit makes us members of God's family. It lets us address God the same way Jesus did, and taught his followers to do, that is, as "Father" (as in the Lord's Prayer; Matt. 6:9–13; Luke 11:2–4). If we share God as Father with Jesus, then as children of God we are members of God's family. Indeed, Paul can even refer to Christ as our "brother" (see 8:29) and as a result call us fellow heirs of God with him (v. 17; see also Gal. 4:5–7).

To be led by God's Spirit therefore means to have changed our future from death to life, to have changed our relationship to God from rebellion to obedience, and to have changed our status from rebellious enemy to beloved child. The evidence of all of this is the fact that within the community of the faithful God can be addressed as "Father." That is the evidence that we have been adopted into God's family as his children. One would therefore give up the privilege of calling God "Father" only on pain of separating oneself from his family and falling back again into the old relationship of rebellion and thus slavery to fear (v. 15).

To be a member of God's family surely promises life and joy in the future, but to be the child of a Father against whom the world stands in rebellion means that the rebellion will also be directed at us. Therefore, if the future holds inexpressible glory (v. 18), the present holds suffering and rejection by the world of flesh we have rejected in being led by the Spirit (v. 17). Yet such suffering presents us the chance to respond to the Spirit's leading in an appropriate way, that is, continuing to follow the Spirit even in the face of persecution. Suffering at the hands of a world dominated by "flesh" is a sign that we no longer belong to that world and that we have become members of a different

138

family. It is just such faithfulness to the Spirit's leading in the face of suffering that will also bring, at the last, our sharing in the future glory promised to all who become members of the family of God.

The lectionary traditions that call for the reading of this passage on Trinity Sunday show keen insight into this passage, since with Trinity Sunday the church year begins its second half, in which we concentrate on our response to the career of Christ. It is that career with which the first half of the church year is concerned, from his birth (Advent) to his resurrection (Easter). Trinity Sunday also points to the uniquely Christian understanding of God, whose presence, though mysterious and challenging, transforms the world in which he appears.

That transformation is demonstrated in a passage like Isaiah 6:1–8, which shows the transformation of Isaiah from observer to prophet. The fire of God's presence cleanses him from sin, and his response is one of obedience: "Send me." A Gospel passage like John 3:1–21 shows the need for a total transformation by the Spirit if one is to enter God's Kingdom. It can be likened only to a rebirth comparable to one's original birth. Again, it is the Spirit that brings about that transformation.

In this context, our verses in Romans 8 display the transformation from living a life dominated by flesh to a life led by God's Spirit. Here the call for transformation which Isaiah feared would mean his own death (cf. 6:5 with Exod. 33:20: to see God is to die), and which caused Nicodemus such perplexity, has become the reality of adoption as God's own children, a reality demonstrated every time the Christian, whether as an individual or within the worshiping community, addresses God as "Father."

It is Nicodemus' perplexity, and Isaiah's fear that point to a second dimension in the passage from Romans: the incomprehensibility of the fact that serving a God who is Father of all humankind should arouse hostility on the part of some. If it is on the face of it incomprehensible that God should welcome rebels into his family (Rom. 8:14–16), it is perhaps equally incomprehensible that such a welcome should subject those who accept it to persecution (v. 17). Yet as the passages from Isaiah and John show, the world in which God appears is simply turned upside down. Nicodemus, "the teacher of the Jews" (John 3:10) is unable to understand what God's presence means, and what it demands. Or perhaps Nicodemus' perplexity is due precisely to the fact that he does begin to comprehend the total transformation about which Jesus is speaking! Isaiah's reaction also demonstrates the apprehension of the prophet at the presence of God. No one who faces the living God can remain as he or she was before.

It is that same mystery to which this passage in Romans points. Those who by calling God "Father" enter his family are transformed in such a way that their former world is no longer their home. Ruled by flesh and its rebellion against God, that world cannot understand those who are at peace with God through Christ, and typically for that world, what it cannot understand it seeks to destroy. That is why Paul mentions persecution in this passage which is primarily concerned with the joy of finding a new family. The transformation wrought by God's Spirit is such that one becomes a foreigner to the culture to which one once belonged. Yet that is a small price to pay for the privilege of belonging to God's very own family.

Such a unity within God's family is finally the solution to the problem of the hate-filled divisions of humanity. That division was begun according to the Old Testament when human languages were multiplied and earth's peoples were scattered abroad (Gen 11:1-9). The resulting confusion, resolved with the coming of God's Spirit (Acts 2:5-21; note the new comprehensibility of all languages, vv. 7-11) and the origin of the church, is what Paul speaks of in this passage on belonging to God's family. Only when all peoples are visibly united will persecutions cease and peace reign. In this passage, Paul shows us a foretaste, in the fellowship of Christ's church, of that blessed state.

The teacher can use this passage as the occasion for a discussion of the nature of the church. To compare the Christian community to a family means one must bring the same expectations, love, and patience to fellow Christians in the church that one should also bring to members of one's own family. Attitudes that destroy a family—uncaring disregard on the part of one spouse toward another, selfish ignoring of the needs of children by parents or of parents by children, preoccupation with one's own interests at the expense of consideration of others in the family—will also destroy a church. The class could discuss not only how the family provides a model for the way the church ought to function but could also use this passage to discuss how the family of God provides a model for the way the human

140

family ought to function. What does Paul say about our relationship to one another within the family of the Father that helps us see how the human family ought to function? For additional information the class may want to consult other passages where Paul speaks of the church (e.g., I Cor. 12:4–27 and Rom. 12:4–8).

Those same passages (I Cor. 12 and Rom. 12) present another analogy for the church, in addition to the analogy of the "family of God," and that is as the "body of Christ." This figure of the church as the body of Christ again throws light not only on how the family of God is to function but also aids in understanding how a human family is to function as well. In both instances, the supportive interaction, whether of parts of the body or members of a family, shows what is necessary for the church to function in its intended way as it also shows what is necessary for a family if that family is to function for the good of its members.

Another angle of discussion could probe the uniqueness of the Christian fellowship in terms of the church as God's family. That uniqueness is precisely the privilege of members of the church to call that God "Father," who as Creator is their unquestioned Lord. It would be useful at this point to discuss ways in which one's relationship to God is different from one's relationship to one's human parents. If one were to accord to one's human father or mother what is appropriate to accord to God as Father, namely worship and adoration, one would fall into idolatry. The class could well discuss other points where it appears that the analogy between membership in the human family and in the family of God proves inadequate. In that way, a clearer picture of the uniqueness of our relationship to God and to our fellow Christians may be developed.

Romans 8:18–30
The Spirit and the Future

The prospect of suffering is never pleasant. Whether because of disease, social stigma, or national defeat in war, suffering rarely adds to the meaning of life and is something most people would gladly avoid whenever possible. Could there be conditions, however, which make suffering not only tolerable but even welcome? Paul thinks that that is in fact the case, and he discusses such conditions in this part of his letter to the Christians in Rome.

This passage does not stand in isolation from its context, however; it follows directly out of the preceding verses. Indeed, verse 18 shows, by its grammar, that Paul intends it to give the reason why we ought to be willing to suffer with Christ in order to be his fellow heirs through suffering. That reason is that our future glory far outweighs any present suffering. In fact, the recompense—glory—is so much greater than the act—suffering —that they are hardly comparable. Surely one should be willing to invest a little to gain a whole lot more!

What that "more" is becomes clear in verses 19–23: It is the redemption of the whole of God's creation. To understand what Paul is saying here, we must recall the episode in Genesis 3, where God spells out the aftermath of the disobedience of Adam and Eve. Among the consequences are the cursing of the earth itself (3:17–18). No longer will it spontaneously bring forth food, but rather thorns and thistles. Creation itself will suffer from the sin of Adam, and that in its turn is a further part of Adam's punishment.

The good news Paul announces in these verses consists in the assurance that that result of Adam's rebellion will also be set right by God in the final transformation of reality. No longer will creation punish and work against human beings. Itself the victim of something for which it was not responsible, namely Adam's disobedience, creation will finally, with the transformation of reality, regain its original goodness. That is the matter to which Paul refers in the rather enigmatic verse 20 in our passage. Creation yearns to be free of the restraint of corruption placed on it by Adam's disobedience, a yearning it shares with all of humanity (vv. 22–23).

That final, freeing transformation of nature will also include the transformation of human nature (v. 23b), and that will be the sign of the final consummation. That is why all creation groans and yearns for that moment of deliverance, like a mother in the pangs of birth yearns for the delivery of her child (that is the figure Paul is using in v. 22).

142

And that, finally, is why any suffering we may now undergo as followers of Christ is small by comparison to that future glory. If one wonders at the "mythology" involved in earth's suffering for human perversity, one can have its truth demonstrated in a quite literal way by seeing what humankind has done by way of the pollution of air and water and the thoughtless exploitation of the natural resources of the world in which we live. Like so much else that on first blush seems fanciful in Paul's writings, more careful consideration of what he says reveals that it has at its core hard reality.

This passage therefore contains the promise that God will restore his violated creation to its original goodness. Yet because the promise of that restoration remains for the moment just that, promise, we have it only in hope. To be sure, that hope is already the beginning of our salvation (v. 24), but it remains at present no more than a beginning, a fact which requires of us yet some patience (v. 25).

Yet the hope we have is more than simply a form of wishful thinking, more than the ability to persuade ourselves that things will surely be better in the future. The hope we have is sure because we already have a foretaste of its fulfillment: the Holy Spirit (v. 23). The reason the Spirit is a foretaste of the consummation is simply the fact that the restoration means above all the restoration of complete communication between God and his creation, and it is the Spirit who is the power of that restored communication. Therefore, such communication as we now have with God through his Spirit is a foretaste of the final consummation. Furthermore, such communication now takes the form of prayer, so it is in prayer that the Spirit provides us that foretaste. Without the Spirit, we are simply at a loss to know how to communicate with God. That is the legacy of human rebellion and sin. If that communication is to be restored, God will have to do it. It is the second announcement of good news in this passage that God has done just that. God has sent his Spirit to open those lines of communication. That is the logic of Paul's discussion in verses 26–27.

What that means, of course, is that we can have confidence in our future with God only because that future is in God's hands, not ours. If it depended on us, we could expect more of the same botching of human chances with which history is replete. Only because God has taken control of our future is our future redemption secure. That is the gist of the final segment of our passage (vv. 28–30).

The assurance of verse 28 is not some Pollyanna unwillingness to admit evil even when it slaps us in the face. It is the confession that because we are in God's hands, the kind of God who sent his own Son for us (remember 5:6–10), all things will finally resolve into good. Apart from confidence in such a God, heaven knows we would have no reason for optimism about human fate. Left to our own devices, we humans will again snatch evil from the jaws of goodness. No, our confidence is sure precisely because our future is not in our hands and does not depend on our faithfulness or ability to be true to God. Rather it lies in God's hands. Redemption is the powerful act of a loving God, Paul has been insisting, and part of that love is not to allow us to botch it up.

That is the point of verses 29–30, as it is the point whenever Paul uses words like "foreknow" or "predestine." As Paul uses them, they do not refer in the first instance to some limitation on our freedom, nor do they refer to some arbitrary decision by God that some creatures are to be denied all chance at salvation. They simply point to the fact that God knows the end to which he will bring his creation, namely redemption, and that that destiny is firmly set in his purposes. God has already set the destiny of creation: that destiny is redemption, as Paul has just told us (v. 21). In that sense Paul can speak of "pre-*destination*." It means, just as the word says, that the *destiny* has already been set; and that destiny is the final redemptive transformation of reality.

The third announcement of good news in this passage is therefore the fact that our destiny lies no longer in our own hands but in the hands of an all-powerful and loving God, whose purpose is redemption. That is what the presence of the Spirit within the community of those faithful to Christ means. That is why its presence is a foretaste, but more, it is a guarantee of the good fate to which God has set us. As the first sheaves of grain indicate what the harvest will be like (that is the figure Paul uses with his word "firstfruit" in v. 23), so the presence of the Spirit in the faithful, prayerful community of Christians shows what that final consummation is to be.

Two topics are mentioned in this passage which provide the teacher with an excellent opportunity to engage the class in a profitable consideration of Paul's understanding of the faith. They are Christian hope and predestination. The fact that they are used together clarifies the meaning of each. The nature of Christian hope as the foretaste of our final salvation needs to be stressed, so that that hope is not seen as some sort of "pie in the sky by and by." Christian hope is grounded in the sure promises of God. It is exactly those sure promises that underlie hope which also inform Paul's understanding of predestination. The coordination of predestination with hope rather than judgment is important for understanding why Paul finds reason for confidence, rather than fear, in the fact that our destiny is under God's control. The fact that the future is in God's hand's, where we neither put it nor from which we can take it away, Paul understands to be the basis of confidence and joy, rather than of fear and pain. For that reason Paul speaks of predestination in the context of hope. That relationship between hope and predestination could be explored in some detail by the class, based on what Paul says about both in this passage.

A discussion of the meaning of Christian suffering could also be undertaken on the basis of these verses. While few people in the United States suffer because of their Christian faith, there are people in other parts of the world who do. What would be our reaction if we were called upon to do so? Could we find the same comfort in Christian hope which those who are called upon to suffer say that they do, a hope which according to Paul is so much grander than the suffering that suffering pales by comparison? Such hope is an aspect of a faith that, as Paul presents it here, seems anchored in the future. How is that future assured by God's past acts for humanity, such as the choice and guidance of his chosen people and the death and resurrection of Christ for human redemption? How does that future already affect the present? Discussion of that kind of question will aid the class in gaining perspective on what Paul intends to say when he casts his letter to the Romans in apocalyptic terms, terms as Paul has adapted them which emphasize both the greater grandeur of the future and its invasion already of the present.

If the Pentecost season of the church year is the time when the church reflects on its appropriate response to the career of Jesus of Nazareth, our risen and regnant Lord, and on the results brought about by that career, then these verses from Romans 8 are ideally suited to that Pentecost season. Taking into account the suffering that following Christ may entail, this passage puts that suffering in the larger perspective of the future that awaits us because of Christ. Our present participation in that future and the certainty of the triumph of goodness also figure prominently in this passage.

There are a variety of ways in which these themes can be

145

highlighted through their relationship with other biblical texts. The theme of a future related to the present but hidden from its view is the point of some of the parables of Jesus. That appears to be the point, for example, of the parable of the sower in the field (Mark 4:1–9), where only the resplendent future harvest gives significance to the otherwise mundane activities of the sower. Similarly, the importance of the future is emphasized in the two parables in Matthew 13:24–35 (wheat and tares, the mustard seed), both of which make the point that the future holds the clue to the meaning of the present. The future will see the separation of wheat from tares, as the future will show the importance of the insignificant mustard seed. However confusing, confused, and opaque the present may be, as it was to many who saw and heard Jesus, the future will give it meaning and purpose, as Jesus' resurrection did and as his future coming will. Similar emphasis on the fact that the future is in God's hands is found in passages like Isaiah 44:6–8 or 44:24–28. The companion emphasis found there, as in the whole of Isaiah 40–55, on God's control of the whole of his creation finds its echo in Romans 8:19–23. Indeed, the theme of the return to God of his rebellious creation is a major emphasis of Paul's total argument in this epistle.

Another episode in the Old Testament which, seen in conjunction with these verses from Romans, lays stress on God's ability to redeem the future from an unpromising present is the call of Moses (Exod. 3:1—4:17). If anything is clear in that story, it is Moses' own dismal assessment of his value to God's future. For every task God has for Moses in the redemptive future of Israel, Moses has a reason why he could not possibly be a part of it. Yet it is precisely that Moses who becomes the instrument by which God brought to reality that future redemption of Israel which he promised to Moses. However dismal present possibilities may appear for God's brighter future, he can nevertheless use them to accomplish his saving purposes.

In that context, Romans 8:18–25 show God's control of the future which gives meaning to an otherwise confusing present (v. 18!), but in addition, these verses in Romans give us a glimpse not only of the kind of redemption that future holds, but also the certainty of its coming. Since it is God's creation, nothing in it can thwart his purposes. It is on that assurance that Christian confidence in God's better future rests.

The statement of the Christians' inability to pray as they

146

ought will strike a familiar chord in the hearts of many contemporary Christians. A sermon on prayer could be a useful employment of this passage. Light on correct prayer could be found by combining these verses with the account of the prayer of Solomon when he became king (I Kings 3:4–14). When Solomon prayed for the ability to govern wisely, God noted it as an unselfish prayer. If the kind of prayer of which Paul speaks in Romans 8:26–27 is also prayer God heeds, then it too will be characterized less by petitions for personal good than for the good of the community of God's people. Solomon's prayer is also identified as good because he did not ask for things to gratify himself but gave up the chance to ask for such things in order to ask for good for God's people.

That is not to say Christians may not pray for themselves, yet that prayer must be cast in terms of God's purposes rather than our own. Jesus spoke of the need to give up all else, this time for the sake of entering God's Kingdom, in such parables as the hidden treasure and the fine pearl (Matt. 13:44–45). In the case both of Solomon's prayer and these parables, what is praised is a willingness to forego, even risk, some present benefit for the sake of God's greater future. That in its turn may also provide clues about the way we are to think of prayer: less for our selfish desires than for the good of God's people, and his Kingdom.

There is another parable of Jesus appropriate to this passage from Romans, particularly the last three verses, 28–30, and that is the parable of the catching and sorting of fish (Matt. 13:47–50). It is a parable of final judgment, when good is separated from bad. To those who find in Jesus the expression of God's faithfulness to his commitment to the redemption of creation, anticipation of such a judgment is a matter of joy rather than fear, since such judgment is another expression of the certainty of the future being in God's hands. That of course is the point emphasized in Romans 8:28–30. Judgment that apart from Christ can only induce fear can, with the guarantee of his presence provided by the Spirit, be a cause of joyful anticipation. Taken together, these two passages tell us of a coming judgment (Matt. 13:47–50) which we may face with confidence (Rom. 8:28–30). Indeed, the verses in Romans urge us to have confidence in a future under God's control and to shape our present acts in light of such confidence.

This passage in Romans therefore points to God's future

147

which already gives meaning to our present and assures us that we already enjoy a foretaste of his final redemption. We are like people on a drought-parched land, who hear the distant thunder of the approaching storm. The freshening wind brings with it the smell of rain and the first few drops of moisture. We rejoice as we stand on that barren land, knowing it will soon be washed with the life-giving rain whose presence we already sense. So we stand in our parched and barren present, looking forward with confidence to God's redemption we see begun in Christ, a redemption sure to come because with the Spirit's presence, we already feel those first showers of God's own healing love.

Romans 8:31–39
The Spirit and Christian Assurance

It may seem strange to us that Paul should place one of his most eloquent passages of Christian comfort and assurance immediately following a discussion of God's foreknowledge and predestination, yet from Paul's perspective, nothing could be more appropriate. God's foreknowing and predestining us in Christ is the way he saves us. The question with which Paul opens this section—"What then are we to make of all this?"— is intended to sum up more than simply the preceding three or four verses. It is intended to introduce the conclusion the reader is to draw from the discussion in the whole of chapter 8, which is supremely Paul's chapter on the surety of God's grace.

The theme of these verses is set in the words following that introductory question: If God is on our side, who or what could possibly mount any effective threat to us? The demonstration that he is on our side is of course the gift of his Son for us. If God was willing to grant us that, is there anything he would withhold from us? The remainder of the passage clearly shows the answer to that question to be a resounding No! Perhaps this is one of the most comforting of all the many No's in the Bible!

Because our earliest manuscripts contain no punctuation marks—indeed people in Paul's time never put them into their writings—we cannot tell whether verses 33–34 are to be understood as alternating questions and assertions, as in the New English Bible, or as a series of questions, as in the Revised Standard Version. Because the last member of the series (v. 35) does not make sense as question and assertion—Paul hardly wants to affirm that tribulation or distress or the like do in fact separate us from God's love—it is perhaps best to understand the verses as a series of three questions, each of which is answered by an absurdity also placed in the form of a question. The passage would then be understood in this way:

> (33)Who is there who will bring an accusation against God's elect? Will it be God, who has in fact rectified our relationship with himself? (34)Who is there who is going to condemn? Will it be Christ Jesus who died, indeed who was raised, who sits at God's right hand and who actually intercedes for us? (35)Who or what is there that can separate us from Christ's love? Will it be any of those perils that characterize the age that is already passing away, (36)which to be sure still happen to us? (37)Of course not! Rather, no matter what befalls us, we are made more than conquerors by the God who loves us.

Such a construction shows that the only ones who have the power to accuse or condemn us—God or his Son—are in fact the very ones who protect us. If the only potential accusers of any significance are in fact our benefactors, then truly we have nothing to fear from any quarter. In that case, whatever happens to us that we might construe as showing God's rejection —tribulation or anxiety, persecution or famine, poverty or war—has lost its power to mean that, because God is on our side. Gone forever the temptation to assume ill fortune is evidence of God's rejection of us! Banished once and for all the temptation to conclude that when things go badly, it means God has deserted us. God is for us. Nothing significant can therefore be against us.

Paul gives the reason for this astonishing confidence in verses 38–39, perhaps the most compelling statement of the basis for Christian confidence in all of Paul's letters. These verses are elegantly translated in the New English Bible. That translation makes Paul's intention clear: No dimension of reality one can imagine has the power to frustrate God's care and love for us. What Paul is listing are categories of creation—natural 149 and supernatural—which in his understanding of the world could be candidates for exercising power over us (similar forces and powers are mentioned in I Cor. 3:22; 15:24; Eph. 1:21; Col.

1:16). No creation, not even time or space, can ever separate the Creator from those whom he loves. What Paul means by such a statement is the assurance that finally there is no other power than God's which can affect our final destiny. No creaturely power—the only other power than God's, since there are no other gods—can affect our lives in any but a temporary way. It is for that reason that nothing that happens to us during our life as creatures of God can have any negative effect on God's loving care for us.

Perhaps the greatest comfort here lies in the fact that we too are creatures. If *no* creature can separate us from God's love, then in the end even our own almost limitless ability to rebel against God is overcome; and we are saved from our last and greatest enemy, ourselves. God has known us from the first and set us on the path of a destiny surrounded by his love. Armed with that knowledge, we can face the future with hope and confidence, knowing that the Lord of all creation is a lord of love and that he is for, not against, us. There, laid bare, is the basis of our Christian confidence: the surety of grace.

The teacher will find here an opportunity to counter the wide-spread idea that personal misfortune can only be the result of God's disfavor. It is a normal reaction for the Christian to assume that, since God is in control, when sickness strikes or tragedy befalls it must reflect God's rejection of the person so afflicted. As this passage makes clear, however, that is not the conclusion the Christian is to draw from such events. To be sure, God continues to exercise his judgment, as Paul made clear in 1:24–30. It is further the case that until the transformation of reality at the end of time, the kinds of things mentioned in verse 35 will happen, that kind of thing and more. Yet these verses provide Christians with the assurance that despite whatever suffering and afflictions they may encounter, such things do not mean God has abandoned them. Suffering and affliction are not God's last word, as his raising Christ from the grave has demonstrated. That act by God lets Christians know that their destiny lies irremovably in his hands. For that reason Christians are enabled to surmount those difficulties, precisely because they now know such misfortunes do *not* provide evidence that God has abandoned them. Evil exists. It is not to be denied, it is to be resisted. Yet evil is not the wave of the future, God's loving care is. The basis for that central Christian assertion is given in this passage.

150

The emphasis in these verses that with God we have all we need, and lack nothing, is frequently made in terms of the metaphor of abundant food. The presence of God's prophet assures the widow of Zarephath an inexhaustible supply of food (I Kings 17:8–16), and the promise of God's future brings with it the promise of food and water so abundant one will not have to buy it (Isa. 55:1–3).

That metaphor becomes reality in the account of Jesus feeding the multitude (for example, Matt. 14:13–21). Again, there is enough and to spare (Matt. 14:20). Yet the reality of the feeding in that narrative is itself a metaphor of the final transformation of reality when Christ comes again. That Old Testament metaphor which becomes reality in the presence of Jesus, a reality which is itself a metaphor of Jesus' final presence with his people, is in its turn celebrated each time the church gathers about the table of its Lord. It is that mixture of metaphor and reality which comprises the mystery of the sacrament of the Lord's Supper, which remembers Christ's life, celebrates his presence, and anticipates his return, all in the metaphorical reality of feeding the people of God.

In that context, the theme "enough and to spare" is given added dimension in our passage in Romans. The superabundance of God's care for his creatures is shown in the power he gives them, through his love, to overcome all dangers. God's love is power enough to overcome all obstacles (v. 37), power enough and to spare. Thus the power of God's future transformation of reality, a transformation motivated by his love, makes itself felt in the present wherever the reality and meaning of his act in his Son is recognized.

Those traditions that link these verses in Romans with the story of the binding of Isaac (Gen. 22:1–18) and Jesus' words on the cost of discipleship (Mark 8:31–38) find in that combination yet another dimension in this passage from Paul's letter. The passage in Genesis raises the question of what one must be ready to do to heed God and obey him (22:2). It also answers the question of what God will do for those who do heed and obey him (vv. 12, 16–18). The New Testament readings together echo those two themes in the account of the binding of Isaac. The Markan account of Jesus' correction of Peter's confession, given in the form of Jesus' words on discipleship, shows what we must be ready to do to heed Jesus and obey him. The passage in Romans, in that context, shows what God will do for those

151

who heed his Son and thereby obey God. Indeed, the verses in Romans make clear that God himself is the one who makes it possible for us both to heed and to obey him. His power it is that allows us to overcome all obstacles, even ourselves (v. 37). It is the passage in Romans therefore that makes it clear that Christians heed and obey God by God's own grace rather than by some power of their own.

PART THREE

God's Lordship and the Problem of the Future: Israel and God's Gracious Plan

ROMANS 9:1—11:36

Paul has concluded the second major section of his letter (4:23—8:39) to the Christians in Rome, a section concerning their present situation, with a massive assurance of God's unfailing love and omnipotent grace. Nothing in all creation, Paul assures his readers, can separate them from that loving grace, since it is the Lord of that creation who is the author of such grace. Where the reality of that grace, incarnate in God's Son and present in the gift of his Spirit, is recognized and allowed to work, there the redemptive power of that grace is already transforming the reality of the community of the faithful. Within that community therefore the future redemption of God's total creation has become visible in anticipatory (proleptic) form. The followers of Christ already know the contours of God's glorious future.

That glimpse of the future, however, puts into sharp relief a question that has been in the background of Paul's whole discussion, as it must be in any discussion that seeks to detail God's ways with human beings and his plan for their redemption. That problem is the persistent unbelief of God's chosen people. They have rejected the very Christ who was born from their race and for their redemption, as he was born for the redemption of all humanity. Is not God's plan for the redemption of all creation through Christ thwarted by their rejection of that plan? How can God's redemption of all creation be complete without them? Can Paul's massive declaration of the surety of grace be anything more than whistling in the dark, or vapid optimism, in face of this persistent rejection of that very grace? How much comfort is there in being told that nothing

153

can separate us from God's love when there is apparently something quite capable of separating the chosen people from God's love? Or is it their final fate to remain separated? What is the future of the chosen people in God's plan for the redemption of humanity? It is to that kind of question that Paul turns in this third major section of his letter to the churches in Rome.

God's Grace and Israel's Rejection

ROMANS 9:1–29

The problem of the rejection of God's plan for redemption through Jesus Christ encompasses more than simply the problem of what is to happen to Israel, the chosen people. What is at issue is the surety of God's grace for anyone who trusts him, because what is at issue is nothing less than the reliability of God's word and its ability to bring God's plans to fruition. The reliability of that word had been celebrated in Isaiah 55:10–11. Yet if God's promised blessing to Abraham and his descendants (see Gen. 12:2–3), a blessing which Paul knows to have come to fruition in Christ (see Rom. 4:11–12), is rejected by those descendants, namely Israel, then God's redemptive word has been defeated. And if God's word can be defeated by Israel's rejection, then what assurance do we have that God's redemptive word, spoken in Christ, may not also finally fail for us? *That* is the issue Paul is addressing as he laments Israel's rejection in the opening verses of chapter 9.

Before we look at Paul's argument in more detail, there are two further points that must be kept in mind if we are to understand chapter 9 and its place in this third part of Paul's letter to Rome. The first is the fact that Paul is addressing the problem of Israel as chosen people and its relation to Christ, present and future. Paul is *not* addressing the fate of some individual—a modern Christian, for example—who may, from time to time, distrust God's redemptive word in Jesus Christ. The context of this discussion, namely the fate of Israel as chosen people, must be honored, especially in verses 6–13 and

154

24–29, or what we hear from these chapters will be quite different from what Paul wants to say. We must also keep in mind
that Paul has not abandoned his conviction in these verses that
God's activity is finally motivated by grace. That point, which
Paul emphasizes in verses 22–24, must not be forgotten when
we read verse 17, or again, what we hear will be far from what
Paul is saying.

The second point of which we must be aware as we consider these verses is the fact that Paul is speaking here of predestination, not predeterminism. The philosophical notion of predeterminism means that every act and every thought a person
has are dictated by forces beyond that person's control. A pro-
grammed robot in a factory is predetermined. Its every act is
dictated by the computer program to which it responds. That
is not what Paul is speaking of when he discusses God's choice
of destiny for peoples in chapter 9 (note again, of peoples, not
of individuals). Predeterminism allows no room for any free
acts. Predestination, on the other hand, simply sets the final
outcome of a process, without determining the route by which
it can be reached. An automobile trip to another city is predes-
tined: The goal of the journey is set, although the actual route
taken may vary depending on choices made in response to road
and weather conditions, for example. Paul in chapter 9 is speaking of predestination, not predeterminism. We will have more
to say on that when we come to verses 14–29.

Romans 9:1–13
God's Word and God's People

"But it is not as though the word of God had failed" (v. 6)
—that is the point Paul intends to address in these verses, and
that is the conclusion he must demonstrate. Paul himself is not
uninvolved in this discussion, however. One can see that from
the way he begins the discussion in verses 1–3. Indeed, the
personal pain Paul expresses there has misled some into thinking the discussion in chapters 9–11 bears importance only because of Paul's personal background as a Jew and has little else
to contribute to Paul's larger design of his letter. It will become
apparent as Paul proceeds that that is not the case, but it in no

155

way lessens the emotional intensity of Paul's distress at the unbelief of his "kinfolk by race" (v. 3). But that is not Paul's major concern, and he moves from his own pain (vv. 1–3) to the historical incredibility of such rejection by Israel of God's plan in Christ (vv. 4–5). In moving to that point, Paul resumes the logic and the themes of an earlier discussion of Israel's unfaithfulness to God's plan for her (3:1–8). Here we learn in greater detail, for example, what the advantages were which the Jews enjoyed. In 3:1–2, Paul mentioned only their possession of the "oracles of God." Here we have enumerated the whole range of redemptive elements which are theirs by prior right as God's chosen people: adoption, covenants, law, worship, promises, patriarchs—even Jesus himself. If people in such advantageous position reject God's plan, can it mean anything else than that God's plan which involved Israel as chosen people has here met with failure?

To answer that question, Paul resumes a second theme he had also discussed earlier (2:28–29): The existence of a true Israel is not a matter of racial descent, as though, being biological, it were out of God's hands. Rather, the existence of a true Israel is a matter of the continuing gracious election of God. The history of Israel is thus not the history of a race, it is the history of a choice, a choice made by God which includes his intention one day to be gracious to all humanity through Israel. Being a member of the chosen people is thus not a matter of biology or parentage (vv. 7–8a) but a matter of God's continuing gracious promise (8b). That is why Abraham's line continued through Isaac, the child of promise, rather than through Ishmael, the firstborn child of Abraham's flesh (vv. 7–8; see Gen 21:1–18).

That is also the logic that informs Paul's use of Rebecca's sons in verses 10–13. Again, the same point is emphasized: The line of true Israel is by God's choice, not biological necessity. Here it is particularly clear because we are dealing with twins! Both share an equal biological heritage ("by one man, our forefather Isaac," v. 10b). Surely if true Israel were a matter of physical descent the line would have to go through Esau, because again, he was the firstborn son. Yet the line went through Jacob, by God's choice, and it was clearly a choice made by God alone, since it was made before either of the twins had yet been born or had done anything to merit such treatment (vv. 11–13). The inference is plain, as Luther noted: "It follows irrefutably: one does not become a son of God and an heir of the pro-

156

mise by descent but by the gracious election of God" (p. 266).

That is the point Paul is making. Paul is showing that God's purpose of blessing all humanity through an elect people cannot be frustrated when some of those who belong physically to that people reject that purpose. The course and destiny of the chosen people are a matter of God's election, not biological descent, and so that destiny remains in God's hands, not their own. What that implies Paul will spell out further in the next passage.

The preacher will find in the movement from despair at the apparent failure of God to the certainty that he will accomplish his redemptive purposes (cf. 9:1–3 with 9:6) a theme which regularly resounds through the Bible. How appropriate it was for Paul to initiate a discussion on the fate of God's chosen people in this manner can be illustrated by seeing reflections of that theme in the story of God's people. Seeing those reflections will in turn aid us in gaining perspective on the problem Paul broaches in this part of his letter to the Christians in Rome.

There is the terror of the Israelites in the face of God's apparent failure to deliver them from the pursuing armies of Pharaoh (Exod. 14:5–12). That terror is met by Moses' assurance that God has not failed them, and that they will yet be delivered (v. 13). That assurance becomes reality when they cross the sea and the pursuing armies are destroyed (vv. 14–31).

There is the despair of an abandoned Elijah on Mt. Horeb, persecuted by the wicked queen Jezebel, and hounded by the priests of Baal (I Kings 19:1–10). The remainder of Israel has abandoned God and forsaken the covenant, Elijah alone is left, and his life is all but gone. Can there yet be hope? Have the chosen people failed God, or, more to the point, has God failed in his attempt to have a chosen people? In the midst of such agony Elijah, sustained by God's care (vv. 5–8!), is assured that God has not failed in his promise to uphold his chosen people (vv. 11–18).

That same theme is cast in story form in the account of Jonah, desperate in his attempt to flee the call of God. From the belly of a fish, a place Jonah compares to the realm of the dead, he nevertheless sings in a psalm his certainty that the pursuing God will yet rescue him (Jonah 2:1–9). It is a certainty which is immediately confirmed (v. 10)!

157

The stories in the Gospels tell again and again of the failure of the disciples: failure to understand, and failure to act. One can take as illustrative of them all the story in Matthew which tells of the disciples alone in a storm and Peter sinking in the sea while attempting to reach Jesus (Matt. 14:22–33). Has Peter failed Jesus, or more to the point, has Jesus failed his followers as they battle the storm, and as Peter sinks into the sea? And are these failures not simply a foretaste, for Jesus' followers, of that final failure of Jesus' mission, when he dies in disgrace on a cross?

Yet Peter, despite his lack of faith, is saved at the critical moment to continue his life of discipleship, as Elijah and Jonah are sent back once more to their prophetic calling. What these stories already imply will be shown conclusively to be the case when Jesus rises from the grave: God's power is such that no failure, however desperate, can thwart his redemptive plan.

It is in that context that these verses from Romans are to be seen. They show us something of Paul's despair at the unbelief of Israel, God's chosen people. He would willingly suffer the condemnation they deserve could he but change their fate. Yet his despair, too, is overcome by the conviction that God cannot be defeated. All these passages thus turn on the theme of God who has rescued, and will rescue, his people from the midst of despair and potential destruction. That theme is a useful one to sound in the midst of God's people who live in a world threatened by sudden and total atomic destruction. God remains in control and will yet accomplish his redemptive purposes.

The teacher will find in this passage clues to the way Paul understands the nature of "chosen people" and therefore how Paul understands the Old Testament history. The choice remains in God's hands and is not delivered over, once it is made, to the vicissitudes of history or the accidents of biology. God remains in control of his plan, guiding it, whatever our response may be, to the goal he has set for it.

A good illustration of this point will be found in Matt. 3: 7–10, where John the Baptist confronts some religious authorities. John announces that they too face destruction at the final judgment if they do not repent; and in verse 9, John anticipates a statement those authorities could make to counter that argument. They could claim "We have Abraham as our father," the implication being that, since we are the children of Abraham to whom God promised blessing, God cannot destroy us or he will have no one left with whom to fulfill that promise. To destroy

158

Abraham's children in judgment would thus mean God's promise, his word, would fail. *The conclusion:* God needs Israel to fulfill his purposes and hence cannot condemn it in the final judgment, whether or not it has repented. *John's answer:* God is not dependent on Abraham's physical descendants, since "God is able from these stones to raise up children of Abraham." Because God created Israel, he can recreate it and is thus not dependent on the present biological descendants of Israel.

That is very much the point that Paul is making about the true nature and reality of Israel as chosen people. That reality continues to be determined by God's choice, not Israel's biological inheritance. God did not start his chosen people on its way with Abraham and then abandon it to the vicissitudes of history. Rather his gracious purposes have continued to be at work throughout the history of Israel. For that reason Paul can see a continuity between Israel, which existed by God's gracious purpose, and the followers of Christ, who are also constituted a community by God's gracious choice. God's plan thus involves a continuity between Israel as chosen people and God's choice of Christ as the instrument of the redemption of his fallen creation.

Romans 9:14–29
God's Grace and God's People

Paul has set out a radical proposal: Membership in the true Israel, God's chosen people, is not a matter of genetic descent from Abraham but a matter of being chosen to belong to that people. The substance, the essence of that people therefore does not rest on biological inheritance, on birth, but rather on God's promise that there would be such a people (9:8). To make clear that God's people depend on his continuing choice for their existence, God chose only one of twin brothers to be the one through whom his people would continue (9:11).

It is with the nature and existence of the true people of God that Paul continues to occupy himself in these subsequent verses. The question Paul uses to introduce this segment of his argument is a familiar one: "What then shall we say?" He used that same question at 6:1, 15, and 7:7, where it introduced three segments of Paul's discussion; and he will use it in the same way again at 9:30, where the next segment of his discussion begins.

The point toward which Paul is moving in this portion of his argument comes clear in verse 24. Paul is speaking about how the same principle of election and choice which began Israel and which sustained it (see vv. 7–13, 17–18) has continued to work in the expansion of the chosen people brought about by Christ. It was in fact this final goal of an expanded chosen people, Paul argues, that God had in mind all along. That expanded people of God now includes gentiles, who once were not part of that people (vv. 25–26). Paul is quoting some verses here from Hosea (2:25, 1 in that order) which Hosea had addressed to Israel, indicating to them that their existence as a people had nothing to do with natural ethnic origins but with God's express act of choice. When Paul now uses these verses to refer to the gentiles who have been included in God's new people, he means to say that the inclusion of those gentiles in God's people is no different from the original designation of Israel as chosen people: In both instances, apart from God's choice, there would have been no chosen people at all. Just as Israel owed its nationhood to God's election of them as chosen, as Hosea said, so God's new people owes its existence as a people to that same kind of election.

But more, God had intended from the beginning that only a part of Israel, a "remnant," should be included in that new people (vv. 27–28). Indeed, the fact that even such a remnant remains which can be included in God's new people is due to the direct intention of God (v. 29). Paul's quotation from Isaiah 10:22 (see its context in Isa. 10:20–23) in verses 27–28 and from Isaiah 1:9 in verse 29 indicates that Paul sees those prophecies fulfilled in the inclusion of only a portion of Israel among those who have accepted Jesus as God's Messiah, as his Christ.

What all of that means is simply that when God chose to create a new people for himself, based on trust in Christ as the one through whom human beings can find their relationship to God rectified, he continued to act in a way consistent with the original choice of Israel as chosen people. Indeed, the process begun with that choice is now fulfilled. Since the origin of Israel, as well as its continuation, was a matter of God's choice and not of genetic heritage (vv. 7–13), no one, least of all the Israelites, should be surprised if God continues to constitute a chosen people by his own act of choice.

160

One cannot read what Paul says in this passage about God's dealings both with Israel and with the gentiles without having a variety of questions arise. Some of those questions are raised by the content of what Paul has to say, while others are raised by misunderstandings that generations of interpretation have introduced into these verses. If we are to be clear on what Paul means in these verses, so that our questions deal with what he is really saying and not with what we imagine him to be saying, three points need to be kept firmly in mind.

The first point concerns Paul's clear understanding that God is the creator of the world and the ruler of its history and that he therefore disposes over it as sovereign Lord. That is especially clear in verses 19–21. Calling the Creator to account for the way he has created his world, or the way he has disposed over its history, lies outside the competence of a creature. Questions we have about that aspect of Paul's discussion therefore are questions raised by our creaturehood and the limitations that that creaturehood inevitably places upon us. This is to be sure not a line of argumentation unique to this part of Paul's letter. Paul has been clear from the outset that it is precisely rebellion against God because of human creaturehood that has gotten the world into its present mess (recall the discussion of idolatry in chap. 1 and of Adam in chap. 5), and a continuation of the illusion that we can rise above such limitations means simply a continuation of our troubles.

What Paul gives us in this part of his discussion is a strong dose of reality, something which, as is the case with any strong but effective medicine, some patients tend to resist. But we are in fact not gods. We are in fact not capable of any sovereign disposition over reality, as the history of humankind demonstrates convincingly enough. What humans have done to each other and to their environment ought to constitute irrefutable proof of that fact. Resistance to God as God, as sovereign Creator, lies at the heart of human rebellion and sin; and it is precisely such resistance that underlies much of what we tend to find distasteful in these verses. But we are, and we remain, creatures; and until we come to terms with that fact, which means until we admit we need God's help to act as creatures in a responsible and loving way to our fellow creatures, little of what Paul says will be convincing.

161

Part of the good news of the gospel is that we are in fact not gods and that therefore the future does not lie in our manifestly incapable hands. That good news constitutes part of Paul's argument in these verses, and we must be aware of that fact.

The second point we must keep in mind if we are to be clear on what Paul intends us to find in this passage is the fact that the God who disposes over his creation as sovereign Creator is a God of mercy. It is within that overarching framework that these verses must be understood or they can only be misunderstood. That the framework is God's mercy comes clear in verse 15, for example, where Paul begins his answer to the sort of questions that inevitably arise as the result of the kind of discussion he is here undertaking. Note carefully Paul's quotation from Exodus 33:19*b*. It speaks exclusively of God's decision to be merciful. It is not neatly balanced, as though God had said he would be merciful to whom he chose and wrathful to whom he chose. Such symmetry between grace and wrath, between mercy and condemnation, is missing here, as it is missing throughout this passage. The whole discussion is marked rather by the asymmetry of a dominating grace. That same point is clear in verse 22, where Paul, speaking of "vessels of wrath made for destruction," comes as close as he ever does to what is popularly called "double predestination" but which would, in its popular understanding, be more accurately called "double predeterminism." It is the notion that grace is balanced by wrath, that God saves some and condemns others and that neither group has anything to do with its own fate. It is precisely that kind of symmetry between grace and wrath that Paul will have none of. Look carefully at verse 22; note the fate of those "vessels of wrath." They are not destroyed, they are "borne with much patience." To what end? To show the riches of God's mercy! If ever there were a place in Paul's letters where he could have expressed the terrible symmetry of grace and wrath, it is surely here. Yet he does not. In fact, he has carefully avoided it. That he has done so indicates that for Paul such symmetry does not exist.

That same point is clear even in verses 17–18. The language with which verse 17 is introduced (Greek *gar*, thus) indicates Paul means that verse to be understood as an example of what is stated in verse 16: The fate of the chosen people depends on God's mercy. Again, if, as Paul's language makes clear, the logical result of verse 17 is verse 18, which once more affirms God's right to dispose over history as he sees fit, that

162

logical result is nevertheless once more set within the framework of mercy. That framework is provided not only by the immediate literary context (i.e., vv. 15–16), it is provided by the historical context as well. The result of Pharaoh's hardening was Israel's exodus from Egypt, so that God's purpose of blessing all humanity through a people descended from Abraham could be continued. It was from this people, as Paul pointed out, that Christ himself came (v. 5), the Christ who is the redeemer of all who trust him, whether Jew or Greek (1:16). The hardening of Pharaoh is thus for the final purpose of redemption, even of the offspring of Pharaoh! If one finds this hard to comprehend, one has the company of Paul, who will sum up his whole discussion of God's plan for the redemption of humankind in 11:33 where, in an outburst of happy bafflement, he describes the mysterious ways of the God of mercy.

The further good news therefore in what Paul has to say here lies in the fact that the Lord of creation is a merciful Father, who does what he does to serve the end of his gracious mercy for his rebellious creation.

The third point that we need to keep in mind is the fact that Paul is dealing in this passage with the place of Israel in God's plan of salvation. He is not dealing with the fate of individuals. What he says of God's gracious purposes in effecting that plan has significance, of course, for us as individuals; but the passage will be misunderstood if its message is taken in individualistic terms. If the passage contains nothing of a symmetry of grace and wrath in terms of inclusion in, or exclusion from, the people of God, it certainly contains nothing of that kind of symmetry in relation to individuals. One will not find here in Paul's intention anything of the "double predestination" of individuals, and that for the two reasons we have mentioned: First, the passage is not concerned with individuals; and second, Paul speaks of the asymmetry of God's grace, not the symmetry of grace and wrath. Everywhere in Paul's argument to this point grace has held the upper hand: It comes to those who do not deserve it (3:22–24; 5:8–10), it is more abundant than sin (5:20–21) and breaks its power (6:22; 7:6), and there is nothing anywhere that can thwart it (8:38–39).

Paul knows, to be sure, of the danger which exists if one resists God's gracious offer of mercy to us rebellious creatures. If we reject that offer of mercy, we run the risk that God will

163

honor our choice. But nowhere does Paul hint that such refusal is willed, let alone predetermined, by God. Were it so, the apostolic office would be a sham; and the proclamation of God's gracious act in Jesus of Nazareth and its call to trust in the One whom Jesus called "Father" would be a snare and a delusion.

Rather, the purpose of God is grace and redemption. Even in that strange movement of Paul's reflections where, acknowledging the total sovereignty of God, Paul can entertain the thought that even human rebellion is encompassed in God's plan, it is finally for the purposes of mercy (see 11:32). Indeed, the only things Paul knows to be irrevocable are God's gifts and his calling which constitute his chosen people (11:29).

That is finally the good news of the gospel, to be found even in the kind of passage here under consideration: God is finally and disproportionately a God of mercy and grace, who does what he does for the good of his creation and its final healing and redemption. God deals with us not on the basis of what we are but on the basis of what he is: a merciful Father.

Because of the kind of misunderstandings that can cling to this passage, particularly among those who stand in the Reformed tradition, the teacher must take care that students understand what Paul is really saying in these verses. Careful attention must be paid in particular to the three points outlined above, so that some at least of the popular misapprehensions about Paul's thought can be avoided. These verses *must* be understood within the larger context of grace and should probably be dealt with only in situations that permit the development of an understanding of that larger context. Considered in isolation, or against the background of the fate of individuals, these verses will almost inevitably be misunderstood.

The difficulty lies in the fact that those who have understood these verses to be statements of eternal truth about how God deals with each individual, rather than a statement of how God has dealt with Israel in pursuing his plan for the redemption of his rebellious creation, have also tended to understand these verses in terms of a rigid and symmetrical predeterminism. In such a predeterminism, God had determined before each individual was born whether or not that person would be saved or damned. Nothing that individual could do would alter that fact. Those who were damned got what they deserved as rebellious creatures. Those who were saved were saved only by grace. But the symmetry of grace and wrath was unbroken: As

164

God acted in grace toward some persons, he acted in wrath toward others.

That is simply not what Paul is saying in this passage. He is not writing about the fate of each individual. He is making a statement about how God dealt with Israel, and continues to deal with it, even when it rejects his Son; namely, he deals with it in mercy, even when it deserves wrath. That is why one so badly distorts Paul's point if one assumes these verses tell me about my fate, or anyone else's, before God: damned or saved. Rather, what these verses tell me is that the same gracious purpose at work in the election of Israel is now at work in a new chosen people to whom I can now also belong, by that same gracious purpose of God. The passage is therefore about the enlargement of God's mercy to include gentiles, not about the narrow and predetermined fate of each individual. We gentiles can now be part of his gracious purpose, we can be part of his people, chosen by grace through Christ Jesus. *That* is the point of this passage.

These verses are rich in preaching resources and can be pointed in different ways, depending on the needs of the congregation. The verses would be appropriate for a sermon on the grace of God, particularly on the way in which the coming of Christ has broadened the scope of that mercy to include gentiles as well. Any one of the Old Testament passages from which Paul quotes would be an appropriate lesson; and such a passage as Matthew 15:21–28, with its expansion of God's mercy in Christ also to gentiles (because of faith, v. 28!), would be a suitable Gospel reading.

The passage would also be appropriate for a sermon on the nature of the church as the people of God, enabling a congregation to understand itself in its continuity with the people of Israel. As fellow-members of God's chosen people, as well as fellow-heirs of Abraham in faith, Christians will see they have no room at all for any kind of anti-Semitic sentiments. For most church members, participants in a culture not notable for its knowledge of or regard for its heritage from the past, this passage would provide insight into the long history to which one becomes heir when one enters the community of faith. As Christians, we have Abraham as our father as well, and the story of the patriarchs and prophets is our story too. It is a story we need to know, and of which we may be proud.

165

Grace, Faith, and the Purpose of the Law
ROMANS 9:30—10:21

In the previous section (9:1–29) Paul discussed in more detail a topic he had treated at an earlier point in his letter, namely, the status of Israel as chosen people (cf. 3:1–8). In this next section of his letter, Paul will expand on another topic he treated earlier, namely, the problem of the basis and purpose of the law (cf. 3:31—4:22). These two topics are closely related. If the law God gave to Israel as his chosen people, indeed as the evidence of their chosen status, did not keep Israel from rejecting God's Christ, what can we say about Israel's relationship to that law or, even more fundamentally, about the purpose of that law? Did God's law fail by leading Israel to expect a righteousness different from that to be found in Christ? And what can we say about the relationship of the law and Christ? Are they opposed to one another? Yet both come from God. Does the expansion of chosen people to include gentiles have a bearing on all of this? These are the kind of questions to which Paul turns in this section.

It would be easy to dismiss this sort of discussion as perhaps having some historical interest but of no real concern to us who no longer have to worry about the law. Yet the issues are of burning importance, because they concern the way one has a rectified relationship with God. If we no longer rely on fulfilling Israel's law for that relationship, we nevertheless are subject to the temptation of assuming that we can rely at least in part on our contribution to that rectified relationship. After all, what we do must at least contribute *something* to God's looking with favor on us and choosing us to be members of his new people in Christ. The idea that we are partners with God in the matter of our salvation is not foreign to the way some people understand the Christian faith even today. Yet it is an understanding which, in Paul's view, is completely at odds with the way our relationship to God is to be understood. That is the issue that is under discussion in this passage; and for that reason, we must pay close attention to this part of Paul's argument.

166

Romans 9:30—10:13
Law and Faith

The words which begin verse 30 show that Paul is ready here, as he was in verse 14, where that same question occurs, to draw out the implications of what he has been discussing. That discussion has pointed to the startling conclusion that "chosen people" now includes more than physical descendants of Abraham. The chosen people has been broadened, by the same means it was originally created, namely God's choice, to include gentiles as well. Indeed, the physical descendants of Abraham now constitute only a small part of God's new chosen people (vv. 27–29). What are we to make of that fact?

Paul tells us in this passage. The astonishing upshot of the whole matter is the fact that while the gentiles were originally excluded from the chosen people, and were not given the instrument of God's grace and instruction, the law, they nevertheless are the ones who have accepted the rectified relationship with God based on trust in him. The Israelites, on the other hand, possessing as a birthright the law which was intended to uphold that relationship (the "law characterized by righteousness" of v. 31), have not achieved the same trust, which was the purpose of the law. The reason? They thought the law pointed to the contribution they had to make to that relationship with God ("as though by works") and hence lost the point of the law, which was to engender trust in the God who had chosen them. That had as its inevitable outcome the result that when Christ came as the one who personified the call contained in the law to trust in God, the chosen people rejected him. That which was the cornerstone of the chosen people— trust in God—became instead a stumbling stone (v. 33).

The tragic point in all of that centers around the fact that the rejection did not occur because Israel was not religious enough. They were very religious, and that perhaps brings us close to the root of the matter. They were so religious that they did not want to settle only for something God could give them. They wanted to be religious enough so that they could become partners with God in the matter of their salvation. God chose them, and now they would prove that the choice was a good one

167

by becoming a very religious people, deserving by their own religious goodness what God had given them by grace. In setting out to merit God's grace, they ignored that grace and shifted the area of trust from God's goodness to their own goodness. That is the point of 10:1–3.

The tragedy is that such zeal for goodness, for godliness, if one will, is in its own way a subtle form of rebellion, of idolatry. It means being unwilling to subordinate oneself to God as Creator and to trust that he is good enough and strong enough and well disposed enough to uphold our relationship with him. Just in case he may prove less reliable, or less generous than he claims, it would be good to have something of our own virtue to fall back on. How we do want to be lovable! How we do want to think that our relationship with God is due, in some small measure at least, to our own religious value, to our own worth in God's eyes! And in that moment, the sin of idolatry has flared back to life, and God has once more been rejected as God.

That also demonstrates the inability of the law to resist that primal sin of idolatry. We saw earlier how the law was taken prisoner by sin, forced to do sin's bidding (see the discussion of 7:7–25). What the law intended—a rectified relationship with God—it was unable to bring about. It was not until Christ came that sin's power was broken, and the law was freed from that power. That is why Christ is both the fulfillment of the intended role of the law in the relationship of creature with Creator and the end of its primary function in that relationship. Paul means both when he says "Christ is the end of the law" (v. 4). Christ is the end, the goal for which the law was established, namely trust in God (see 3:31). But Christ is also the end of the law as the primary means of a relationship with that God. Paul shows that Christ is the end of the primary role of the law in verse 5. He shows that Christ is the goal of that law in verses 6–13. We must attend carefully to both of the ways Christ is the "end of the law."

Paul comments on Christ as the end of the primary role of the law in the matter of righteousness in verse 5. The whole problem with the law is that if one depends on fulfilling the law as the basis for one's relationship with God, that is the only basis that relationship will have. Since that relationship then depends on one's own trustworthiness ("works of the law") rather than on God's trustworthiness ("faith"), it will not be a stable or even a real relationship. Such a real relationship can only be based on total trust in the trustworthiness of God, a trust Christ came to elicit. Because Christ, not the law, is now the basis for trusting God, Christ is the end of the law as the means of salvation.

Yet Christ is the end of the law because he is also the incarnation of the goal of the law—the demonstration of God's faithfulness to his creation—and Paul concentrates on that in verses 6–13. The substance of verses 6–8 are taken from Deuteronomy 30:12–14, a passage in which Moses assures the Israelites that God's law is truly accessible to them. It is not remote, or isolated. When Moses described the law in those terms, Paul implies, Moses was describing the reality of the law which has now been realized in Christ. That is why the law is no longer the primary way to trust in God. Its reality has now been embodied—incarnated!—in Christ. And that, Paul concludes, is precisely what the gospel he preaches is all about (v. 8*b*).

Paul's interpretation (his "midrash"—Paul is here employing a Hebrew mode of interpreting Scripture) continues in verses 9–10, where Paul interprets Deuteronomy 30:14. Trusting God totally ("in your heart") and acknowledging such trust through public confession ("with your mouth"), are what Christ as fulfiller of the law can and does bring about. Seeing in the events of Jesus of Nazareth the guiding hand of God himself— that is what the Christian faith is all about. Above all, the demonstration of God's trustworthiness is to be seen in Jesus' rising from the dead. It is important to note that the emphasis in verse 9*b* is on the fact that *God* raised Christ from the dead, not on the event of resurrection as such. Jesus' resurrection is important because it shows God can be trusted even to overcome death. Trusting in that God from the heart is what leads to a rectified relationship with him, and acknowledging that trust with our lives is what leads to our sharing in God's final deliverance of his creation from its bondage to corruption and evil (v. 10).

Paul is ready to conclude his argument. All of what he has said so far Paul finds summed up in a verse from the book of the old covenant, the covenant of the law. Why from the covenant of the law? (Paul quotes here from a prophet, but he quotes often enough from the law itself to make one wonder.) If the religious function of the law has been ended by Christ, how can Paul continue to quote from it? He can do so because, now that Christ has come to make clear the true purpose of the law, we can finally see what the law is all about (see II Cor. 3:12–16, where Paul says exactly that). Seen in relation to Christ, and the

169

trust in God to which he summons us, the law can now function as an aid in the understanding of our rectified relationship with God. That is why Paul can continually quote from the book of a covenant whose primary role in our salvation has been taken over by Christ. Freed from a burden it could not bear—to be the primary means of salvation—the law can now illumine that true means of salvation, Christ.

The verse Paul chooses to sum up his argument points to trust in God as the only way to a relationship with him that will not in the end prove illusory and disappointing (v. 11). That is also why the chosen people now includes gentiles as well as Israelites. There is finally no distinction between them (v. 12). The same God is Lord of all races. The same God lavishes the riches of his mercy on all peoples alike. The same God proves his trustworthiness by delivering from their bondage to sin and rebellion all who call upon him in the trust that he is trustworthy and he will maintain them in his love (v. 13).

The teacher who undertakes a session on this passage will find here the key to Paul's understanding of the law and its purpose in relation to Christ. It would be well to review for the class the logic of Paul's argument. Paul points out in verses 31–32 that the law was to engender trust in God on the part of Israel. The law was therefore to be a matter of trust. Israel rejected that and chose instead to understand the law as a matter of works. Paul then argues in verses 2–3 that Christ came to engender trust in the God who sent him. Christ was therefore to be a matter of trust. But Israel rejected Christ and did not trust in him, as it had rejected the law as a matter of trust. Since therefore both law and Christ point to trust in God, Christ is the goal and end (Greek: *telos*) of the law. The tragedy is that the same rejection of the purpose of the law (trust in God) also led the Israelites to reject Christ (who similarly called for trust in God).

What Paul is dealing with here is two contrasting ways of viewing the law: seeing it as a summons to uphold our relationship to God with our good works and seeing it as a summons to trust in God to uphold that relationship as an act of sheer grace. Paul knows that the law, understood in the first way, leads to a false sense of our ability to meet God's trustworthiness to his promises with a trustworthiness of our own. Such a false estimate of our own ability makes impossible any real reliance on Christ as the sole basis of our relationship to God. Informing

Paul's whole discussion is the question of the extent to which we really need to rely totally on God for our relationship to him. Paul insists that anything other than total reliance is another manifestation of idolatrous rebellion. This passage will aid the teacher in making clear the meaning of faith as the abandonment of any claim to goodness on our part, as the abandonment of all "works of the law."

The preacher who follows the tradition that sees in these verses an appropriate Epistle reading for the Lenten season of the church year will find additional perspectives on them as they are read with other lessons. A comparison of this passage, which contains an explicit reference to Christian confession (10:9) and its results (vv. 10–13), with an Old Testament confession such as the one contained in Deuteronomy 26:5–11 yields a new perspective on the passage from Romans. In this perspective, the Christ described in Romans 10:5–13 is the culmination of the story of the chosen people which is recited in those verses from Deuteronomy. In that passage, gratitude for God's gifts from the land he gave to Israel is to motivate a grateful recitation of the story of God's redemptive dealings with Israel from the very beginning. Seen in that perspective, the verses in Romans become the climax of that grateful recitation: The goal God had in mind with the beginnings of his chosen people and their law is now embodied in Jesus Christ. As Israel was summoned to grateful recitation of the providence of God, so we in Christ are summoned to a grateful recitation of the fulfillment of God's promise, namely the Christ who fulfills and opens to all peoples the blessing of his grace.

In the context of Lent, such insight opens the way to understanding the true motivation for confession of sin and self-examination: not in an attempt the better to deserve God's grace but in sheer gratitude that our relationship to him rests on his trustworthiness, not ours. Self-examination that probes our insistent desire to put at least some of the burden of our rectified relationship with God on something other than total trust in him is an appropriate self-examination for Lent in light of these passages.

Combined with a Gospel reading like Luke 4:1–11, which portrays an attempt to get Jesus to be something other than the suffering redeemer God wishes him to be, our verses from Romans illumine our own temptation to be something other than the trusting and grateful creatures we are meant to be. The story of the temptations of Jesus does not turn on some attempt by Jesus to prove to himself or to Satan or to anyone else, for that matter, that he is God's Son. The Greek in which the questions are framed will not permit that interpretation. Rather, Satan, admitting what both he and Jesus know to be true ("Since you are the Son of God . . ."), tempts Jesus to use that sonship in ways other than the only appropriate way: as suffering Son of God. The third temptation identifies the problem: It is a matter of tempting God, of testing his purpose and his resolve. That is not an appropriate mode of conduct for his Son.

Nor is it an appropriate mode of conduct for the followers of his Son. Seen in light of Luke 4, the verses from Romans have a bearing on the temptation of Christians who, feeling Christ is somehow remote from them and depends for his accessibility on something they must do to bring him nearer, undertake to make themselves "worthy" of that nearness. It is the temptation Christians undergo when they feel they must, and can, earn Christ's presence. Yet he is in fact as near as heart and mouth, and he calls us, not to help him become available, but only to acknowledge his ready availability. It is finally a matter of trusting God, this Christian life, a trust open to all and at hand to all. Lenten self-examination that remains preoccupied with self, rather than with moving on to loving trust in God, comes dangerously close to a narcissistic idolatry of self. We are called to trust the God who will deliver us from that bondage of preoccupation with self. The self-examination which involves a contemplation of that bondage will resist the temptation to be something other than it ought to be only when trust in God alone is its final outcome.

Romans 10:14–21
Proclamation and Faith

The advertising campaign for a major American corporation centered around the foresight of that company in teaching its workers how to listen. Unless one hears what is being said, the ads suggested, there is not much point in speaking. If Madison Avenue advertising executives had needed a New Testament text for those ads, these verses from Romans would have served admirably. Whatever else this passage may be about, it is uniquely about the great importance of hearing. Paul emphasizes in these verses that the trust which is the only adequate response to the God who gave the law comes from hearing the good news about what that God has done for us in his Son. The pivotal verse in this passage is therefore verse 17, where verses 14–16 find their summation and verses 18–21 find their theme.

This pivotal verse helps us understand why Paul is so terribly serious about his responsibility to preach the gospel to the whole of the world he knows. Where Christ is not proclaimed, faith as a response to God's gift in Christ cannot arise. For that reason Paul writes to the Romans, so that they can support his further mission to the western Mediterranian world (15:24). That is why Paul is compelled to carry out his apostolic call: God himself is the one who has commissioned him to announce what God has done, and to open the way, through that announcement, for the response of trust in such a gracious God (II Cor. 5:18–20). That is why the divine woe is upon Paul if he shirks this task: He will be failing in his part of God's redemptive purposes for all human beings if he does not tell them what God has done for them in Christ (I Cor. 9:16).

It is necessary at this point to recall that when Paul lived there was no New Testament as we know it. Paul could not therefore assume that those who did not hear the apostolic proclamation about God's act for humanity in Jesus could at least read about it in the New Testament. But even had the New Testament been available so that people could have read it, that would not have served as a substitute for the apostolic preaching. That was true for two reasons. First, Paul of course did write material others could read—his letters—and they did become part of the New Testament when it was collected in later years. Yet even he did not feel his letters were a substitute for his presence in the matter of the proclamation of the gospel. His opening words to his readers in this letter make that clear enough (see 1:9–13).

Second, there was in fact material which could be read which informed the reader of God's will and his purposes, namely the writings contained in what we know as the Old Testament. Even if in Paul's time no final agreement had been reached on everything that was to be included in that collection, the materials were nevertheless available. Paul was con-

173

vinced that a careful reading of those writings would also inform the reader about God's promises fulfilled in Jesus Christ. Yet the problem there, as Paul well knew, lay in the fact that it was all too easy to miss those promises of the redemption God was to bring in Jesus of Nazareth. That was due in part to the fact that that redemption was of a different sort than Israel had imagined it would be. Jesus was not the divine restorer of national pre-eminence many were looking for. It was also due in part to the veil which, Paul felt, lay over the eyes of those who read Scriptures apart from a knowledge of Jesus Christ. Until that veil is lifted, one does not fully understand the witness to Christ in the writings of Israel's law, her prophets, and her wise men and women (see II Cor. 3:14–17).

That is why Paul put such a great emphasis on hearing. Reading the Old Testament, which contained God's promises fulfilled in Jesus Christ, or even apostolic letters such as Paul wrote, could not be a substitute for hearing the proclamation of the apostolic message. Paul knew from experience that faith was awakened by *hearing* the apostolic message. Trust in God was awakened in those who heard the apostolic announcement, which was to be carried to all people everywhere, the announcement that the gracious intentions of God which culminated in Jesus Christ had been present from the beginning of his creation of the world, as they were present throughout his dealings with his chosen people. That is the message with whose proclamation Paul had been entrusted, and he took his charge to preach that message with great seriousness.

With that understanding of the importance for Paul of the preaching and hearing of the good news of God's act in Christ, we can readily follow the logic of the passage we are considering. If trust as the proper response to God's grace comes from hearing the apostolic message which summons one to such trust, perhaps the reason Israel had not responded properly was due to the fact that she had never heard the apostolic message. After all, how could one call upon a God in trust about whom one had never heard, and how could one hear unless the news were announced, and how could the news be announced if no one had sent a messenger to announce it (vv. 14–15a)?

174

That would be a valid line of reasoning were it not for the fact that God has sent his apostles (the word "apostle" itself is derived from the Greek word for "send with a message") precisely to make that announcement. That is the way God does such things. He does not leave his people in the dark about his plans for them. Isaiah had already known that when he announced to Israel her impending freedom from her exile (v. 15b), and that same kind of announcement of deliverance was now being made by God's apostles. Thus the problem lay not in any failure on the part of those making the announcement, it lay rather in a failure on the part of those who ought to have listened to it and heeded it.

Any excuse that Israel might make that she had not heard this good news would therefore be invalid. As the psalmist had foretold (Paul quotes Ps. 19:4 in v. 18), the announcement of God's gracious redemptive act in Christ has gone to the far reaches of the inhabited world. Had Israel read its own Scriptures therefore it would have known it ought always to listen carefully for God's Word, since God never keeps his good news secret.

But perhaps Israel has not understood what that announcement means for her, and that is why she has withheld her trust in Christ. Again, Paul says, the answer must be negative, because again, Israel's Scriptures, carefully considered, would have made clear what is going on in Christ, namely the creation of a chosen people that now includes peoples who formerly had not known Israel's God nor had they sought after him (vv. 19–20; note here the similarity to the theme stated in 9:20). Yet once again, Israel has refused to accept what God has done for her and to trust that those acts will result in her redemption (v. 21).

This second part of our section has made clear that if preachers bear the burden of responsible preaching, hearers bear the burden of responsible listening! If the only way one can learn how to respond appropriately to God's grace is by listening, one had better listen carefully! One's relationship to God may depend on how carefully one listens and understands what is being said! Our passage therefore clearly implies a warning against careless hearing, since hearing is the key to trust in God.

A sermon based on this passage could well point to the need for careful hearing. How one hears is of utmost importance to one's relationship to God and to his Son Jesus Christ. An appropriate Gospel reading to accompany these verses would be the parable of the sower and its interpretation (Mark 4:1–20), a passage which points to the perils and rewards of careful attention to what Jesus says. The Old Testament lesson could profita-

175

bly be drawn from Deuteronomy 11:18–21, a passage which reports Moses' emphasis on the need to heed carefully what God has told his people. The preacher will of course have to take the texts seriously if the sermon is to be a responsible one, since preachers must surely be careful and responsible listeners before they can be careful and responsible proclaimers. One ought to bear in mind that the proclamation of the gospel is itself a part of God's redemptive act in Christ (II Cor. 5:18–19). *That* is why preaching is so important a part of the life of Christian community.

The teacher will note that this passage is a further link in the chain of Paul's discussion of the place of Israel in God's future. Paul continues in these verses his discussion of Israel's rejection of God's act of mercy for them and for all human beings in Jesus Christ. Why has Israel rejected the Savior? In the first instance, because they misunderstood their nature as chosen people. Failing to understand that the basis of their existence lay in God's choice and their necessary response of trust, they assumed "chosen" had to do with genetic inheritance and the performance of the individual commands of the law (9: 1–29). In the second instance, clearly growing out of the first, Israel misunderstood the purpose of God's law. Thinking the law pointed primarily to what they had to do, rather than to the trust they were to place in God, Israel could not see that what the law intended had in fact been fulfilled in Christ, so that henceforth the chosen people would be the people of Christ rather than the people of the law (9:30—10:14).

In our verses, Paul turns to a third concern, namely the question of whether the Israelites acted as they did because they were ignorant of the fact that Christ fulfilled and thus ended the law. Perhaps they simply did not know that the law was intended to point to trust in the God who gave it rather than to the performance of its individual commands. That that is not the case Paul makes clear in this passage.

The teacher can make use of a second point in a lesson on this part of Paul's letter to the Christians in Rome. The burden of these verses, as we have seen, is the need for careful listening to the apostolic message. Since what we know of that apostolic

message is contained in our New Testament, the passage is a call to careful and attentive reading of those Scriptures, as it is to careful and attentive listening to its message when it is proclaimed in the context of worship. The importance of hearing the message of the Bible, which can bring again to reality what is otherwise past and gone, is worth pondering with a class. Perhaps that is why the Bible puts so much emphasis on God's Word and on those who hear it and then must announce it. Perhaps that is the only way a redemptive act which occurred in the past can continue to become present for us, namely in the telling and in the hearing of it. If we do not hear it, how will we know how to respond to God?

Israel and
Her Future with God

ROMANS 11:1–36

With this chapter, Paul reaches the climax of the discussion he began in the very first chapter. The sordid story of human sin and rebellion, a rebellion in which gentiles and Jews alike shared; the new beginning with Abraham and his descendants; the redemption in Christ now possible for all who trust God, with the final breaking of the cruel bondage to sin and law; the creation of a new people through whom the good news of God's redemptive action is to be spread abroad—this whole story finds its culmination in these chapters. Fittingly enough, since the story of the rescue of God's creation began with Israel, the chosen people, it will also conclude with them, with this difference however—their belonging to the chosen people is now on the same basis as the gentiles: on the basis of trust in Jesus Christ.

This chapter also displays Paul's understanding of the reason for, and the outcome of, Israel's rejection of Christ as God's gift of grace, and hence of the basis of their chosenness. That reason is on the one hand to create space in God's plan for the inclusion of the gentiles and on the other hand to recreate space in that plan for Israel herself. Paul's conclusion to all this is in keeping with the whole tone of this letter, indeed with the whole tone of his theology: All of this happened for the purpose of the redemption of creation from its rebellion and the ensuing corruption.

177

Paul is able to summarize the whole purpose of God's redemptive plan in one sentence: God has brought disobedience upon all humanity for the purpose of showing his grace to all (11:32). One could advance reasons why that should be: Human weakness is such that unless God has grace upon all no human being could be saved; all needed to be taught the fearsome outcome of disobedience if they were finally to understand and accept the God of grace. Yet finally such attempts to divine the reasons for the acts of a God whose ways are not our ways, and whose thoughts are not our thoughts, must end in failure. Yet not in failure; rather in unbounded, almost speechless, adoration of a God who has as his final overarching purpose the redemption of his wayward creation. In the end, the only appropriate response to such a God is confession and adoration. Paul knew that well, and he ends his considerations of the ways of the God of mercy with his rebellious creatures in an outburst of praise:

> O the depths of God's riches, and his wisdom, and his knowledge. How unsearachable are his judgments, and his ways, how past finding out.
> "For who has known the Lord's mind,
> or who has been his counselor?"
> "Has anyone ever given him something beforehand,
> so that God was in that person's debt?"
> It cannot be, for all things are begun, sustained, and brought to their conclusion through him, to whom be glory through all the ages. Amen (11:33—36).

It is our task now to trace the logic of Paul's argument as he moves to that hymnic conclusion of his understanding of the ways of God with humanity.

Romans 11:1–12
Israel and God's Plan

At issue is the fairness of God. Paul has confessed that God disposes over his creation as he sees fit. Some creatures he fashions as vessels of mercy, some as vessels of wrath (9:22). On some he showers mercy when they turn to him, others he hardens in their rebellion against him (9:18). Some he chooses, some he does not (9:10–13). That sort of confession fairly shrieks for explanations. Why does God act that way? What is his reason for so differentiating between creatures equally tainted by the rebellion of Adam, and equally at war with their Creator? What is the reason for all such activity? In the end, as Paul must have known when he began his discussion, he would have to deal with such questions, and that is the task to which he turns now in chapter 11.

We have learned that all things work together in accordance with God's plan. We have also learned that Israel has rejected God's mercy in his Son. Does that have as its consequence that God in his turn has rejected Israel? That is the question with which Paul begins his discussion in this passage, and his answer is a strong No! To justify that answer, Paul turns not to theory but to historical reality. That is to say, he does not answer with a doctrine or a confession, but rather with a recitation of historic event, a manner of argument he has been pursuing from the outset of this letter. Paul cites two examples which justify the negative answer he has given to the question. The first example is Paul himself. He is himself an Israelite; and if God had rejected his people, Paul as a member of that people would never have been called as an apostle. The second example is Elijah, who, reading the signs of his times, concluded that God must surely have rejected his people. Elijah was wrong. God had preserved for himself a remnant in Elijah's time, and, Paul affirms, he has preserved for himself a remnant in Paul's time (v. 5).

God's motivation in all this? Grace! Paul apparently cannot overemphasize that point. He returns to it again and again. Grace has nothing to do with human performance; if it did it would not be grace (v. 6). Such ignoring of human performance, of human abilities, is itself an act of grace, since no performance by a creature, a weak and soiled and rebellious creature, would stand the test of divine scrutiny. Only if God deals with us in grace will we survive. Those who would have it another way thereby seal their own fate. Yet God will not have it so. He is a God of mercy, and his mercy *will* prevail. That is the gist of this whole chapter.

The nagging question persists. God is in control. He hardens whom he will. Israel has been hardened. What other conclusion is there than that God has hardened them? No other, and Paul is ready to concede that point (v. 8). Indeed, how could he not concede it, since Scripture itself, to which Paul so readily attributes authority in these matters, says that very thing. God has hardened a part of Israel (vv. 8–9). He has dimmed their

179

eyes and stopped up their ears, and the inevitable result is that they have missed the import of God's act in Christ.

A loving, merciful, gracious God, who renders his chosen people unable to recognize his loving, merciful, gracious deed in his Son Jesus Christ? Is it not a contradiction in terms to describe such a God in such terms? If that is what it means to be "chosen people," would one not prefer to forego that honor? If the chosen people failed by God's own choice to accept the promised redeemer (v. 7a; cf. 9:30), what purpose did their chosenness serve? Was Israel God's chosen people only to serve as a negative example to the gentiles? Would that not in the end show the gentiles to have in fact had the inside track over Israel as chosen people all along? Those questions are valid, and Paul will deal with them, one by one, in the verses that follow. In these verses, he deals with the first of them: What was the purpose of the hardening of Israel? Were they hardened so that God could have an excuse to condemn them? Did they, as Paul frames it, "stumble in order to fall" (v. 11)?

The answer to that question is clear, and it is final: No! Were that the case, God's final purpose would not be grace, and his election would serve purposes other than redemption. Rather, Israel's stumbling was the occasion for redemption to be opened to gentiles. There is almost a spatial analogy here. Only if some Israelites are cleared out will there be room for gentiles. Paul is reflecting here the missionary experience of the apostles. What had occurred was that when Israel rejected the gospel of Christ, the apostles turned to the gentiles with their message of reconciliation. And the gentiles responded! That is the reality that underlies Paul's discussion here, and one can read about it in Acts (e.g., 13:44–52; for the problems that raised, see Acts 15:1–29).

So far so good. The gentiles now hear the good news, and many accept it, many more gentiles than Israelites, in fact. But where does that leave the Israelites? Granted their stumbling served the purpose of mercy for the gentiles, what does it do for the purpose of mercy to Israel? Is Israel to be sacrificed for the good of non-Israelites? What good would that do Israel?

Paul hints at an answer he will develop more fully in the next passage: When Israel sees the mercy they have rejected become reality in the new chosen people who confess Christ as their Lord, they will become envious of that grace and return to become a part of that new chosen people. The main point

180

Paul wants to make here, however, is simply this: Even the hardening of Israel serves the purposes of mercy. And it serves the purposes of mercy not only for gentiles but for Israel as well. If Israel's impoverishment means the enrichment of others, what do you suppose, Paul asks, the subsequent enrichment of Israel will mean for others? If in Israel's poverty she has enriched the gentiles, what can Israel's enrichment do but enrich gentiles beyond all bounds? Clearly, as Paul's subsequent argument will show, he thinks that will be the case: Israel's enrichment means further enrichment for all, Israel as well as gentiles. How that will be the case is the burden of Paul's further argument in this chapter.

The teacher who has been engaged with Paul's letter to the churches in Rome will find in this passage some of the answers to the kind of questions that inevitably arise from a consideration of 9:14–21. What we found implied there, we find expressed here: What God does, he does for the purposes of his mercy. The idea of "remnant" is also a key concept in this passage (v. 5) and picks up a theme with which Paul has also been dealing in the previous chapters (esp. 9:27–29). Lessons on this and the remaining parts of Romans 11 present the teacher with the opportunity to review the course of the argument in Romans and to see its fulfillment in God's purposes of mercy on his rebellious creation.

Although this passage is not complete in itself, and understanding it depends on seeing it within its context, it does deal with a problem which a class could well discuss. That problem is one with which most Christians have wrestled: When things go badly, can we still affirm that God remains in control? It is evident in this passage that just as these verses must be seen in their larger context to be understood, so things that seem to go badly must also be seen in their larger context to be understood. It is just that larger context that Elijah had missed which led him to assume that God had given up on his purposes for Israel. This passage gives us the larger context within which to view the events that seem to go counter to God's redemptive purposes. The class could discuss specific examples of times when things go badly and view them in the larger context of grace seen in this passage. These verses make clear that the reality of God's gracious purposes may not always match the appearance of the events we see.

Despite the incomplete nature of the discussion contained

181

in these verses, the passage nevertheless bears rich freight for the preacher. Verse 7 presents the opportunity to clarify the nature of grace. Grace is in no way the reward of good works, not even in its smallest part. Such a sermon would make the congregation aware that were their fate to hang from their own performance, the future would indeed be bleak. Yet what is on one side judgment on our worth is on the other side comfort in a God who overlooks that judgment for the sake of his mercy. In the end it is better to be able to rely for redemption on God than on ourselves, and a sermon on that verse should help make that clear. A passage from the Gospels such as Luke 18:9–14, and from the Old Testament such as Isaiah 31:1–3, will help throw light on the need to place one's reliance on God and on the perils involved in placing it on someone or something else.

There is also the opportunity to fashion a sermon from these verses on the purposes of God. God has in the past worked with a faithful remnant. Should anyone therefore be surprised if the Christian community continues to be a minority, a "remnant," in our own culture? The passage from I Kings 19:10–18 from which Paul quoted will throw light on this idea, and Jesus spoke of the little leaven that leavens all the dough and of the tiny seed that becomes a great tree (Matt. 13:31–33). Could that be the fate of chosen people now, as it was their fate in Paul's day? Are we too to be impoverished for the enrichment of others, as Israel was, and as indeed Christ himself was (see II Cor. 8:9)? A sermon in such a vein could help a congregation gain perspective on its role in the larger culture and by the same token help it to interpret its own experience as a community of the chosen people.

Romans 11:13–24
The Olive Tree: The History of Grace

The olive tree says it all. Grace may be free, but it is not to be presumed upon, is not to lead to arrogance, and above all it is not cheap. The God of grace remains the Lord of his creation, a fact one forgets at one's peril. Lest grace lead one to overlook that fact, Paul places his discussion of grace under the rubric of the absolute Lordship of the Creator, who continues to dispose over his creation as the gardener disposes over his olive trees. For that reason, the olive tree says it all.

To be sure, the analogy of the olive tree is an analogy of grace. The point is clear: In this olive tree, *all* branches have been engrafted. The wild branches (gentiles) have no claim upon this tree, which is clearly God's chosen people; and so if they are engrafted into it, it cannot be by right, only by grace. The natural branches (Israel) have been broken off by their rejection of Christ; and if they are regrafted, it is now on the same status as the gentiles, that is, by grace and not by right.

Grace is therefore the point to be found in the analogy, the grace which has motivated God in his dealing with his creatures, Jew and gentile alike. That leads to a second point in this analogy about which we must be clear, and that is the fact that the analogy of the olive tree is an analogy of history rather than of doctrine. It tells of the successive steps in the history of God's chosen people, beginning with God's choice of Israel (that decision to choose a people is the "holy root," v. 16) and moving through their rejection of Christ (the "breaking off" of some branches, v. 17), which caused the apostles to turn to the gentiles. When the gentiles accepted Christ they became members of the chosen people ("wild olive branches" grafted in, vv. 17, 24). So far the course of history. But Paul sees beyond current history to the future culmination of this plan of God for his chosen people. In the end, Israel, whose rejection of Christ provided the motivation for the apostolic proclamation to the gentiles, will return to Christ and join again God's chosen people ("natural branches" will be regrafted, v. 24). The analogy of the olive tree is thus the analogy of God's gracious purposes for Israel and gentiles alike.

There is more, however. If Paul wants to speak of God's grace by means of this analogy, he wants also to use it to speak of human responsibility. Paul speaks of two aspects of such responsibility. One aspect Paul addresses overtly, the second by implication. The aspect of human responsibility of which Paul speaks obviously and overtly is the responsibility to refrain from assuming one has been shown God's grace as a matter of right. That holds equally for Jews as it does for gentiles, but in this passage it is pointed primarily at gentiles (so v. 13). Inclusion in 183 the story of God's grace is a matter of the choice of a gracious God, a God who continues to dispose over his creation as he sees fit. He can break out ingrafted branches as he broke out natural branches. The gentiles are therefore not to take credit for God's gracious choice of them, as though that choice depended on their worth. It does not. The choice depends on God's grace alone. The God who is kind in election can also be severe against those who play fast and loose with his grace (v. 22). The God who has created a people with the death of his Son is not a doting and permissive Daddy, who greets the irresponsible activity of his children with bemused tolerance. God remains Creator and Lord, and one forgets that at one's peril.

In fact—and this is the covert aspect of the human responsibility with which Paul is dealing—grace demands the response of trust. To presume upon God's kindness is dangerous (recall 2:4). God may allow to stand one's decision to reject rather than to trust him. Grace is not permission to do as one pleases. Such permission, as Paul told us earlier, is not a manifestation of God's grace, it is a manifestation of his wrath (1:24, 26, 28). Rather, grace is the summons to respond in trust to the God of grace and to shape one's life by the structures of that grace. God's redemption of his creation in Christ is a matter of utmost importance; and to reject it, or to fail to take it seriously, must surely bring unfortunate consequences in its train. God's kindness to us is an invitation we reject only at our own peril (vv. 20–22). That is also the point of the analogy of the olive tree.

Yet here, as always, the last word is grace. God freely accepts those rebels who turn once again to him (v. 23). In the end, Israel will accept God's act for her in Christ and will return to her natural place within God's chosen people (v. 23). If grace summons a response from the graced, it is also grace alone that makes that response meaningful. God's choice to be gracious to his creatures is the primary, indeed the only, thing that allows those who respond to find grace. The response is important, on that point Paul is clear; but it is grace alone that makes that response what it is, a response to a God who seeks to redeem his lost and rebellious creation. In the end, the priority belongs to grace.

The teacher will find in this passage the key to Paul's understanding of the future of Israel. Clearly, Israel has not been finally rejected. In fact, the language of verse 15, which is so strongly reminiscent of the description of the meaning of Christ's act for us in 5:10, suggests that Paul may see in Israel's fate (rejection equals death; acceptance equals resurrection) a recapitulation of Christ's fate. For that reason, and because

184

Christ is humanly from the people of Israel (see 9:5*b*), they will not finally be rejected. This of course makes plain the utter folly of anti-Semitism on the part of any Christian. Any such sentiments are clearly akin to those about which Paul warns gentiles in verses 17–21. Such arrogance over against the Jews is clearly an example of responding to God's kindness in unfaith. There is no indication here that Jews are to be ignored and not told of the good news in Christ. But any evangelization of Jews must take a different form from that of the evangelization of non-Jews. Evangelization of Jews must take the form of recalling members of the family to their own home, and it must be done in the humility of adopted children bringing pleas of return to those who have prior claim on the family inheritance. Every Christian may not have the opportunity for such evangelization, but every Christian can and must resist and reject every form of anti-Semitism in whatever form it occurs. Any other reaction is inappropriate to the history of God's grace.

These verses are also useful for a discussion of the problem of grace versus works. If we are to respond to God's grace in trust, is not that trusting response a "work" without which we cannot be saved? And if it is a necessary "work," how can we say we are saved by grace alone and not also by works, that is, by what we contribute? As these verses make plain, the response of trust is only effective due to the prior invitation of grace. The acceptance of an invitation to a party is only effective because the invitation has been offered. Those who have not been offered an invitation can accept as vigorously as they please, but it will do them no good because there is no invitation to which they are responding. It is the invitation that gives to the response the effectiveness it has.

In the same way, our trusting response to God's gracious offer of redemption in Jesus Christ is effective only because God has offered us his redemption. Had he not done that, we could trust him as faithfully as we please, and it would be to no avail. It is the offer of grace that makes our response of trusting acceptance of it significant. In fact, to respond in trusting acceptance to God's redemption of us by grace in Jesus Christ is to admit that one can be saved only by the grace which God gives, not by the works which we contribute. The "work" of trust is therefore the admission that no work we do is adequate to aid in our salvation. Otherwise, as Paul said in 11:6, it would not be grace. Our sole "contribution" to our salvation is the rebellion

185

against God which made our redemption necessary and the admission that that is the way things are. A class discussion on this question could help clarify the relationship between grace and works as Paul understands them.

The preacher who essays a sermon on this passage will be helped to see how closely Paul has formulated his thought to prophetic insight in relation to Israel. Zechariah 8:20–23 announces the universal worship of God among all nations, and Isaiah 56:1–8 speaks of grace to gentiles as well as to wayward Israel. In fact, to read the passage from Isaiah is virtually to reread Paul's analogy of the olive tree. They are so similar in outlook that one must wonder if that passage from Isaiah was not the passage that gave shape to Paul's own thought. Clearly, what Paul is saying in these verses echoes what Isaiah had said much earlier. That in itself is an evidence of the constancy of the purpose of the God of grace. A sermon on the faithfulness of that God to his purposes of redemption surely suggests itself from that striking parallel of thought.

God's grace to gentiles finds expression also in the Gospel stories, particularly in those that show Jesus' willingness to bless those who are not counted among the children of Israel. Jesus' gift of healing to the Geresene demoniac (Mark 5:1–20) or to the Centurion for his servant (Luke 7:1–10) illustrate this. Even more striking is the story of Jesus and the Syro–Phoenecian woman in Matthew 15:21–28, where Jesus at first denies the appeal for grace (v. 24). This story gives added emphasis to several points in our passage from Romans. As the woman clearly illustrates, faith is the only proper response to Jesus, and it is her persistent unwillingness to take No for an answer from Jesus that clearly demonstrates her faith.

The Gospel story also adds emphasis to Paul's understanding of the historical priority of Israel in God's plan of redemption. They were the first to be chosen, and their existence depended on God's acts to begin it and sustain it (see e.g., Exod. 15:1–18; 16:2–15). That sustaining choice by God remains an ineradicable advantage (recall Romans 3:1–2). If God's plan of redemption includes gentiles as well as Jews, the priority nevertheless remains with the Jews. On Jesus' own admission, they have first claim on him (Matt. 15:24, 26), a point that makes clear the inappropriateness of any boast, or any despising of Israel. It is clear once again that anti-Semitism is not a possible Christian attitude.

186

Romans 11:25–36
God's Plan Is Grace for All

From the stuff of human disobedience, God has shaped the means of his mercy (v. 32). That is the conclusion to which Paul comes in this passage, and it may well be his intention to have that conclusion stand as the summation of his entire discussion so far in his letter to the churches in Rome. Mercy is God's response to disobedient Israel as it is his response to disobedient gentiles. If it seems a strange way to go about the redemption of creation (Paul admits as much in his hymnic conclusion, vv. 33–36), it is surely a striking example of the omnipotence of God. The very acts of his creatures which were intended to thwart him become the means by which God's plan for them is carried through. If opposition becomes the very means of accomplishing what is opposed, what is there left that could possibly thwart God's plan? Nothing! Nothing in all creation! That is the point Paul has been making in this chapter, and he sums it up in these final verses.

What Paul has been expounding he now terms a "mystery." Our word "mystery" comes from the Greek language and has as its root meaning the idea of being initiated into something. Until one has undergone that initiation into the secrets of some lodge or some other group, for example, what that group does will remain impossible to understand, that is, it will be a mystery. The hidden secret (Greek: *mysterion*) is therefore known only to the initiate (Greek: *mystes*). Paul tells us in these verses that he will now initiate us into this mystery of God. One should therefore not be surprised that one is surprised by what Paul has been saying! A "mystery" cannot be figured out by the non-initiate, by an "outsider." A mystery is available only to those who are given the information (see Mark 4:11, where *mysterion* is used the same way). Precisely because God's plan is such a mystery, it is incapable of being penetrated by any empirical means. Observation of the course of nature, or of history, however systematically made or acutely analyzed, will not allow one to fathom the purposes of God. It is not the sum total of reality that reveals the purposes of God, but rather those

187

events by which God sets forward his purposes. It is such events —the choosing of Abraham, the exodus from Egypt, the career of Jesus of Nazareth—which are the keys to understanding God's purpose for his creation.

But not even the meaning of those key events, or even their identification as key events, is open to rational deduction. Only the final consummation of God's plan will make incontestably clear which were the key events. As in a murder mystery on the stage, where we do not learn what the key clues were until the end of the play, so it is with God's plan. Not until his kingdom becomes empirical reality in the transformation of the age will the key clues, and their meaning, become known to all.

Yet a God whose plan is grace will not leave his creatures without knowledge of that plan, and it is an apostle's function to make clear that knowledge. That is what Paul is doing when he now declares to his readers this "mystery." The revealing of God's plan through the apostle is in itself an indication of his gracious dealings with his creation. And what is the content of that "mystery," that hint of the plans of grace? It is—the hardening of Israel!

Clearly, Israel's rejection of Christ is open to a variety of interpretations. One interpretation: They rejected Christ because when Christ came, God was through with them, and so their call proved to be only temporary. Another interpretation: Israel's call never was valid, and their claims of a special relationship to God the Creator were self-serving illusions. Yet another: In the end God rejected them because of their rejection of his Son. All are possible, indeed even plausible—and all are wrong. The reason for Israel's being hardened in its rebellion against God's Son? Grace! Grace for gentiles, and finally, grace for Israel as well! God's plan, says Paul, runs from God choosing Israel, to his hardening Israel to save gentiles, and then to his saving gentiles in order finally to save Israel.

God hardens the very people he intends to save! Rebellion serves the purposes of salvation! Recall the hardening of Pharaoh (9:17–18) which served the purposes of God's gracious plan, a plan which included the very descendants of Pharaoh because it included in its redemption gentiles as well. Recall the hardening of vessels of wrath for the purposes of showing mercy (9:22–24)! Recall the hardening of Israel, done for the purposes of God's mercy to that very Israel (11:15–16)! Consider the total rebellion of all creation, done for the pur-

188

pose of the mercy to be shown to that creation (11:32). That is the mystery of which Paul speaks. That is the wisdom of God so past searching out. If, in hardening, God takes rebellion seriously, it is only for a specific period of time. Hardening cannot alter the final purpose of God's election, which is grace. If, in God's plan, redemption for the gentiles needed the hardening of Israel (v. 28*a*), that hardening is not a permanent condition. God will not rescind his promises to the Patriarchs (v. 28*b*). That choice of Israel by a gracious God will not be revoked (v. 29). Hardening in disobedience is temporary and serves the purposes of grace; that is the mystery Paul announces (v. 32).

Because that is so, because God can use even rebellion and disobedience in his plan of mercy on all, we may have utter confidence in that God, however his plan may seem to be going awry. Nothing, not even the rejection of his own Son by his own people could affect God's purposes of grace. If God's ways are past finding out, his mercy is past any impeding. God is faithful to his purposes of mercy, and he is capable of carrying out his plan, whatever the reaction of his creation may be to those purposes. Trust in such a God is an eminently reasonable act, since he is reliable and unwavering in his purpose of mercy for his creation and is totally capable of bringing that mercy to reality. It is that assurance that Paul sings forth in the closing hymn of verses 33–36. God is the source, sustainer, and goal of all things. What a glorious God!

Sermons derived from this passage will perforce deal with the heart of the biblical understanding of the ways of the God of grace with sinful, rebellious humanity. The God who avenges sin and requites injustice does so in the end because of mercy. The God who punishes disobedience does so finally because of grace. That God's response to disobedience is mercy is the theme that runs like a red thread throughout the prophetic literature and is summed up in a passage like Isaiah 59, where a litany of human shortcomings is climaxed by God's declaration of his unending covenant faithfulness, or Jeremiah 31: 31–37, where the climax of God's judgment against Israel (see 8:4—9:11) is a new covenant which will not be broken as was the covenant of former times. It is surely not by chance that Paul quotes from both these passages in 11:26–27.

189

That the ultimate act of rebellion—killing God's own Son on a cross—is met by the ultimate act of redemption—God raising his Son from the dead—demonstrates the centrality of this theme for the Christian faith as well, providing as it does the climax of Jesus' career during which he constantly announced God's mercy to sinful men and women (Matt. 9:10–13; Mark 10:42–45; Luke 6:27–36 are only a few examples). God's response to disobedience is mercy; a sermon on that theme will go to the very core of that faith.

Paul's final hymn (vv. 33–36) is also rich in sermonic possibilities, particularly for an age that finds even the notion of a unique and absolute God to be all but incomprehensible. Rather than arguing against such a notion, Paul celebrates it in these verses. God's incomprehensibility is the very basis of trust in him, since his difference from human perfidy and inconstancy lies in his constancy and faithfulness.

Inability to understand God was no different, however, in the time of Israel. The attempt to create a more manageable, visible God runs from the time of Israel's creation as a people (Exod. 32:1–6) to the post–exilic time when they still needed warning against such an attempt (Isa. 44:12–20; 45:18–22). Yet there again, it was that very difference that made it possible for God to be deliverer and redeemer (Isa. 55:9–11).

Nor was it different with Jesus himself. From the time he was a young man (Luke 2:41–52) to the mocking that greeted his crucifixion (Mark 15:29–32), people found him difficult if not impossible to comprehend. Yet in him we see the ways of almighty God with his sinful creatures on the earth. In the very death of Jesus caused by uncomprehending Roman and Jewish officials, Christians see the supreme act of the redemption of a gracious God. That is the kind of divine inscrutability Paul celebrates in these verses in Romans. Whether for Christmas, with the mystery of God born as a babe in Bethlehem, or for Easter, with its incomprehensible rising of Jesus from the dead as God's promise of redemption to all creation, this theme is appropriate for any who would announce to rebellious creatures the source of their redemption.

The lectionary tradition that finds in these verses the epistle lesson for the Pentecost season of the church year gives another perspective on them. If God is inscrutable in his purposes, those purposes are nevertheless working themselves out in the world, and perspective must be gained on how and where that happens.

Combined with a Gospel passage like Matthew 16:13–20,

190

our verses in Romans point to the place where the unsearchable ways of that triumphant God do begin already to become reality in our present world. It is within the church, called into being by God's Son and grounded in the faith of the apostles, that such reality can be found. A passage like Isaiah 22:19–23 clarifies the power of keys: The deposing of a prime minister, where his symbols of office are taken away, includes removal of the keys. The keys are the symbol of the greater power whom one serves. The story in Matthew of the giving of the keys therefore tells of the assignment of God's redemptive power to the church based on that apostolic witness.

The way in which the unsearchable paths of God which Paul hymns in the passage from Romans invade our sphere of reality is clarified in three ways in this passage from Matthew, and so it helps us to think of them in more concrete terms.

First, the knowledge about Jesus which Peter confesses is not the result of human cleverness. God's way, his plan, is not open to objective discernment or verification. If God does not reveal it, it remains unknown. Second, God's church will be built on the witness of the disciples (see Matt. 18:18; Peter is here their spokesman), as unlikely a crew for such a task as one could imagine. It is nevertheless God's unsearchable decision to build his church on such a foundation. If that church survives, it will hardly be because of the personal abilities of the disciples. It will only be by God's sustaining power. Third, the church has the authority to be God's "prime minister," as it were, with the power of the keys. To deal with the church is therefore not to deal with a social collection of like–minded individuals. It is indeed to deal with the "body of Christ," since it carries Christ's own authority on earth. Let priests and pastors, as well as congregations, pay serious heed: What is done in the church carries with it the responsibility of representing God's own authority. Cause there for both joy and humility!

The teacher will find here the culmination of Paul's line of discussion begun with chapter 9, to say nothing of the entire discussion of the letter so far. For that reason, the teacher is presented in these verses with the opportunity to clarify the core of the gospel as Paul understands it. Verse 32, with the announcement that mercy is shown to human beings in spite of the disobedience of all is of a piece with a theme that Paul has been discussing throughout this letter. That theme is the heart of Paul's gospel, namely that God will restore his lordship over

191

his rebellious creation by means of the mercy he shows through his Son. Paul has said this in a variety of ways. God justifies the ungodly (4:5). God brings something into being where before there was nothing (4:17). While we were sinners, Christ died for us (5:8). In understanding that to be the heart of the gospel, Paul mirrors in his own way what Jesus was illustrating when he sought fellowship with the down and out of society, namely that God's mercy comes to those with no claim to it at all. Jesus associated with that kind of person not because he hated the religious people or those who were successful, but rather, in an enacted parable, Jesus turned to the outcasts to show that when God turns to humanity and shows it mercy he is perforce showing mercy to outcasts because that in the end is what humanity has made itself vis-à-vis God. Even the good have as little claim on God as the socially unacceptable. Paul's statement that Jesus died for us while we were yet sinners is thus a summary of the kind of career of Jesus that is described for us in the Gospels. We do not face the choice therefore of Jesus *or* Paul. As these verses make clear, the same gospel is proclaimed by both Jesus *and* Paul.

Another angle of approach on these verses would be to center in on the fact that God's plan cannot be deduced from the general course of history, whether the natural history of the universe or the history of human culture. If things are not always what they seem, that is certainly true of the relationship of the course of history to its final outcome in God's redemption of it in Christ. Yet that is a reason for confidence, rather than uncertainty or despair: God's power is such that nothing can frustrate his purposes of mercy. A fruitful discussion is possible about what all that says for the way we respond to events, good and bad. How are we to respond to events in our lives, given the knowledge that in the end, nothing can defeat God's purposes? Will it make us indifferent? eager to respond in trust in God? It is Paul's intent that the discussion contained in the final part of his letter (chaps. 12—15) will indicate the proper response.

PART FOUR

God's Lordship and the Problems of Daily Living: Grace and the Structures of Life

ROMANS 12:1—16:27

How the story of God's relationship to his rebellious creation bears on the way Christians are to conduct their daily lives is the burden of the final chapters of Paul's letter to the Roman Christians. That story concerned the past, with its rebellion of humanity against its Creator (1:18—3:20), but a past which also contained a preview of the redemption in Christ (3:21–31) and the way of its appropriation, an appropriation presaged in the trust of Abraham (4:1–22). The story turned to the present (4:-23); and Paul described how Christ had reversed the direction given humanity by Adam (chap. 5), how Christ's death for our redemption could be appropriated so the power of sin could be broken (chap. 6), how that freed human beings from a past dominated by sin and law (chap. 7) and opened them to a present dominated by God's Spirit (chap. 8). The story also pointed to the future. Paul told how from the beginning God's plan of gracious election had been at work (chap. 9), culminating in Christ who brought the law to an end by incorporating its goal in himself (chap. 10). The future return of Israel to God's chosen people is to be the culminating act of God's gracious restoration of his lordship over his rebellious creatures (chap. 11).

If that story was and is the story of the grace of God toward his rebellious creatures, a grace which would not abandon them to a lordship other than his own, the results of that story continue to be a matter of grace. The very fact that Paul can include ethical admonitions in his letter is a further demonstration of that grace. To those still under the power of sin and its tool, the law, such admonitions can serve to do nothing but drive them to further acts of rebellion (see 7:7–11). It is Paul's

193

testimony that only when the power of sin has been broken, only when God's grace has triumphed over his creatures' rebellion, can ethical admonitions serve any function other than the increase of sin. It is therefore a manifestation of the victory of God's grace that Paul can now turn to such ethical admonitions for his Roman readers, and for us who also seek to know the outcome of that grace.

These ethical admonitions therefore display a further reality, in addition to the victory of God's grace over human rebellion. They show that grace is not another form of total permissiveness, in which "anything goes." Such permissiveness on God's part, as Paul made clear in 1:24–32, is not a manifestation of God's gracious care, it is manifestation of his wrath. Grace is thus the opposite of permissiveness. Grace brings with itself specific structures. It brings with itself the power to reshape and restructure our lives in a way appropriate for life under the lordship of God rather than under the lordship of sin. The ethical admonitions therefore illustrate the structuring power of grace. They point human beings to the appropriate response to the Creator to whom they owe their reconciliation. To those freed from the compulsive bondage of sin, ethical admonitions point to the way grace is to order those lives newly freed. The ethical admonitions of chapters 12—16, themselves a further sign of the grace of God, show us examples of the way that grace is to be followed as it becomes the structuring reality in our own daily lives.

Grace and the Community

ROMANS 12:1–21

Paul begins in these verses a discussion of the structuring effects of grace as they come to bear on a variety of circles of human society. The fundamental response to the gracious lordship of God displayed in his Son is to allow oneself to be shaped totally by that new lordship, rather than by the lordship of sin that operates in "this world" (v. 2). Beginning with the Christian

194

community (12:3–13), Paul moves to the wider society (vv. 14–21) and then to the state (13:1–7) in his discussion of the impact of God's structuring grace on human relationships. We will follow that division in our consideration of this material.

Romans 12:1–2
The Structuring Power of Grace

Life under the lordship of God means a life under the structuring power of grace. That power transforms not only individuals, but the individuals' relationships to the community around them. Living by the power of the Spirit, and accepting the gracious lordship of God, the Christian's world has been made new (see II Cor. 5:17); and the task is now to let the structuring power of grace transform that world into the shape of grace.

It is clear from the opening verse that grace is to affect the whole of human life. In language reminiscent of 6:12–13 (the first time Paul mentioned admonitions since it was the first time he discussed the individual's appropriation of liberation from sin), Paul tells his readers that their proper response to their Creator is the shaping of their total lives by his gracious will. Like the burnt offering given wholly to God, the Christian is to be a total sacrifice to God, and that sacrifice is to consist of the whole of life. That, says Paul, is the logical response (the Greek word at the end of v. 1 is *logike* from which our word "logical" is derived) to the history of God's grace he has been reciting.

That logical response consists in shaping our lives to the structures of grace rather than to the structures of the world. Paul reflects that same idea in verse 21, when he again urges his readers not to be shaped by the reality of the world (evil) but to reshape that reality by the power of grace (good). By thus framing his discussion with those two references to the transforming power of grace, Paul points to the importance of this idea. Christians are to shape themselves, their thinking and their doing, comformably to faith. Verse 2 may be translated: "Do not let yourselves be shaped by what everyone else does, but rather let yourselves be transformed by a whole new way of thinking, so you can discern what conforms to God's will,

195

namely what is good, and pleasing, and perfect." That is grace at work: to be able to hear—and obey!—such admonitions. The remainder of chapters 12—15 consists of examples of such conformity to God's will.

Romans 12:3–13
Grace and the Christian Community

In his letter to the Philippians, Paul calls the Christians there a "colony of heaven" (v. 20, Moffatt's translation). A colony in the Hellenistic world, as in later times as well, may be located in a place far removed from the home country, but the life of that home country, its language and its customs, continues; and the citizenship of the colonists remains that of the mother land. That is the reality to which Paul points in these verses. Having been adopted into the family of God by the power of the Spirit (see 8:12–17), Christians are now to conform their lives to their new family, their new citizenship, as it were. How they are to do that is the gist of Paul's admonitions in verses 3–13.

After his general statement on the structuring power of grace therefore Paul in verse 3 directs his admonitions to the most intimate expression of Christian life, namely, the Christian community. If that Christian community responds appropriately to the structuring grace at work within it, what it will display in its life is unity. It is a unity comparable to the unity found in the human body (vv. 4–8) and best expressed under the general rubric of "love" (vv. 9–13). It is that unity which provides coherence to what otherwise may appear to be a random collection of ethical epigrams.

That unity cannot be reduced to sheer uniformity, however. Paul's comparison of the unity of the Christian community's diverse members and varieties of ways of acting to the human body and its various parts rules out any such rigid uniformity. Indeed, that analogy of the body not only allows for, but even emphasizes the necessity of, diversity, a diversity based on the multifaceted abundance of God's grace itself. That rich and multifaceted grace finds expression in the various ways Christians are moved by grace to enact their faith, whether in speech or deed (vv. 6–8). Such "spiritual gifts" refer to the ways

196

God commissions those who trust him to enact that trust in their lives, whether those actions are undertaken within or outside of the gathered Christian community. Grace finds expression in those gifts in variegated ways (v. 6*a*). Yet that rich plurality of gifts is to be used in ways, and with attitudes, that promote unity rather than discord.

That diversity of Christian activity within the necessary unity is not to be dependent on only a few specially-gifted persons. The examples Paul gives of the way such gifts are to be employed (vv. 6–8) clearly imply that every Christian has been given such a gift (Paul makes that implication explicit in I Cor. 12:4–30, where he discusses such spiritual gifts in more detail).

The difference therefore between Christians is not that some have spiritual gifts and some do not. The difference consists in the fact that not all have received the same gift. That means that not every Christian will have the gift of preaching or of teaching or of social action or of caring for church property. But every Christian does have some gift, and part of one's Christian responsibility is to discover what gift one has and then to use it for the glory of God and the good of one's fellow human beings.

Two points need to be taken into account here. First, it is important to note that the list of such gifts Paul gives in these verses cannot be meant to be exhaustive. Some he mentions here are not listed, for example, in I Corinthians 12, and some listed there are not included here. Paul makes no mention here of speaking in tongues, for example, and he does not mention the gift of liberal giving in I Corinthians 12. Paul therefore means us to understand that the gifts he names here are to be taken as examples of the kind of gifts God gives to make the life of his people rich and diverse.

Second, it must be emphasized that while there is a diversity of gifts, there are no negligible gifts of the Spirit. There are no gifts of God the Christian community can afford to ignore. Because all gifts come from God, none confers superiority on the recipient; and therefore no one has a right to boast, or feel superior, because of the gift he or she has received. It is precisely such a notion of superior and inferior gifts that Paul knows has the greatest potential for undermining the unity of the Christian community, particularly at the congregational level. Paul had seen in the Corinthian church the corrosive effects which spiritual pride based on the idea that one gift, in

197

that case speaking in tongues, was better than another could have on Christian unity. Any who pride themselves on their "spiritual gifts" need particularly to pay heed to this point: No spiritual gift makes any Christian superior to any other. For that reason Paul emphasizes the need for a sober, realistic self-estimate on the part of Christians (v. 3). The very faith that enlivens the Christian is the gift of God, a gift to be used for the good of others, not of self.

That problem of mixing ego with grace was evidently as real for Paul as it is for modern Christians. For that reason Paul continues with admonitions that point to such a danger (vv. 9–13). As in his discussion in I Corinthians 13, Paul here points to love as the solution to the problem of pride and over-inflated egos.

The Greek text of verse 9 does not contain the imperative supplied by most English translations at its beginning. The Greek therefore may well be intended as a statement about the nature of love, rather than advice concerning it. In that case, Paul simply declares, "love is not hypocritical" and then draws implications for Christian interaction from that fact. Those implications are what Paul then states in verses 9b–13; they all demonstrate unhypocritical love in action.

All of this, note well, by way of example. Paul is not giving an inclusive law, complete with casuistic differentiations depending on changing circumstances. Rather Paul is giving examples of the way grace is to provide the structures for the activities of Christians in their common life with one another within their Christian community. This is the way we are to respond to the grace that now orders our lives (vv. 2, 21). This is the way our trust is to be shaped. This is the way it is to work itself out in our everyday lives.

Actions conformable to the structure of grace (vv. 1–2): That is what Paul invites us to consider. It is again typical that such a requirement is not something new for the people of God. That Israel was to respond to God's gracious deliverance by conforming its life to the structure of God's covenant was the requirement without which there could be no people of God, no "kingdom of priests," no "holy nation" (Exod. 19:3–6).

198

That such obedient conformity is not a guarantee of immediate comfort or peace, however, is also a dimension of the understanding of our passage about which Christians must be clear. A passage like Matthew 16:21–28, the words of Jesus on the cost of discipleship, emphasizes that conformity to grace is a serious, even costly matter, as grace itself is a serious, even costly matter—it costs the death of God's Son. That high cost was required by Jesus not only of others, but also of himself. What it would cost is already anticipated at the beginning of his life (Luke 2:33–35); his first allegiance lay with God and what God wanted (Luke 2:41–51). The whole of Paul's discussion in the first eleven chapters of Romans shows clearly enough Paul knew about the costly nature of grace. His admonitions here are made with full knowledge of that cost, and the passages from Matthew will help the preacher keep that in mind in any sermon on these verses from Romans.

That same point is equally clear in the Old Testament. Israel as chosen people was not delivered from all vicissitudes or calamities in its national life. Indeed, it was the burden of the prophets to make that point. A prophet like Jeremiah displays the costly benefits of conformity to the grace of God's word (for example, Jer. 15:15–21 or 20:7–9). Jeremiah knew the cost of conformity, as did Paul, and a sermon based on our passage from Romans will benefit if that dimension of Paul's discussion is clarified by its association with passages like those from Jeremiah. (For further sermonic possibilities, see the discussion at the end of vv. 14–21.)

The teacher will find here the opportunity to differentiate Paul's ethical admonitions, understood as indications of the way life is to be structured in response to God's grace, from some legal system, the obedience of which will earn that grace. It would be useful here to recall that such response to grace was in fact the original purpose of Israel's law. That law was to show how life was to be shaped in ways appropriate for God's people as their faithful and trusting response to his gracious choice of them and of his deliverance of them from their slavery in Egypt. The grace of deliverance came before the giving of the law!

In a similar way, Paul is telling his readers how they are to structure their lives in a way appropriate to the way God has dealt with his rebellious creation. Paul has told the story of those dealings in chapters 1—11 and turns now to illustrate how those who have benefited from the events recited there ought to respond. Paul's ethical admonitions are therefore not a way to earn God's favor but rather the way one responds appropriately, in trust and faithfulness, when one has received that

199

favor. Life shaped in the way Paul describes it is therefore grateful response to the God who has delivered us from our slavery to sin. These admonitions are thus not "law" in the sense of requirements we must fulfill if God is to accept us. Paul is not smuggling in the law through the back door, as it were, in his ethical admonitions. The admonitions are not contrary to grace, they are the response to a grace taken seriously enough to shape one's life accordingly. That relationship between grace and concrete action is very important for anyone to understand who wants to understand Paul's thought in Romans, and it will be a useful passage for a teacher who wants to clarify that relationship.

Romans 12:14–21
Grace and the Secular Community

If the structuring power of grace is to shape the lives of Christians in their intimate association with one another in their Christian community, however, that structuring power of grace is not limited to the visible Christian community. God's grace is given to rebellious creatures (recall 5:9–10), and so its structuring power is to be allowed to work not only in the Christians' relationships to other Christians but also in their relationships within the secular world. If unity is the mode by which grace structures life within the Christian community, peace is the mode by which grace structures the Christians' relationships within the larger society. Verse 18 is the key. We recognize here the same careful literary construction we found in verses 3–13. There the theme of unity (vv. 4–5) followed the call to shape one's intentions conformably to grace (v. 3). In like manner, we have here the theme of peace (v. 18) following a similar call to shape our intentions conformably to grace (vv. 16–17). The consistent, almost punning use Paul makes of the Greek word for "shape intentions" (Greek: *phronein*) in verse 3 is repeated in verses 16–17. Although it cannot be reproduced completely in English, the New English Bible does a better job of suggesting it than the Revised Standard Version: (v. 3) " . . . do not be conceited or think too highly of yourself; but think your way to a sober estimate . . . (vv. 16–17). "Care as much about each other as about yourselves. Do not be haughty, but go about with humble folk. Do not keep thinking how wise you are. Never pay back evil for evil. Let your aims be such as all men count honorable." The parallel construction of the two passages (3–13; 14–20) therefore confirms the content of the verses: Christians are under the same obligation to shape their conduct by the structuring power of grace in the secular world as they are to shape their conduct by that structuring power in the Christian community.

Grace therefore is the structuring power that shapes the life of the Christian; and as is the case with all structures, grace contains within itself limits as well as permissions. The whole of Paul's ethical discussion is to be seen under the rubric of verse 2, which as we saw is repeated as summation in verse 21. Again, the very arrangement of Paul's prose—admonitions enclosed by verses 2 and 21—reflect the intentions of the content of that prose. All that Paul says, he says within the limits stated in verse 2. Peace, for example, is not to be purchased at the price of conformity to "this world." There is always the temptation to absolutize one or another of these admonitions Paul gives here, and elsewhere, and assume that all else is to be subsumed under it. It is just that kind of aberration Paul seeks to combat by placing these admonitions under the control of verse 2. Christians are called to a new reality, often at odds with the world in which they live, and no virtue, however appealing, which leads one to conform to that world reflects the structuring power of grace.

The limits imposed by the structuring power of grace have a further effect. They prevent Christians from confusing the structuring power of their personal desires with the structuring power of grace. An example Paul cites is personal revenge (vv. 19–20). The temptation is there for devoted Christians, smarting under some attack, to take upon themselves the task of avenging that insult to a faithful servant of Almighty God. Such an act is not to be undertaken, however. If there is any wrath to be administered, leave that to God (v. 19). Humans are too prone to identify as God's enemies those people who displease them. Rather, the Christian's task is to embody that grace to enemies which is the way to reconciliation and peace (recall again 5:9–10!). The offer of peace to enemies is one way to bring about repentance (v. 20; recall 2:4). That is what Paul intends to say here. When he speaks of caring for an enemy's needs

201

which heaps coals of fire on that enemy's head (Paul is quoting Prov. 25:22), he is not giving advice on a better way to get back at one's enemies! Rather, such treatment is intended to get the enemy to turn from enmity to friendship. Gracious deeds thus burn away the hate within. Such treatment of opponents has as its goal reconciliation and peace, not another's defeat and suffering. That is the way God dealt with us when we were his enemies. That is the way God deals through us with those who continue to oppose him.

None of this means withdrawing from all contact with secular society. It means continuing to live within that society, but with a different set of values and different goals. One is to take active part in that society, sharing in its joys and sorrows (v. 15). One is to search out what is good within that secular society and conform to that (v. 17b). One is not to be surprised that such a secular society, though often at odds with God, yet contains much that is good. That society, after all, is part of God's good creation. Small wonder that much of that good remains. That secular society is under the power of sin does not mean everything within it, its values and actions, are totally evil and without good. The problem is not that there is no good alongside the evil. The problem is that secular society is unable to discern the difference, often confusing what is bad with what is good. That is exactly the problem Paul discussed in chapter 7. The Christian, with the renewed way of seeing reality which grace has brought, can see more clearly what is good within secular society than can those who see in that society the highest good! Christians are called upon to see, and support, those elements of their secular society that are conformable to the structuring power of grace. By working for those impulses within secular society, Christians can give visible shape to the responsibility to "overcome evil with good" (v. 21).

Paul has continued his discussion of acts conformable to God's grace made visible in Jesus Christ. That is the agenda to which he calls his readers for their interaction with fellow Christians and with the wider society within which they live. Sermon possibilities abound in the chapter as a whole and in the final segment on life in secular society. A sermon on Christian unity, and the humility with which spiritual gifts must be exercised, will find solid foundation in verses 3–8. It is precisely spiritual pride which most frequently lies behind congregational dissension where "charismatics" have appeared, and these verses make clear no gift confers superiority, whether that gift be preaching, teaching, or even speaking in "tongues," a gift Paul did not think important enough to include here. If tongues are a manifestation of God's Spirit, as I Corinthians 12:4–11 makes clear, a Christian congregation can have a full life even in the absence of that gift, as verses 3–8 make equally clear. Such gifts are neither to be forbidden nor required, but when present, must be used without pride or they are abused.

The need for Christians to live in harmony with their secular society is also emphasized in these verses. If Christians run the risk of persecution for the faith (v. 14), they are by no means to court that persecution, as though faith without persecution somehow could not be genuine. Verses 14–21 are in fact advice precisely on how Christians can conduct themselves in order to live in harmony with all people, so far as that harmony depends on the attitudes and actions of the Christian (v. 18). But when the boundary is reached beyond which harmony means conformity to the world (v. 2), or overcoming good with evil (v. 21), the Christian must desist. Then if persecution comes, it must be borne without rancor. An all but impossible task, such conduct, yet the history of the church bears evidence that the structuring power of grace makes even such conduct possible.

(For comments on teaching this passage, see the discussion at the end of the section on vv. 3–13).

Grace and the State

ROMANS 13:1–7

Is the Christian under obligation to support whatever policies the governing authorities may deem appropriate, whether those policies are for the good of the people or simply for the purpose of keeping those governing authorities in power? Is that what these verses mean? That is the interpretation given to them in the late thirties and early forties of this century by a group within the Protestant church in Germany, who for nationalistic reasons called themselves "German Christians."

203

By means of this passage they justified their claim that Christians owed allegiance to Adolph Hitler. For further support, they cited Luther's interpretation of this passage. Luther had written: "Christians should not refuse, under the pretext of religion, to obey men, especially evil ones" (p. 358). Is that in fact what this passage means? Does Paul here place on Christians the obligation to obey all edicts of whatever government happens to hold civil power over them? Is the ability to take over governing power, by whatever violent means some group is willing to employ, sufficient demonstration that the governing power they have assumed has been granted by God? Does every government, however established and however maintained, have equal claim to the divine sanction these verses confer on governing authorities? Such are the kind of questions this passage poses for us. How are we to answer them?

First of all, this passage rather clearly means that Christians may not frivolously disregard civil authority, as though the freedom from law won for them by Christ's death included freedom from all civil law as well. Part of the good order of God's creation, which was itself established by the overcoming of primeval chaos (see Gen. 1:1–2), is the ordering of human affairs. If, to paraphrase Reinhold Niebuhr, that goodness makes civil order possible, the corruption of human nature by sin makes such civil order necessary. The first premise Paul lays down therefore is that order is established by God (v. 2), because chaos and disorder are God's enemies. To oppose such order is in fact to oppose God by supporting those forces which are at enmity to him (v. 3). The Christian's freedom from law therefore does not mean freedom from civil law. The believer is just as obligated to obey traffic lights as the unbeliever!

The second point to be noted here is that while governing authorities are God's servants for order, and are hence to be obeyed, that obedience is not dependent on the governing authorities either acknowledging or even being aware of that fact. One cannot relativize these verses in that way. The governing authorities to which Paul was referring surely did not understand themselves as servants of Paul's God. Governments can evidently serve God's purposes whether those in government intend to do that or not.

204

Since, then, governing authorities promote the good and punish evil (vv. 2b–4), they are to be obeyed as the servants of God's purposes. They are also to be supported by the payment of taxes (v. 6). This passage, in opposing chaotic civil life, therefore relativizes the freedom of individuals for the purpose of a good and decent society. Social order has behind it the authority and purposes of God himself.

Yet the language of this passage, at the same time that it calls for obedience to civil governments, also relativizes that governing authority. In the first place, since governing authorities are in fact God's servants for the promotion of civil order, those governing authorities cannot claim for themselves divine prerogatives. A government that claims for itself the total and absolute devotion which a creature can give only to its Creator, ceases in the moment it makes that claim to be an agent of divine order, or a divine servant. It has become instead an idolatrous opponent of the living God. Governments that claim for themselves divine prerogatives are hence no longer the kind of governments of which Paul speaks in this chapter. The early Christian reaction to that kind of government can be seen in Revelation 17:1—19:10.

In the second place, Paul describes governments as agents of good, which are to promote civil good and punish evil and disorder. That is of course their task as God's servants. But what happens when a government reverses those roles and begins to reward evil and punish people who do what is good? Again, clearly enough, that would no longer be the kind of government about which Paul here speaks, as Calvin saw. He wrote: ". . . tyrannies, and unjust exercise of power, as they are full of disorder, are not an ordained government . . ." (p. 479). These verses therefore not only describe what governing authorities are, they also prescribe what those authorities are to be. They speak as much to governing authorities about the limits of their power as they speak to the governed about their duties of obedience.

If then a government claims for itself the kind of devotion proper only to God and demands of its subjects that they perform evil rather than good, and if it punishes those who disobey such demands to do evil, that government no longer functions as a servant of God and is therefore no longer to be obeyed as such. So far so good.

Yet the fundamental problem remains: How does one decide at what point a government has passed from the ranks of God's servants to the ranks of his opponents? On that matter this passage gives no specific advice. That decision will have to

205

be reached on the basis of the larger content of this letter, and indeed of the whole of the Bible. Such a decision about governing authorities cannot legitimately be based on personal desires or personal advantage, however. Nothing in Paul's writings, or the remainder of the Bible, gives justification for a decision on such a basis. Yet the limits of civil authority are clear in these verses, and any use of them will have to take that fact into account.

In the final analysis, these verses point to the fact that there is no dimension of life that is beyond God's concern or outside of his power or control. God's lordship, which in Christ has begun to be re-established over his rebellious creation, is not limited to certain areas of human life which have to do with "religion." That lordship is exercised over the whole of creation; and nothing in that creation, religious or secular, is beyond the power and purposes of God. Those who govern are finally answerable to God, because there is no area of reality which can exempt itself from his sovereign power.

In many ways, this passage carries the same message as Jesus' words about what one must render to Caesar and what one must render to God (Mark 12:13–17); and the preacher can approach it from that perspective with profit. Both passages make clear that one has an obligation to the civil authorities (Caesar) as well as to God. If the obligation to God clearly does not rule out an obligation to civil authorities, neither can any obligation to civil authority rule out the obligation to God. If the implied point of comparison in Jesus' statement is the image of Caesar on the coin (Mark 12:16) and the image of God in which human beings were created, then the obligation to God is by much the more far reaching than the obligation to human authorities. Yet the obligation to human authorities who rule for the purposes of restraining evil in human society, and promoting good, may not be ignored; and the preacher who chooses this passage in Paul will need to keep both in balance in the sermon. Obedience to civil authority is a Christian duty, but it is to be exercised within the framework of the Christian's more far-reaching commitment of obedience to God.

The teacher will find in this passage an opportunity to involve the class in a discussion of the extent of the Christian's obligation to civil authority. The entire movement of civil disobedience in the United States, whether dealing with the issue of civil rights or the issue of nuclear weapons, falls within

206

the scope of such a discussion. The teacher will want to emphasize the fact that because God is a God of order and not disorder
(see I Cor. 14:33), anarchy is not a possible Christian stance, nor
is it permissible in the name of the Christian faith to provoke
disorder for its own sake. The democratic form of government,
unknown to Paul, also provides opportunities of redress which
can be taken long before governments assume a shape which
is at odds with their status as divine servants for civil order. A
discussion of what is the "good" the government is to foster
could also involve this whole fourth part of Paul's letter (chaps.
12—16), as the class seeks to determine what Paul understood
that "good" to be. Is it personal comfort? Devotion to God?
Loving action toward fellow human beings? Such questions will
help the class get to the heart of the meaning of this passage for
life in our contemporary world.

Grace and the Neighbor: Love in Action

ROMANS 13:8–14

With this passage Paul moves from secular society writ
large—the state—to that society as represented by its smallest
unit—the neighbor. There is no romantic notion here, however,
that careful attention to this smallest unit of society represented
in the neighbor renders less necessary or even eliminates careful attention to the larger unit of society represented in the
state. The Christian has an obligation to the state, to live as a
good citizen by obeying its laws and by supporting it through
the taxes it levies. The Christian is to render whatever the
appropriate response may be to the various levels of government: respect, for example, to those charged with administer-
ing and enforcing the law; taxes in whatever form they may be
levied; honor to those officials to whom by their conduct, or by
statute, it is due. Good citizenship is part of good Christian
conduct.

207

Yet the Christian's obligations to his or her fellow human
beings are not totally discharged simply by observing such legal

requirements with regard to them. There is a larger obligation which underlies all that a Christian is expected to do. It is the obligation to act in love toward those fellow human beings.

Romans 13:8–10
The Neighbor and the Actuality of Love

That Paul should regard love as the key to one's relationship to one's neighbor will not come as a surprise to the reader of Romans. Paul wrote of its centrality already at 12:9. In these verses, however, Paul carries his observations about love a step further. To understand love as the basic requirement for the Christian who lives under the grace of Christ is to understand such Christian life as the fulfillment of the law God gave to Israel. As Christ is the one to whom the law of Israel had pointed and in whom it found its culmination and thus its end (recall 10:4), so in the love that same Christ commanded as the primary obligation of one human being to another (see Mark 12:28–31) one is also to find the culmination and hence the end of the law (Rom. 13:8–10). Paul emphasizes that point by framing his discussion with the explicit claim that such love is, as Jesus had said, the fulfillment of the law (vv. 8*b*, 10*b*; cf. Mark 12:31*b*).

Love is thus to be the rule of the Christian life. But can love be a "rule?" Indeed, can love be commanded at all? Emotions are not that much under our control. To be commanded to love therefore appears to be totally unrealistic; and it will lead either to frustration, since we are being asked to do something we cannot do, namely love a person we find unlovely, or it will lead to sham and hypocrisy when we pretend to love someone we really do not love at all. How then are we to understand this command to "love?"

The beginning of the answer lies in understanding the kind of perversion the word "love" has undergone in our society, in our "world," as Paul would put it. The problem is that the word "love" has been so captured by Hollywood producers and the romantic novelists that it has come to mean either sheer sentimentality or else the feeling that comes over a person when an attractive member of the opposite sex comes into view. Love has therefore come to be identified with an emotional state.

That is not what the New Testament means by "love." That God loves us hardly means that he gets a warm feeling inside when he thinks of us. We know God loves us not because of the way he *feels* about us but because of what he has *done* for us: He gave his son for our redemption.

What Paul and the rest of the New Testament mean by love therefore centers not on emotions but on actions. To love someone is actively to promote that person's good. To be commanded to love one's enemy means that one is commanded to work for that person's good, not harm. To love an enemy therefore does not mean primarily to change one's emotional state toward that person so much as it means to do good for that enemy, regardless of what one's emotional response to that person may happen to be. Love acts for the good of another. *That* is the love that Paul speaks of here, and that is the love that fulfills the law. As verse 9 makes clear, such love means to cease actions that harm another person and to do what promotes that person's good.

This dimension of the biblical understanding of love is one that must be present in any sermonic treatment of that subject, and the preacher will aid in securing that dimension by combining this passage with other biblical passages which make it clear. Such an Old Testament passage, for example, as Ezekiel 33:7–9, which speaks of the duty of the watchman to warn fellow citizens of approaching danger, says nothing about love. Rather it speaks of the duties of a watchman as the analogy of the prophetic task of Ezekiel. Yet the watchman who carries out his duties of warning at the approach of danger, as the prophet who carries out his divine commission, is in fact acting for the good of those entrusted to his care. In that situation, the watchman and the prophet love their fellow human beings by *doing* something to promote their good: They warn their people of impending danger. That of course is true of all prophets and all apostles who carry out their God–given task of proclaiming God's will to God's people. Warning of dire consequences to those who rebel against God is thus an act of love, done for the good of those who hear, not an act of hate or vengeance. The preacher's love for the congregation he or she serves will on occasion have to take that sermonic form as well.

Again, a Gospel passage like Matthew 18:15–20 does not contain the word "love." The passage records Jesus' advice on how one is to go about recovering an erring fellow Christian,

209

and the great import attached to the responsible exercise of that task. Yet the description of such a recovery is surely the description of an act of love on behalf of the erring fellow Christian, just as Jesus' telling how such recovering is to be done is an exercise of love on his part. Jesus, the embodiment of God's love, exercises that love in this passage by telling his disciples how they are to embody that love. Again, love consists in doing something for the good of others.

Jesus, the incarnation of God's love, thus acts out that love in all he says and does. He is a love that warns as well as comforts, that promises as well as fulfills. But above all he is a love that gives itself freely for the good of others, even if that means death on a cross. But he is also, and finally, God's redemptive love when he rises victorious from the grave. In that way we see that love is act, not sentiment, and sermons on love must make that clear to those who hear.

(For comments on teaching this passage, see the discussion of 13:11–14.)

Romans 13:11–14
The Neighbor and the Dawning Day

It is obvious that Christian love will have an impact on how Christians are to act toward their neighbors. It is not so obvious that the impending consummation of the age, with the visible establishment of God's gracious lordship, also will have an impact on how Christians are to comport themselves with their neighbors. Yet it is this latter topic to which Paul turns in this passage.

There is more connection between the impact of love and the impact of the future on the Christian's behavior than may at first seem apparent. If verses 8–10 reflect the words of Jesus about love as the fulfilling of the law (see Mark 12:28–31), verses 11–14 reflect the words of Jesus about the impact of the future on present activity (see Luke 21:34; Mark 13:35). If love is the appropriate mode of action now in light of the past, with its law (vv. 8–10), then love is also the appropriate mode of action now in light of the future, with its eschatological salvation (vv. 11–14; esp. v. 11*b*). Thus these verses are simply further examples of love in action; but they turn our gaze from past to future, to that time when the fulfillment for which the Christian yearns, and in whose light the Christian attempts to obey God's will of love, becomes visible reality.

These verses make clear that Paul's ardor for the future and for Christ's return did not cool in the course of his ministry. The almost casual mention (v. 11*b*) that that final consummation was now closer at hand than when he and his Roman readers set out on their course of Christian faith shows that he remained convinced that it was close at hand.

Yet if he did think that, and it is clear he did, then he was wrong. Christ still has not returned, almost two millennia later. Of what good then are Paul's reflections based on a timetable which was clearly in error? Does the value of his ethical reflections, tied to that return of Christ, not diminish in value in proportion to the additional delay of that return?

In some sense of course that is true. We are no longer dominated in our understanding of the Christian faith by our sense of the nearness of Christ's return to the extent that Paul was. And yet, it is precisely that future—God's future—that casts its light into the present and that provides the illumination of the reality by which we are called to live. The conviction that Christ will return is the conviction that God will in fact one day redeem his creation, that he will one day fulfill the promise of restoration and recreation given in the resurrection of Christ. Indeed, it is precisely the fact that that future has already invaded the present, an invasion shown by the presence of the Spirit within the community of the faithful (recall 8:23), that gives to the Christian faith the distinctiveness it has.

To lose sight of the return of Christ, with its promise of God's restoration of his creation, is further to run the risk of thinking that if any such good and any such restoration are to come, we are the ones who will have to produce it. After all, if Christ is not going to return to preside over the final restoration of God's gracious lordship over his creation, then any such restoration which is going to take place will have to be accomplished by us. Yet to think that is to fall back into the idolatry of thinking we create our own salvation. It is another form of the attempt to achieve a renewed relationship to God through our own ability, by fulfilling the requirements of the law or in any other way, in this case fulfilling for God his promises of the future. It is precisely the lively awareness of God's future, promised with

211

the return of Christ, that keeps the Christian from falling back into the slavery of idolatry to self and to what the self can produce for its own salvation.

The self-righteousness of those who believe that unless they do the good it can never be done is a fearful thing, and it is abroad in the world today. Much of the vilification visited by social reformers upon those who do not fully support, let alone upon those who question, their programs is the result of their feeling that unless their version of societal reform is enacted no redemption will ever occur. Such hostility toward those who disagree with their program for goodness bears eloquent testimony to the outcome of such self-idolatry which occurs with the loss of hope for God's future. That the Christian is not passively to accept injustice and evil is patent from what Paul has just said about the Christian obligation to love, and hence to aid, one's fellow human beings. But unless that love is tempered by the hope of God's final redemption, it will turn into an instrument of ideological tyranny and fearful self-righteousness.

Christians therefore, in Paul's view, are creatures of the future, not the past. To it they are to look, and by it they are to act. The centrality of that future-oriented stance of Paul is made clear when we see that verse 13, with its call to live now in conformity with God's future (the dawning day) and not in conformity with the evil past (the night), recapitulates the basic theme Paul laid down for the discussion of chapters 12—13 in 12:2. Do not be conformed to this age, with its evils, he wrote there, but be transformed into the newness which the future will bring. That in its turn means we are not to live for ourselves but for God, and we are to obey his will for our lives. That is what Paul means when he says we are to "clothe ourselves in the Lord Jesus Christ" (v. 14). But that in turn recalls the verse with which the whole discussion began (12:1): We are to live as sacrifices to God, wholly conformed to his will. Thus in the very shaping of his discussion, by the way he links beginning and end, Paul calls attention to the importance of shaping our present in the light of God's future. In the final analysis, that is what the Christian faith and the Christian life are all about. Liberated from the burdens of a sinful past, the Christian strides with confident step into a future which brings ever closer the fulfillment of God's redemptive plan for his creation.

It is the anticipation of that future that dominates the Advent season of the church year, and this passage is therefore

212

highly appropriate for it, as those traditions recognize which assign this passage to be read during that time. Not only does the Advent season illumine the meaning of these verses, these verses also inform and deepen our understanding of the future whose advent Christians celebrate both in the birth and in the return of Jesus Christ. That reciprocal impact of Scripture and church year is strengthened when this passage is considered in light of other scriptural passages which help illumine its varied dimensions. Coupled with Isaiah 2:1–5, for example, our passage, with Isaiah, points to the coming of God's future when all will acknowledge him as Lord. Coupled with Matthew 24:36–44, our passage, with Jesus, warns of the suddenness of the end of this age. Both dimensions are appropriate to the Christian expectation of Christ's return—both promise and warning—and they are highlighted by these two passages. Taken together, they fill out the picture of the impact of God's future on our present with which Paul has occupied himself in these verses.

For the teacher, this passage may be treated either as a unity, with love understood as the new reality introduced into the present by God's future, a reality already pointed to in the law, or the passage may be divided into its two logical parts: love as fulfilling the law and the impact of the future on our present lives. In either case, there is an excellent opportunity here to engage a class in discussion about the nature of Christian love. The passage will be especially appropriate for helping class members understand the kind of perversion our culture has visited on the biblical understanding of the word "love." Other examples of Jesus' activity can be drawn from the Gospels, for example, Jesus' acts of healing or his teaching sessions, and can be analyzed as examples of love in action.

The significance of the expectation of the return of Christ is another important topic about which much confusion has grown up as a result of those who continue to think they can figure out when that future is coming, something even Jesus said he could not do (see Mark 13:32)! Can we continue to look to the God who controls the future, and who will one day fulfill his plan for the redemption of creation, even if the kind of timetable Paul anticipated proved to be in error? Do verses like 11–14 depend totally, or even partially, for their value on Paul's timetable? Or is there another sense in which the knowledge that God will one day redeem his creation, whenever that may

213

be, continues to throw light on the way we are to act in, and shape, our present? Such a discussion will help class members come to grips with some of the basic dimensions not only of Christian conduct but of the faith that underlies that conduct as well.

Grace and Unity in the Faith: The Weak and the Strong

ROMANS 14:1—15:13

Paul turns in this section to a discussion of the dangers posed to the unity within the Christian community by different conceptions of the proper response to the gospel of Christ. He frames his discussion in terms of the "weak" and the "strong" and warns against setting one's own understanding of the proper response to the gospel as the norm against which to judge all other responses. Paul feels there is room within the Christian community for differing ways of responding to the gospel with respect to one's everyday life and warns that any attempt to impose uniformity in those matters will rupture the very unity whose preservation is sought. While Paul addresses the problem of convictions about eating in this passage—what kind of food and drink are permitted to a Christian—it is apparent that what he says could be expanded to cover other forms of the response to the Christian gospel one displays by one's ordinary conduct as well. These verses constitute Paul's plea for tolerance within the larger framework of a responsible and thankful response to God for his gracious gift of redemption in Christ.

The passage can be divided into three sections. The first (14:1–12) deals with the problem of self-righteousness and the harm it can cause within the community. The second (14:13–23) concerns the priority of responsibilities over rights within the Christian community. The third (15:1–13) emphasizes the servanthood of Christ as the final basis for Christian unity. Together they give us an informative insight into the way Paul met practical problems on the basis of his understanding of what God has done for humanity in his Son.

214

Romans 14:1–12
Unity and the Problem
of Self-righteousness

The danger of self-righteousness lies in its tendency to make one's own convictions the measure of the validity of the convictions of all others. Paul frames his discussion in terms of "weak" and "strong" and shows that both groups are in danger of allowing their convictions about proper Christian obedience in everyday matters to disrupt the community of the faithful. There has been much speculation about the identity of the "weak" and "strong." That the "weak," who as Christians felt they could eat only vegetables (v. 2*b*), were not necessarily converted Jews is indicated by the fact that nowhere did the Jewish law forbid the eating of meat as such. It only forbade the use of certain classes of animals as food (see Lev. 11). Nor did that law forbid the drinking of wine, which the "weak" apparently also avoided (see 14:21). Indeed, the question about what it was proper to eat also arose where former adherence to pagan idols, not the Jewish law, was the issue (see I Cor. 8:7–10).

The conflict between "weak" and "strong" is therefore unlikely to have been an argument between Jewish and gentile converts to the Christian faith. There were of course disputes between them (see Acts 15:1–21; Gal. 2:1–13), but those disputes had more to do with the question of whether Christian Jews could share any table fellowship with gentile Christians than with the question of whether it was proper for the Christian to eat meat or drink wine.

It is also interesting to note which group Paul designates as the "strong." It is the group that feels it is permissible to eat whatever they please! It is the "weak" who need to abstain from certain food and drink lest their faith be compromised. It is thus the weakness of the "weak" that leads them to impose such discipline on themselves in the matter of what they eat or drink.

Yet who is weak and who is strong and which group is relatively more faithful to the structures of grace is really not the issue. Paul does not condemn those who feel they must

215

restrict their diet out of Christian conscience any more than he condemns those who feel their freedom in Christ now allows them to eat and drink whatever God has provided for them. In fact, it is precisely such condemnation of one group by the other that Paul condemns. Paul does not take sides on whether "weak" or "strong" are more correct. He is intent rather on meeting the threat to Christian unity posed by the attempts of one of the groups to make its convictions about conduct the sole and exclusive measure of true and faithful response to God's gift of his Son. The advice to both groups is the same: Respect the convictions of the other group.

Paul outlines three reasons why such condemnation by either group of the other is wrong. In the first place, a Christian is a servant of God, and thus a member of God's household; and it is not proper, so Paul avers, to criticize or judge a servant who is a member of someone else's household. If God is willing to accept such a person, whether "weak" or "strong," then no one else is in a position to condemn God's acceptance (so vv. 1–4).

In the second place, the condemnation of fellow Christians whose practices differ from those allowed by one's own understanding of the proper response to God's grace is wrong because, although the practices may differ, they grow from a common root: All are done in order to honor God (vv. 5–6). That motivation for Christian conduct is the only appropriate one, since Christians, as God's servants, do not live for themselves but for God, who through Christ rules not only over their living but over their dying as well (vv. 7–9). What can be done appropriately to honor God may therefore not be condemned by those who would prefer to honor God in a different way.

In these verses (5–6), Paul also extends the application of such tolerance for differing dietary convictions among Christians to include the way one may act on certain days. Apparently Paul felt the Old Testament Sabbath regulations as well as the pagan holy days had been rendered non-obligatory in Christ, just as these verses have shown he felt all dietary regulations had been so rendered (see also I Cor. 8:4–13). Yet he is unwilling to condemn those who differ with that judgment. Christian freedom extends to whatever may be done to honor God.

216

The third reason why it is improper to condemn those who differ in their understanding of appropriate Christian life-style rests in the fact that it is God, and not the Christian, who is the one who judges in such matters (vv. 10–12). To set oneself up as judge is therefore to arrogate to oneself what belongs properly only to God. The danger of self-righteousness is therefore closely allied to the danger of self-idolatry. It is the danger of setting up something other than God as god, in this case oneself and one's own preferences. Besides, Paul points out, since we all will be judged by how we have conducted ourselves as Christians, we ought to have enough to worry about in respect to our own conduct without taking on the additional burden of shaping in minute detail the lives of other Christians!

That all will be judged—even Christians, even faithful Christians—is a regular emphasis of Paul (see 2:6; I Cor. 3:8–15; II Cor. 5:10). It points to the fact that along with liberation in Christ there come responsibilities as well, and the follower of Christ had better take those responsibilities with utmost seriousness, since God also takes them seriously. That is the point of Paul's emphasis on the judgment facing Christians. It is not a judgment by which one is deemed worthy of salvation or not. Such a judgment would contradict everything Paul had said about God's grace to undeserving, sinful creatures. But it is a judgment about the quality and responsibility of one's Christian life, and as such it emphasizes the need for responsible action on the part of Christians (see I Cor. 3:8–15 for the results of such judgment). That is the topic to which Paul turns in the next part of his discussion (14:13–23).

This passage deals with a perennial concern within any Christian community: The propensity of one group to impose its understanding of the Christian faith, and a life-style appropriate to it, on all others in the community. The fact that such attempts are rooted in strongly-held convictions does not make them any less examples of the kind of self-righteousness Paul is combatting in these verses. Clearly the structures of the grace of which Paul writes confer a measure of freedom in respect to how one conducts one's everyday activities. That flexibility within responsible limits nevertheless demands tolerance among Christians for behavior of varying kinds. The need for that tolerance within acceptable limits of Christian responsibility with regard to life-style is a central thrust of these verses, and it is an emphasis which can be used with salutary effect in contemporary congregations.

217

The teacher will find in these verses (14:1–12) an insight into the kind of tolerance Paul sought within the Christian community. His words obviously are not to be construed to mean that once one is Christian, anything goes. Of course there are limits to what is permitted by way of Christian behavior. That can be confirmed by a glance at the list of actions carried on by those whom God has abandoned to their own desires (1:29–31), and who therefore by definition are not doing what God wants. But within the realm of proper response there is freedom, perhaps more freedom in matters of eating and drinking, or of what is done on Sunday, than we are often accustomed to think. Some perceive in such freedom a distinct threat to the integrity of the faith, while others understand such freedom to be the essence of that faith. How is one to decide at what point the exercise of that freedom poses a threat to responsible Christian actions? Paul points to two insights: tolerance among Christians for those who disagree in these matters, which should hinder one from making one's own preferences the norm for all Christian behavior, and the need to do everything one does to the honor of God (v. 6). The class may want to see how those two insights would apply to some problem within their own group.

This passage of Scripture seems all but made to order for those situations where there are divisions within a church based on differing perceptions of the correct way to live out the Christian faith. Can a Christian ever drink an alcoholic beverage? Are there foods a Christian is under no circumstances allowed to eat? What kind of activity is permitted on Sunday? Such questions are not unknown to modern congregations, such questions and more like them. This passage in Romans offers a variety of insights on ways such problems are to be dealt with. One such insight is based on the need to forgive. Coupled with a Gospel passage such as Matthew 18:21–35, which records Jesus' advice that one must be prepared to forgive far more often than seems reasonable (v. 22), a sermon on these verses from Romans will emphasize the need for tolerance within the Christian community. Indeed, to deny to others the forgiveness one has received oneself may jeopardize one's own forgiveness (vv. 23–35). God takes forgiveness seriously!

An Old Testament passage such as Genesis 50:15–21, which emphasizes Joseph's unwillingness to condemn his brothers' malice toward him, since God can turn acts that were meant for harm to his own good purposes, can also highlight a Pauline emphasis in our passage from Romans. God's ability to turn any act, however intended, to his own redemptive purposes, would add a further reason, to Paul's three, why judgment in God's name on what is appropriate is to be avoided whenever possible.

Another way to emphasize Paul's caution against mutual condemnations within a congregation is to combine this passage from Romans with a Gospel passage that emphasizes Jesus' acceptance of the unacceptable. Passages like Mark 9:33–37 or 10:13–16, or Luke 7:36–50 which show Jesus accepting those who in his culture had no social or political standing, symbolic of all the sinners who had no religious or social standing whom Jesus came to call, will help make that point. The parable of Jesus about serving the Son of man by serving those least respected in society (Matt. 25:31–46, esp. vv. 40, 45) will aid in making the same point. The prophets who plead for justice for those who have no one to defend them (Isa. 1:17–23; Jer. 7:5–6) and condemn those who take advantage of the helpless (Amos 2:6–7; 4:1; 5:7, 10–11) are also making that same point. It is God's will that one accept the unacceptable, just as he accepted unacceptable sinners. God really does take forgiveness seriously!

Romans 14:13–23
Unity and the Priority of Responsibilities over Rights

In a time like ours, when there is much talk of rights and little of responsibilities, Paul's words in these verses come with a particular relevance and cogency. The question at issue in this passage is the relationship between the *right* of Christians to use their freedom and their commensurate *responsibility* to use that undoubted freedom in a way that is constructive rather than destructive of Christian fellowship. Paul continues in these verses his discussion of the relationships among Christians within the community of the faithful. For that reason, the discussion is one to which Christians need to pay particular attention.

When Christ fulfilled and brought an end to the law, part

219

of what came to an end was the whole regimen of clean and unclean foods which had been, and remains, one of the distinguishing characteristics of the Jewish faith. Realization that that regimen no longer had any religious authority for them seems to have been rather difficult for those Christians for whom, prior to their conversion, such considerations had been at the center of their religious convictions. After all, one of the ways Israel was to respond appropriately as chosen people to the God who had redeemed and called her was to observe certain dietary restrictions. For former Jews to live in total freedom from such restrictions was obviously difficult, and difficult in proportion to the extent to which they had previously sought to live under the law God had given to Israel. One can see the extent of that difficulty in the story of Peter's vision in Acts 10:9–19. Peter resists the heavenly voice (God!) that tells him dietary restrictions no longer apply (v. 10); and even after being told the same thing three times, Peter still has difficulty absorbing what the vision meant (vv. 16–19).

A similar kind of difficulty was faced by gentile converts to the Christian faith. Many of them had followed religious practices which involved eating meat that had been sacrificed to some god or goddess, or which involved drinking wine as part of their participation in cultic celebrations. For some of them, apparently, the identification of such food and drink with the idols they had formerly worshiped had been so complete that now, as Christians, it seemed inappropriate to continue to consume them. Paul faced a similar problem in Corinth (see I Cor. 8). Obviously, while the religious convictions of these Christian converts had changed, their consciences remained sensitive to those former convictions.

Other Christians, who were not bothered by such former associations, felt their freedom in Christ enabled them to eat or drink anything they pleased for "the kingdom of God does not mean food and drink but righteousness and peace and joy in the Holy Spirit" (v. 17). Is that valid insight to be sacrificed to those unable or unwilling to realize it? Is my freedom to be limited by the ignorance or weak conscience of others? It is that problem Paul is addressing in our passage.

220

Paul has no doubt that all things are "clean," that is, that one does not profane God by what one eats. In this Paul is following what the Gospels recall as the position of Jesus himself (cf. Mark 7:1–23). One is not made a "better" Christian by one's diet. If salvation is not by works, it is not by diet either. No one can tell Christians what they may or may not eat on religious grounds (vv. 14*a*, 20*b*). That is clearly an unrestricted right.

Yet that clear, unambiguous, undeniable right is tempered by responsibility to others. Paul is also clear on that point (vv. 15*b*, 20*a*, 21, 22). What is at issue here is the tender conscience of those Paul has earlier identified as the "weak." They are people who have not yet achieved the maturity of faith to realize that no food in itself can jeopardize one's relation to God. Some of the weak, for example, feel that the Christian is duty bound not to drink wine (v. 21). Paul thinks such a position is wrong; in itself, wine is "clean," and can be consumed, as can any other food (v. 20*a*). What then is the proper, even the unhypocritical, path of action? Should one flaunt one's freedom in the face of the weak? Can I allow my right to witness to the freedom I have in Christ to be limited by the ignorance or weakness of others, whether Christian or not? Do I not on the contrary have the duty, precisely by my acts, to shock them out of their weakness, by showing what Christian freedom really means?

Paul's answer is No. The limits of one's freedom, even the freedom of faith in Christ, is the good of one's fellow Christian. If, as we saw earlier (13:8–10), such active concern for another's good is the definition of "love," then such love is what limits Christian freedom. And that is exactly what Paul says here (v. 15*a*). To flaunt Christian freedom is to abuse that freedom. My rights as a Christian, in short, are circumscribed by my responsibility to my fellow human being. What is at stake here is nothing less than the unity of humankind in Christ, for which he died and for which God raised him. It is precisely the elimination of dietary rules which made it possible for Jews to associate with gentiles, and hence for gentiles to become followers of Christ and thus heirs of the promise of Abraham (recall 4:16–17; it is also the point in Acts 10:34–48). Yet if that freedom that opened the faith to all humankind is then used in a way that offends some of the very people for whom Christ died, that freedom itself becomes a hindrance. The abuse of Christian freedom is therefore to absolutize it, with no regard for the consequences to others. Such abuse of others is hardly the goal of Christian faith or of God's restoration of his rebellious creation (v. 17; see also Gal. 5:13–15).

If love is therefore the external limit of Christian freedom,

221

that is, the limit of what the Christian can do in relation to others in the exercise of Christian freedom, what are the internal limits, if any? What are the limits of what I can do as a Christian when it is not a matter of any impact on others? After all, verse 14a is rather sweeping. Does it mean that whatever Christians claim that they do in faith is therefore no longer offensive to God? Is that what verse 23 means? Is the "sky the limit" in what is acceptable Christian behavior, so long as no one else is harmed?

No, that is not the case. The test of Christian behavior remains what Paul had said earlier it was: Whatever is done must be done to the honor of God (see v. 6). Therefore if love of fellow human beings places external limits on Christian action, love of God places the internal limits on that activity.

There is a further consideration to be taken into account when one considers Christian freedom. That is the fact that the Christ whom the Christian is called to follow as Lord did not act to please himself but acted to please God and for the benefit of his fellow human beings. It is in thankful response to that Lord that the Christian must act, and Paul turns to consider what that means for Christian freedom in the next section of his letter (15:1–13).

A sermon based on this passage presents to the preacher the opportunity to bring Paul's words to bear on a "me first" generation that has tended to claim rights in such a way that the sole responsibility of others is to ensure the untrammeled exercise of my rights. That is where emphasis on "rights" without a commensurate emphasis on "responsibilities" inevitably leads. And just as inevitably it brings with it as a consequence the fragmentation of society into mutually hostile groups. It is precisely such a consequence Paul seeks to prevent in this passage. That there is a limitation placed on my freedom, my rights, by my active concern, my responsibility for your good (i.e., my love for you) is a point most church congregations, as well as most sectors of contemporary culture, need to hear; and this passage presents the opportunity for it to be heard.

Another dimension in this text can be emphasized by linking it with a passage like Mark 7:1–23, or an appropriate selection from those verses. That dimension deals with the kind of activity that does indeed constitute impermissible behavior for a Christian. Freedom from dietary regulations does not mean that nothing Christians do can defile them. It is not what one takes in from outside that is the problem. It is what we do to others because of our inner purposes and motivations that presents the danger of our defilement before God (see Mark 7: 18–23). The dangers in this area of Christian conduct therefore come not from without but from within, and that is a message a modern congregation can also hear with profit.

The teacher can use this passage to engage a class in discussion on the distinctions between those activities the Christian is obliged to curtail out of love for fellow human beings (e.g., preferences in food and drink) and those activities which cannot be curtailed under peril of denying one's faith (e.g., confessing Jesus Christ as Lord). Such distinctions must be drawn with care, since, as we saw, such statements as verse 14 do not mean "anything goes" for Christians even though they are convinced that it is permissible activity for Christians. Another factor to be considered in such a discussion is the responsibility of the "strong" to bring the "weak" to a fuller understanding of the freedom Christ won for them on the cross. Is there a danger in permitting the "weak" to continue to think the consumption of certain foods or certain beverages will jeopardize their relationship to God? How close does such an idea that God requires that I not eat or drink certain things in order to remain pleasing to him border on "works righteouness" and imply a denial of the total sufficiency of grace? A consideration of such issues will give the class an opportunity to explore the implications of these verses for contemporary life.

Romans 15:1–13
Unity and the Servanthood of Christ

Christian unity exists in Christ. It is given to those who acknowledge God's gracious lordship in his Son. It is that Son, therefore, who is also the key to the actualization of that unity within the Christian community. It is he who will overcome the dangers posed to unity by self-righteous self-assertion (14:1–12) and by the emphasis on rights at the expense of responsibilities (14:13–23). What this passage contributes to the discussion of Christian unity between the weak and the strong therefore is the definition of the norm of all Christian acts and attitudes, namely Christ himself. But it is the strong who most need to heed that fact.

The way Christ acted, the Christ who although he was strong yet for our sake became weak, is the way that the strong must also act toward those whose own faith is weak. The self-limitation of Christ for the sake of others thus shows the way the strong are to exercise the freedom they have in the faith: Its exercise is to be limited for the good of others, in this case, the weak. Thus, while Paul's discussion to this point had been directed both to weak and strong, this passage, as its contents indicate, is now directed specifically to the strong. The opening verse of our passage which makes that clear serves both as summary of 14:13–23 and as an introduction to 15:1–6.

The Christian's responsibility to bear with the weaknesses of others is based on God's act of bearing with the weaknesses of his rebellious creation in Christ. Because Christ is our Lord, he is also the model of the way we are to act. The point Paul wants to emphasize here is that Christ acted not for his own good, or his own pleasure, but for the good of others. He bore what rightly we ought to have suffered (the point of the quotation from Ps. 69:9 in v. 3), and in that way acted for our good.

The fact that Scripture, here in the form of Psalm 69, illumines this aspect of the ministry of Christ means that Scripture can continue to illumine the Christian's life under the lordship of Christ as well. Recalling a theme here (v. 4) that he had sounded earlier in 4:23, Paul reminds his readers of the role Scripture plays in strengthening the Christian's hope. The fact that that hope comes by the power of the Holy Spirit (v. 13) gives at least indirect evidence of Paul's notion of why Scripture can be the basis of the Christian's hope: In those Scriptures, the power of the Holy Spirit himself is at work.

The benediction which ends the first part of the discussion in these verses reflects the language Paul used in Philippians 2:1–6 and represents the kind of vocabulary he employs when Christian unity is uppermost in his mind. That of course is the purpose for which Christ came and the purpose for which he died, namely to break down the barriers between Jew and gentile and to unite in himself the whole of rebellious humanity, gathered in by the forgiving love of the Father. That unity then becomes the theme of verses 7–13, the second part of our section.

224

Like 15:1–6, which began with a summary statement that

also set the theme of the following discussion and which ended with a benediction, 15:7–13 also begins with a statement which is at once the conclusion of verses 1–6 and the statement of the theme of the discussion which is to follow. Like verses 1–6, verses 7–13 will also end with a benediction (v. 13). In that way, Paul points not only by content but also by the very construction of his prose to the parallel between the purpose of the Christian's responsibility to neighbor (vv. 1–6) and the purpose of God's enacted responsibility to us in Christ (vv. 7–13), namely the unity of all people based on their mutual welcoming of one another because of God's forgiving love.

As verse 7 makes clear, the basis for the mutual welcoming of Jew and gentile, which makes possible the unity of all peoples, is Christ. On the one hand, Paul points out that Christ's coming fulfills God's promise to Israel. That is, Christ is the basis of the unity of all peoples as far as the Jews are concerned, because by his coming he showed God's truthfulness toward his promises to the patriarchs that through them all of humankind would be blessed. Christ in coming for the redemption of the Jews therefore displays that God's word is true and that he is faithful to his promises. As a result, Jews can trust God and in that trust can welcome others.

On the other hand, Christ is the basis of the mutual welcoming which results in the unity of all humankind as far as the gentiles are concerned because by his coming he showed God's mercy to all peoples so that, gathered now into the whole people of God, gentiles too could praise him. Christ in coming for the redemption of the gentiles therefore displays that God is merciful. As a result, gentiles can trust God and in that trust can welcome others because God in Christ has shown himself to be merciful.

The goal of God's act of grace in Christ is therefore unity among his creatures, a unity which, as this whole discussion has shown, is to become reality in the present in the community of those who acknowledge God's gracious lordship in Christ. If the universal scope of the mutual welcome all peoples are to extend to one another waits the restoration of creation, with its new heaven and new earth, that mutual welcome is nevertheless already to be visible reality within the church. That is the burden of Paul's discussion in these verses.

225

If in the present time that reality still remains a hope, it is a hope grounded in the power of God himself; and that is why the hope is sure. Paul ends his discussion with the benediction in verse 13 that makes that very point. Any human striving toward unity therefore has its sole power from God himself; and just as such striving which is in accordance with his will expressed in the lordship of Christ will surely triumph in the end, so any such striving which ignores that lordship will just as surely fail.

The fact that this discussion, though intended for a time long since gone, still intersects our lives is confirmation of what Paul had said earlier about the function of Scripture. Although, of course, he did not think of his own letters as Scripture—Paul's Scripture was limited to what Christians know as the Old Testament—the experience of the church over centuries has shown that these letters too, by the power of God's Spirit, continue to illumine the lives of Christians and to provide the basis of continuing hope.

Such intersection with our lives of what Paul says here occurs in at least three places. First, what Paul says can lift our vision beyond the problems we face in our individual churches to see that we are part of a larger plan of God. The problems we face are not unique to us, and the solutions that worked in Paul's time will continue to work now. That is why we may have hope that in our time as well people will be able to heed God's call to follow Christ, and thus provide a foretaste within the community of the faithful of that final unity of all creatures at the end of time.

Second, Paul's discussion helps us understand the inclusive nature of God's love. His purpose is inclusion, not exclusion. No area, no people, are in principle separated from his mercy. Whatever therefore that contributes to exclusion from the Christian community, whether social pressures or racial biases or whatever else, works at cross-purposes with the redemptive intention of God as shown in Christ. Christians are representatives of God's plan of the redemptive unity of all peoples and are to act accordingly, both individually and as members of the community of the faithful.

Third, Christian tolerance for those whose understanding of the faith requires from them a different response in their daily lives to the lordship of Christ shares in, and is part of, God's eschatological plan for harmony and peace in his creation. That is the weight placed on the need for unity among Christians, despite the diversity of their response to Christ's Lordship; and

226

it shows that the ecumenical movement is not a luxury but a necessary part of the mature faith of God's people on earth.

It is because these verses show how God's plan informs and illumines the way we are to act under the lordship of Christ that they are recognized by many traditions as particularly appropriate for the Advent season which awaits the coming of that Lord, although they would be appropriate for any sermon on the return of Christ in glory. These verses in Romans announce that the one who comes is faithful (as he is to Israel) and merciful (as he is to gentiles), and therefore we may greet his coming with joy. He comes to restore unity to the broken peoples on the earth. From this perspective, other biblical texts that announce the coming judgment of God take on new light. The announcement by John the Baptist (Matt. 3:1–12), for example, that the Coming One is in fact the final judge, whose decisions will determine the shape of God's new world, may be greeted with happy anticipation rather than with fear-filled foreboding because we know the nature of God's plan for his creation. It is mercy and forgiveness and peace.

Yet even here, the understanding that God's coming means mercy and peace rather than condemnation and destruction is known to the prophets as well. A passage like Isaiah 11:1–10 reinforces the vision of that peace which lies at the heart of the mission of the "shoot from the stump of Jesse," who is, we now know, Jesus. With Jesus the new reality announced in Isaiah has begun. Like Israel, we yearn for an end to evil and the establishment of universal peace. Like those who heard Isaiah speak these words, we rejoice in the hope they provide. Thus the hope announced in Isaiah becomes the anticipation given voice by John the Baptist, and that anticipation becomes joyful acknowledgment with Paul that in Christ that peace has already become reality in the career of Jesus, as it is to become reality in those who bow in joyful adoration to his lordship. Advent for the Christian is therefore a time of expectation and joy, of waiting and of fulfillment. If such waiting is the particular emphasis of the Advent season, it is not limited to that time of the church year, and the preacher will find here rich treasures for a sermon on Christ's expected return, whether during Advent or at some other season in the life of the community of faith.

227

These verses will provide the teacher an excellent opportunity to aid a class in coming to grips with the true purpose of the movement toward church unity, the "ecumenical movement." The notions that it was initiated solely by those who sought a "super-church," or only by ecclesiastical bureaucrats who sought to extend their power, are shown by these verses to be wide of the mark. The need for the unity of all who confess the lordship of Christ is grounded in God's own plan for his creation. A useful discussion can be organized around the question of what elements in present church structures and activities promote, and what elements hinder, further unity among Christians. What characteristic activities of those who acknowledge the lordship of Christ are due more to social or economic pressures on them than to the nature of the Christian faith? What kind of activities are essential for an acknowledgment of that lordship within our contemporary society? Such questions, discussed in light of Romans 15:1–13, can help class members probe the essentials of their faith and its daily expression in their lives.

Grace and Paul's Apostolic Plan

ROMANS 15:14–33

Are there to be second-class citizens within the people of God? Will the church take seriously Paul's apostolic message that Christ is God's gift of reconciliation to all peoples, not simply to the Jews (Jesus was, after all, a Jew) and not now only to gentiles (the Jews have, after all, rejected God's reconciliation through his Son)? If not, then the church as the people of God will be fundamentally divided into two (or more) classes of Christians; and it will then be working at cross purposes to God's intended restoration of the unity of all peoples in Christ (see 15:7–13). That is the issue in this passage, and it may well be the primary reason why Paul has written this letter to the Christians in Rome. For that reason we must look very carefully at these verses.

228

Paul begins his discussion of this most crucial topic, surprisingly enough, by outlining three sets of travel plans. One set concerns his journey to Rome and his visit with the churches there (vv. 22–24, 28). That of course recalls a discussion at the beginning of the letter (1:10), where he also mentioned his long-standing desire to make such a visit. The second set of travel plans, closely related to his visit to Rome, concerns his further journey to Spain. Paul understood his apostolic call to consist in opening new frontiers for the Christian faith, and he felt he had completed that task in the eastern Mediterranian world (15:19*b*–20, 23; cf. I Cor. 3:10; II Cor. 10:16). The third set of travel plans concerns a journey to Jerusalem with an offering for the Christians there which he had collected among his churches in Greece (vv. 25–33). It is that journey about which Paul expresses the most concern. It is in regard to that journey, in fact, that Paul makes the only direct personal request of his readers in the entire letter: He asks them to pray for him as he undertakes it (v. 30). That shows the significance of the journey and reveals Paul's great dedication to the unity of the people of God.

Paul asks their prayers for two concerns. The first is that he be delivered from his enemies in Judea. That that would be a concern is easy enough to imagine. Those enemies had already sought once to put him to death (II Cor. 11:32–33; cf. Acts 9:23–25), and the continuing hostility of the Jewish leaders to one whom they must have regarded as a religious traitor is not hard to imagine. That Paul would solicit prayers for his deliverance from their evil designs is therefore not surprising. But secondly, Paul also asks for his readers' prayers that his offering may be accepted by the church in Jerusalem; and that request is surprising. After all, the authorities in Jerusalem had requested the gift (see Gal. 2:10); and it is hard to imagine why they would be reluctant to accept it. The reason for that possible reluctance lies, not in the gift itself, but in what the gift symbolizes. It is that symbolism which is the key to understanding the potential difficulty, and it is therefore to that symbolism that we must now turn our attention.

Paul is clear that the original promise of God to bless humanity had been given to the Jews. It constituted their irrevocable advantage (recall 3:2; 9:4–5; 11:29). When Christ, born from that people, opened the way for gentiles as well to enter the chosen people (the burden of Paul's apostolic mission to those very gentiles), it meant that Jews were now sharing with gentiles their own precious call. Gentiles thus were given a share in Israel's spiritual blessings (15:27). As a result, gentiles now

229

stand indebted spiritually to the Jews. What can the gentiles do about that obligation? What can they do as a gesture of gratitude, and as a way of equalizing the indebtedness so it becomes a matter of mutual giving and sharing?

That is where the offering comes in. The offering of the gentiles to the church in Jerusalem is the gift the gentiles are giving to the Jews. The gift is therefore a gesture of unity and equality. Accepting the gift is therefore tacit admission by the Jewish Christians that Jews and gentiles now stand on equal footing with respect to each other. Yet there is even more to the offering and the acceptance of the gift than that.

We know that Paul understood his mission to be the preaching of Christ to the gentiles. Yet in these verses we see another dimension of that mission. Paul understood his apostolic commission in priestly terms: it was his task to bring the gentiles as an acceptable offering to God (v. 16; the NEB captures the priestly flavor of the language better than the RSV). As the priest has the responsibility to see that the offering he brings is acceptable to God—it cannot be blemished or profane, and it must be offered in the proper manner (see Lev. 22)—so it is Paul's responsibility to see that the "obedience of the gentiles" (i.e., their faith, v. 18) is configured in a manner acceptable to God (for Paul's use of similarly priestly language to express his apostolic task, see Phil. 2:17).

In addition to bringing the gentiles as an acceptable offering to God, a further part of Paul's priestly service as apostle to the gentiles was his responsibility, by preaching Christ to them, to actualize the unity of God's people, both gentiles and Jews, which had been established in Christ (see vv. 7–12). That, after all, is what God's reconciliation of human beings to himself in Christ was all about. That unity has constituted a major theme of this letter, and it was apparently a major element in the way Paul understood his apostolic commission.

It was in the service of this second part of his priestly function as apostle to the gentiles, namely the unity between gentile and Jewish Christians, that Paul is about to take the offering to Jerusalem. When we realize that that offering was not merely a friendly gesture, but was part of Paul's priestly ministry as an apostle, we can also understand the heavy freight of meaning that that offering bore. If the church in Jerusalem accepted the offering, it would be an acknowledgment that just as they have rightfully received a share of the material blessing

230

of the gentiles so the gentiles have rightfully received a share of the spiritual blessings of Israel. That would mean that they are mutually indebted to one another and are on an equal footing within the people of God. More than that, the acceptance of such an offering would be a clear acknowledgment that Paul's apostolic mandate is valid and that his ministry can continue, with the blessing of Jerusalem as well as of Rome. The acceptance of the offering will therefore mean Paul can come to Rome, joyful in the knowledge that his proposed mission to Spain will contribute to the unity, not the division, of the people of God (v. 32).

That is why the offering is of such great importance to Paul and why he solicits the prayers of his fellow Christians in Rome for its acceptance. He is asking for nothing less than their prayers for the unity of the people of God. And if the people of God is unified, then there are in fact no second-class Christians. Then racial origin will make no more difference than one's gender or social standing as far as one's Christian status is concerned: All will be one in Christ (see Gal. 3:28).

All of that has more than a little relevance to the way the life of the people of God is carried on in our world as well. Distinctions within a congregation which are based on social status or racial origin or gender are on the same level as the rejection by the Christians in Jerusalem of Paul's offering from the gentile churches. It means a denial of the unity of God's people and their equality in his eyes. That does not mean everyone in the church is to have the same tasks and the same responsibilities. Paul made that clear enough in 12:6–8. Different people have different spiritual gifts, and as a result they have different functions and tasks within the church. Yet any ranking or importance of superior/inferior on the basis of those gifts and functions is to be eliminated. That is what is at issue for Paul.

A further perspective on that aspect of equality within God's own people will be gained if the preacher combines these verses with a passage from the Gospels such as the parable of the laborers in the vineyard (Matt. 20:1–16), where the workers hired early think the kind of work they have done entitles them to preferential treatment. That parable speaks directly to the problem of different rankings on the basis of different functions and makes clear that all are accepted by God's generosity, his grace. Function does not entitle one to preferential treatment before a God who treats all on the same basis: his mercy.

231

Another appropriate Gospel passage would be Luke 5: 29–32 where people fuss at Jesus for associating with those who are beneath his—and their—social level. In light of our passage in Romans, one can begin to understand why Jesus associated with such persons as a matter of course. It was precisely to demonstrate the total absence of second-class status within the people of God. Jesus welcomed all who were outcast, whether for reasons of illness, economic status, or social rank, to show God's care for them as well. There are no second-class people in God's eyes. Clearly enough, what Paul sought to accomplish with his offering to Jerusalem was identical to what Jesus had announced God's new people to be: a people among whom no group, of whatever social or cultural origin, was of lesser importance.

The perspective is broadened yet further when one considers the witness already contained in the Old Testament to the special attention God gives to the helpless and to the outcast. Psalm 146:6–10 or Isaiah 10:1–5 show God's concern when ill treatment is visited upon those who have no wealth or social position to call upon in their own defense. Clearly, there were to be no second-class citizens in Israel, God's people, and those who sought to establish such rankings found God himself as their opponent. That continues to be the case. The preacher will find in that context—Prophet, Jesus, Paul—that the theme of God's equal concern for all people runs through the entire Bible, and it is a theme that speaks with force to the contemporary church.

For the teacher these verses provide an opportunity to review the career of Paul and the way he understood his mission. The peculiar significance he attached to the offering illustrates the significance he attached to his mission to the gentiles within the total plan of God for his creation. In an incidental way verses 30–32 also show the confidence Paul placed in the power of prayer. Instead of a request for someone to accompany him to Jerusalem, or even a letter of recommendation on behalf of the collection, Paul requests their prayers as the way they are to become participants in this struggle for the unity of the people of God.

232

If the class has been studying Romans for a series of lessons, this passage will serve as a means of linking Paul's concern for the unity between weak and strong within the church in Rome (14:1—15:13) with his concern for unity between Jew and gentile within the church at large. It also enables the teacher to highlight Paul's emphasis on salvation through trust in Christ as the way into the people of God for "all who trust, for the Jew first and also for the Greek" (1:16). Paul's great concern for the unity of the people of God thus brackets the entire letter, from the opening verses to its conclusion in our passage.

REFLECTION:

Chapter 16 and Paul's Letter To Rome

Is the letter of Paul to Rome as we have it in our New Testament the letter as he wrote and sent it, or have some things been added to it which Paul did not include in his original communication with the Roman Christians? The issue around which that question turns is fundamentally the question of the original destination of chapter 16. While there is general agreement among scholars that the remainder of the letter as we have it is essentially as Paul wrote it, there is no such agreement about the sixteenth chapter.

The problems related to this question have been a matter of scholarly debate for over a century. Both the content of the chapter and the history of the transmission of its text raise that problem. There is more involved here, however, than simply a question of the genuineness of chapter 16 in relation to Paul's letter to Rome. Whether or not the example of division between "weak" and "strong" in chapters 14—15 reflects Paul's knowledge of an actual conflict among the Roman Christians or whether Paul chose that as a general example, drawn from, say, his experiences in Corinth also depends at least in part on how we answer the question of the origin and intention of chapter 16. Because this issue in biblical scholarship has a potential impact on the interpretation of at least part of Paul's letter to Rome (14:1—15:13), we may survey the kinds of argument advanced by those who contest the originality of chapter 16 and those who support it.

Those who question the original joining of chapter 16 to the first fifteen chapters of Romans point for evidence to the names mentioned in the chapter to whom Paul wants to send greetings. There are twenty-six individuals in all, far more than Paul

233

greets in any other letter. It is unlikely, so the argument runs, that Paul could have known that many people in a church he had never visited.

On the other hand, if Paul had sent a copy of this letter to one of the churches he himself had founded, and had added these greetings to that copy, it would more easily account for so many names. According to Acts 18:2, Paul had met the Prisca and Aquila mentioned in Romans 16:3 in Corinth. Paul had founded the church in Corinth and had spent considerable time there. Perhaps Phoebe (see Rom. 16:1), who herself was from Cenchrae, a town very near Corinth, had taken a copy of Paul's letter to Rome, made up of the first fifteen chapters of our present Romans, to the Christians in Corinth so that they too could benefit from Paul's theological reflections. To that copy Paul would then have added these special greetings to the people he knew there.

If the difficulties Paul had had with the Christians in Corinth make it unlikely that he would have wanted to send them a copy of his letter to Rome, another possible destination for such lengthy personal greetings would be Ephesus. Paul had spent more time with the Christians in Ephesus than with any other group of converts, according to the narrative in Acts, and he would surely have known people in the numbers represented in chapter 16. Further evidence for a destination in Ephesus is found in the mention of Epaenetus (Rom. 16:5), who as the first convert in Asia could well have lived in Ephesus, one of the major cities of the Roman province of Asia.

In addition to such reflections based on the content of chapter 16, there is also some manuscript evidence. One of those early manuscripts of Paul's letter to Rome omits the sixteenth chapter altogether. In other manuscripts, the benediction that now appears at the end of chapter 16 (vv. 25–27) appears at the end of fifteen. Would that not indicate that the letter had originally ended there and that at some later time, when Pauline material was being collected, what we know as chapter 16 was added to the original fifteen chapters of the letter? Such are the arguments of those who feel that chapter 16 was not part of the original letter Paul sent to Rome.

234   Yet that manuscript evidence is not so persuasive as it might seem. The doxology that we find in our New Testament at the end of chapter 16 is found not only at the end of chapter 15. In some manuscripts it is found at the end of fourteen, in

others it is at the end of both fourteen and sixteen. One manuscript omits the doxology altogether, although there is a space after chapter 14, perhaps indicating the copyist knew some manuscripts that put the doxology there. The manuscript evidence is therefore so ambiguous that it scarcely allows us to come to any firm conclusions about the original form of Romans.

Nor does the presence of the twenty-six names in chapter 16 argue decisively against the presence of that chapter in Paul's original letter to Rome. If Paul was writing to Christians in a city he had never visited, it would surely be to his advantage to mention all those he had learned to know in his other churches, and who had since moved to Rome, to show that he was not that much of a stranger to that Christian community. Those whom Paul knew there could also have vouched for him to those who had not yet met him. But could that many people have moved to Rome between the time Paul had met them elsewhere and the time he wrote this letter? That is in fact quite possible. Rome was after all the capital city of the Mediterranean world, and the system of roads Rome maintained to the far-flung borders of its empire made travel relatively easy. We know from other records that such travel was common and that masses of people flocked to Rome from all parts of the empire. Such movement of people to Rome was therefore quite possible.

There is a further event that would have made such movement likely. The Roman emperor Claudius had ordered the expulsion of all Jews from Rome about the year A.D. 49 because of constant agitation among them. That agitation was perhaps caused in part at least by the coming of Christian Jews to Rome who were engaging in religious disputes with the Jewish population of the city. Because the Romans at that point had not yet learned to differentiate Jews from Christians—Christians looked like nothing more than another Jewish sect, like the Essenes or the Pharisees—Jewish Christians would also have been affected by Claudius' edict. In fact, Acquila and Prisca were in Corinth precisely because of that edict (Acts 18:2). If Paul, as seems likely, was writing his letter to Rome sometime in the late fifties or early sixties, people whom he had met on his missionary journeys, who had been exiled from Rome, would have had time to return; Claudius' edict was not very long-lasting in its effects. It was not the first such expulsion of

235

a group from Rome, it would not be the last, and the affected groups learned how to cope with them. If that were the case, it is not hard to imagine that Paul could easily have learned to know all the people he named in chapter 16 during his travels, people who in the meantime had returned to Rome.

How one decides the question of the place of chapter 16, whether it belonged originally to Romans or not, has implications that range wider than simply that chapter, however. For example, what one decides about chapter 16 will have an impact on how one understands the discussion of "weak" and "strong" in chapters 14—15. If one decides that chapter 16 is a later addition to the letter, sent originally to some city other than Rome, one will no longer have any evidence to assume that Paul knew anything about the situation of the Christians in Rome. One will then understand the discussion of the problems between "strong" and "weak" as a general treatment of the kind of problems Christians in an overwhelmingly non-Christian culture are likely to face. The similarity between the problems discussed in I Corinthians 8 and Romans 14:1—15:13 will tend to confirm such an idea. In that case it would also be an exercise in futility to try to identify who the "weak" and who the "strong" were. Any such attempt at identification is not only doomed to failure but wrong in intention, since Paul, lacking knowledge of the Christian community in Rome, would not have been aware of their own internal disputes.

If on the other hand one assumes that chapter 16 was part of the original letter Paul wrote to the Roman Christians, one will then be more inclined to seek for cultural and religious clues that would help in identifying the background of the "weak" and the "strong," since Paul, knowing so many people there, would also have had the chance to learn from them of the situation there. Lack of conclusive evidence has forced such attempts at identification to remain largely conjectural, but those who hold to the genuineness of chapter 16 will continue the attempt to identify the two groups within the congregation at Rome, rather than understanding them as two idealized groups constructed from Paul's experience in other gentile churches.

236   Until new and decisive evidence is uncovered, there seems little chance that the debate will be resolved. In the end its resolution may be less important than it would first appear to be for our understanding of Paul's advice to the "weak" and the

"strong," since his advice is the same to both: They are to tolerate one another in the exercise of Christian love. Understanding that point may be more important for understanding chapters 14—15 than resolving the dispute about the original destination of chapter 16 and its implication for Paul's knowledge of the actual situation among the Christians in Rome.

For further information: More detailed discussion of the problem can be found in an introduction to the New Testament. One of the most detailed and complete is W. G. Kümmel, *Introduction to the New Testament.* Commentaries also give detailed discussion of this problem. C. K. Barrett's *The Epistle to the Romans* or Ernst Käsemann's *Commentary on Romans* would be good places to look. For the attempt to interpret the passage on the assumption that Paul did know about specific problems within the Christian community in Rome, and was addressing specific groups as "weak" and "strong," one may read Paul Minear's *The Obedience of Faith.* A strong argument for the authenticity of chapter 16 as part of Paul's original letter to the churches in Rome will be found in Harry Gamble, Jr., *The Textual History of the Letter to the Romans.* Several articles in *The Romans Debate,* edited by K. P. Donfried, also deal with this subject, particularly those by Donfried and Robert J. Karris. A good attempt to reconstruct the course of the Christian community in Rome from its origins through the early second century will be found in Part Two of *Antioch and Rome* by R. E. Brown and J. P. Meier. Each of the books mentioned contains additional bibliography for those who wish to pursue the problem further.

Greetings and Summation

ROMANS 16:1–27

Paul's letter to the Romans ends with one of the great benedictions in biblical literature (16:25–27). It is appropriate that the letter end with such a celebration of God's plan of salvation, announced by prophets, fulfilled in Christ, and

237

opened now to all nations, since that is also the way the letter began (1:2–5). Thus framed, the whole of Paul's discussion can be seen within the perspective of God's accomplishing in Christ what he had purposed to do: exercise his redemptive lordship over his rebellious creation and reconcile it to himself. The rectification of that relationship through trust in the Son of God ("justification by faith") can thus be seen in its proper perspective within the larger framework of God's redemptive care, his grace, toward his creation. A benediction to God's completion of his grace-filled plan to heal the breach sin opened between himself and his creatures is thus a most appropriate way to conclude the letter.

The short section of admonitions in verses 17–20 also summarizes the theme that had preoccupied Paul not only in his section on admonitions (chaps. 12—16), but which also underlies the whole of his theology, namely the unity in Christ of Jews and gentiles, a unity which is part and parcel of the rectified relationship between God and humanity. The reconciliation and peace among all human beings mirrors and is part of the reconciliation and peace to be achieved in Christ, a reconciliation and peace already coming to reality by the power of God's own Spirit within the community of the faithful (recall chap. 8). Thus verses 17–18 resume the theme of the unity of God's people, which was the topic of chapters 14—15, by warning against the kind of divisions which make such unity impossible to achieve, and verse 19 points to the kind of attitude to good and evil which makes possible the unity in the faith for which the Romans are justly well known (recall 1:8b). Verse 20 points to the only power which in the end makes any reconciliation and peace among human beings possible, as it makes any rectified relationship to God possible, namely his power to crush the forces of evil arrayed against his good creation. In God, Satan has met his match; and his final defeat will be accomplished in what, compared to the eternity of God himself, can only be regarded as "quickly."

Framing these two passages are Paul's greetings to individual Christians. On the problems these greetings have posed for Pauline scholars, the reader is referred to *"Reflection: Chapter 16 and Paul's Letter to Rome."* What these greetings show is Paul's consciousness of being a part of a larger Christian fellowship within which God's Spirit is at work to accomplish God's plan. The phrases Paul uses to characterize these individuals—

238

"fellow workers in Christ Jesus" (v. 2); "Mary who has worked hard among you" (v. 6); "men of note among the apostles" (v. 7); "our fellow worker" (v. 9); "Persis who has worked hard in the Lord" (v. 12); "Rufus, eminent in the Lord" (v. 13)—indicate Paul's awareness of the fact that he was one of many whose trust in God through Christ led him to work for God's new reality in the world. If being an apostle conferred special responsibility, it did not confer special rank—that is clear from these greetings. Paul's overriding concern is not himself but the Lord Jesus Christ (see II Cor. 4:5), and that is demonstrated in the generosity of his characterizations of those whom he greets. That generosity toward others in itself is a clear, if unintended, witness to the kind of attitude which is appropriate for the unity of human beings. It is also the only proper response to God's act of grace and reconciliation in his Son.

In short, verses 17–20 and 25–27, placed in the midst of Paul's personal greetings, sum up the core of what Paul has wanted to communicate to the Romans in his desire to share with them his gospel of God's redemptive care for his creation in Christ Jesus. And the greetings themselves, among which those verses appear, confirm in their own way what Paul has said about the appropriate response to the new relationship God has offered his rebellious creatures in Christ.

All of that helps make it clear why the concluding verses of this chapter (vv. 25–27) are regarded by many traditions as appropriate for the Advent season of the church year. In Advent, Christians recall the first advent of the key figure in God's plan for humankind, Jesus Christ, and they await his return. That rhythm of remembering and awaiting can be given added substance by joining these verses to an Old Testament passage like II Samuel 7:1–16, which announces the place in God's plan for David's royal descendants. David speaks of building a temple, something he can do for God, but God's prophet announces a succession of kings, something God will do for David, and indeed, in his descendant Jesus, for all humanity. The preacher will recall Jesus' statement about himself that "greater than the temple is here!" (Matt. 12:6). As in Christ, so in the announcement to David of God's plan, the temple is superceded by the coming Greater One.

239

In the Lukan account of the annunciation of Jesus' birth (Luke 1:26–38), the angel Gabriel announces to Mary the fulfillment of the plan which the prophet Nathan had announced to

David, making this an appropriate passage to combine with the verses from II Samuel and Romans. Mary's child will be the heir of David and will fulfill God's plan. And he will fulfill it by the power of the same divine Spirit to whom he owes his conception.

It is that Victorious One whose return the church anticipates, an anticipation given clear focus in Advent. With his return he will bring to final completion the plan Paul has described in his letter to the Christians in Rome, and which he summarizes in the concluding verses of that letter. The descendant God promised to David the angel announced to Mary: Jesus, whose very name means salvation for his people (Matt. 1:21).

That final benediction in Romans thus contains nothing less than the proclamation of the final victory of God's grace: the restoration of his gracious lordship over his redeemed creation. In light of those verses, the Christian's life can be a time of assured expectation, since God brings to completion what he has promised. The Christian's life can also be a time of joyful expectation, since the fulfilled promise of God is nothing less than the restoration of creation to its rightful relationship of love and devotion to its Creator and Lord. Rectified by a trust in that Lord, a trust grounded in confidence in his Word, the Christian may recall with joy that first advent of Christ and await with quiet confidence his second advent, when God's plan for his creation will become visible reality. That is the message to which these readings give voice and to which they invite the preacher to devote his or her proclamation, whether during Advent or at any other time during the church year.

The teacher will find here the opportunity to review the whole course of Paul's discussion in the letter to the Roman churches, if the class has studied the whole of the epistle. Verses 17–20 will provide a good opportunity to review what Paul has had to say about the relationship among Christians to one another (the "weak" and the "strong" in chaps. 14—15), as well as to those outside the Christian fellowship (chap. 13).

Study of chapter 16 will also provide the opportunity for the teacher to discuss with the class the problem of the original destination of chapter 16 (see *"Reflection: Chapter Sixteen and Paul's Letter to Rome"*). If chapter 16 was originally sent to another destination, and later attached to Romans, does that affect its usefulness for us? Were it not for the collection and combination of materials from many sources in the early church, we would not have our New Testament today. Paul's letters were written to many different places, and the four Gospels were not all written in the same place or used in the same churches. That means all of the writings we have in the New Testament were assembled by the early church. That insight could lead to a good discussion by a class on the extent of our debt to the early church for its collection of the New Testament and the significance that work by the early church has for the way we understand the Christian faith today. What would our faith be like without the New Testament? How dependent are we for our faith on those decisions of the early church about what should and should not be included in the New Testament? Such a discussion will aid a class in understanding how our faith depends not only on the New Testament but on the early church as well. We stand in a tradition of faith that began with the apostles like Paul and continues to the present day. That is why we study writings like Paul's letter to the churches in Rome!

BIBLIOGRAPHY

1. For further study

BARTH, KARL. *The Epistle to the Romans,* translated by Edwyn C. Hoskins (London: Oxford University Press, 1950).

BEST, ERNEST. *The Letter of Paul to the Romans.* CAMBRIDGE BIBLE COMMENTARIES OF THE NEW ENGLISH BIBLE, VI (Cambridge: Cambridge University Press, 1967).

CRANFIELD, C. E. B. *A Critical and Exegetical Commentary on the Epistle to the Romans,* I and II (Edinburgh: T. & T. Clark, 1975–79).

HARRISVILLE, ROY A. *Romans* (Minneapolis: Augsburg Publishing House, 1980).

HUNTER, A. M. *The Epistle to the Romans* (London: SCM Press, 1955).

LEENHARDT, F. J. *The Epistle to the Romans: A Commentary,* translated by Harold Knight (London: Lutterworth Press, 1961).

MALY, EUGENE H. *Romans.* NEW TESTAMENT MESSAGE, IX (Wilmington, Del.: Michael Glazier, 1979).

NYGREN, ANDERS. *Commentary on Romans,* translated by Carl C. Rasmussen (Philadelphia: Muhlenberg Press, 1949).

SMART, JAMES D. *Doorway to a New Age: A Study of Paul's Letter to the Romans* (Philadelphia: Westminster Press, 1975).

THROCKMORTON, B. H. *Romans for the Layman* (Philadelphia: Westminster Press, 1961).

2. Literature cited

BARRETT, C. K. *A Commentary on the Epistle to the Romans.* HARPER'S NEW TESTAMENT COMMENTARIES (New York: Harper & Row, 1957).

BEKER, J. CHRISTIAAN. *Paul the Apostle* (Philadelphia: Fortress Press, 1980).

BORNKAMM, GÜNTHER. *Paul* (New York: Harper & Row, 1971).

BROWN, R. E. and J. P. MEIER. *Antioch and Rome* (New York: Paulist Press, 1983).

CALVIN, JOHN. *Commentaries on the Epistle of Paul the Apostle to Romans,* translated by John Owen (Grand Rapids: William B. Eerdmans, 1947).

DODD, C. H. *The Epistle of Paul to the Romans* (New York: Harper, 1932).

DONFRIED, KARL PAUL, editor. *The Romans Debate* (Minneapolis: Augsburg Press, 1977).

GAMBLE, HARRY, JR. *The Textual History of the Letter to the Romans* STUDIES AND DOCUMENTS, Vol. 42, I. A. Sparks, editor (Grand Rapids: William B. Eerdmans, 1977).

KÄSEMANN, ERNST. *Commentary on Romans,* translated by G. W. Bromiley (Grand Rapids: William B. Eerdmans, 1980).

————. "The Righteousness of God in Paul," *New Testament Questions of Today* (Philadelphia: Fortress Press, 1969).

KITTEL, R., editor. *Theological Word Book of the New Testament,* translated by G. W. Bromiley, II (Grand Rapids: William B. Eerdmans, 1964), pp. 174–225.

KÜMMEL, W. G. *Introduction to the New Testament,* translated by Howard Clark Kee (Nashville: Abingdon Press, 1975[16]).

LUTHER, MARTIN. *Lectures on Romans.* LIBRARY OF CHRISTIAN CLASSICS, XV. Wilhelm Pauck, editor and translator (Philadelphia: Westminster Press, 1961).

MAYS, JAMES L. *Hosea: A Commentary.* OLD TESTAMENT LIBRARY (Philadelphia: Westminster Press, 1969).

MINEAR, PAUL S. *The Obedience of Faith* (Naperville, IL: Alec R. Allenson, 1971).

REUMANN, JOHN H. *Righteousness in the New Testament: With Responses by Joseph A. Fitzmyer and Jerome D. Quinn* (Philadelphia: Fortress Press, 1982).

SANDERS, ED. P. *Paul and Palestinian Judaism* (Philadelphia: Fortress Press, 1977).

SANDAY, W. and A. C. HEADLAM. *The Commentary on Romans.* INTERNATIONAL CRITICAL COMMENTARIES (New York: Scribners, 1896).

SCHRENK, G. "δίκη (etc.)" in Kittel, R., ed., *Theological Word Book of the New Testament,* translated by G. W. Bromily. Vol. 2, 174–225. Grand Rapids: Eerdmans, 1964.

STENDAHL, KRISTER. "The Apostle Paul and the Introspective Conscience of the West" and "Call Rather Than Conversion" in *Paul Among Jews and Gentiles* (Philadelphia: Fortress Press, 1976), pp. 78–96 and 7–22 respectively.

STOWERS, STANLEY K. *The Diatribe and Paul's Letter to the Romans.* SBL DISSERTATION SERIES 57 (Chico, CA.: Scholars Press, 1981).